ORANGE MADNESS

ORANGE

MADNESS

The Incredible Odyssey of the Denver Broncos

Woodrow Paige Jr.

THOMAS Y. CROWELL, PUBLISHERS

Established 1834

New York

FIRST EDITION

Designed by C. Linda Dingler

Library of Congress Cataloging in Publication Data

Paige, Woodrow, Jr.
  Orange madness.
  1. Denver Broncos (Football team)—History.
I. Title.
GV956.D4P28   1978   796.33′264′0978883   78–4767
ISBN 0–690–01776–6

78 79 80 81 82 10 9 8 7 6 5 4 3 2 1

For Woodrow Paige Sr.

CONTENTS

Photo sections follow pages 100 and 190.

Acknowledgments

In 1974 I drove an old Chevy to Oklahoma City, took a right, and ended up in Denver. I moved to Colorado, as so many others before me, because of the mountains, the climate, the attitudes, the good life, and the job opportunity. What I found was a football team—the Denver Broncos. The city, the state, the whole region, if you will, breathed Broncos. A religion existed. In the South everyone was a Baptist; in Colorado everyone was a Broncomaniac, win or lose. And it was almost always lose. My first impression was that if the Denver Broncos ever became victors, the golden dome on the state capitol building would turn orange, the peaks would tumble, and the populace would go crazy. But I didn't fret. There was no danger of the Broncos becoming conquerors. That is, until 1977. And when the Broncos did win—and reached the Super Bowl— Orange Madness overtook an entire region and then the country. The mood of a football team and a city which had been waiting so frustratingly long had to be captured and recorded. It was like none other elsewhere. So a book was born.

I must initially thank the citizenry of the Rocky Mountains, who didn't make this book possible, but rather necessary by its incredible response to an athletic team. Every fan and loyalist made it worthwhile and enjoyable, and all cooperated with me to the fullest.

Most important, though, was my editor, Nick Ellison, who realized early on that he was guiding a village idiot through this experience and did it with ultimate tact, skill, and understanding. This belongs to him, also. I will forever be grateful.

Denver coach Red Miller suffered through several hundred sessions, explaining what it all meant and what was happening on the inside, and I am most appreciative. The assistant coaches, staff members, office workers, and especially the players provided insightful contributions, but I must single out public relations director Bob Peck, who was most informative in the midst of a hectic time; quarterback Craig Morton, who had to survive the Super Bowl and then talk repeatedly to me about it, and defensive captain Billy Thompson, who had spanned the bad times and good.

The library staff at the *Rocky Mountain News* endured the countless research queries and always came through, thank goodness. The two major Denver daily newspapers—the *News* and the Denver *Post*—were of great benefit, and particularly writers Joseph Sanchez, Dick Connor, Steve Cameron, and Bob Collins. I thank Bobby Jones and Michael Balfe Howard for permitting me the freedom and the time, and John Swagerty, who came up to my desk one day and suggested that I might want to hang around the Broncos for a while.

And I thank Ginia.

W. W. P. Jr.
July, 1978
Denver, Colo.

ORANGE MADNESS

1

BATTLE OF NEW ORLEANS

The end.

The Super Bowl is the end.

It's the end of the line, the end of an achievement, the end of the rainbow, and, mostly, the end of the season.

THE SUPER BOWL.

Ah.

The words rolls off the tongue.

The
Super
Bowl

No other event in this country captures the imagination, interest, and intrigue of the populace like the Super Bowl. While only a game, it's still, to this country, the coronation of the Queen, Macy's Thanksgiving Day Parade, Mardi Gras, Twenty-Four Hours of LeMans, presentation of the troops in Moscow—much of some, some of each. They call it football.

On a single day in January everything comes to a halt in the United States. The streets are clear, and movement is at a minimum. Outside it appears as if the world has been abandoned. All eyes and ears have turned to the Super Bowl. The National Football League didn't know what it had created in the beginning, but now it does. For sure. And the league plays up the game for everything it's worth. In 1978 the Super Bowl would become the highest-rated television show in history. It was being played in the biggest possible indoor television studio, aptly named the Superdome. Super, super, super.

The NFL championship contest brings together the two best professional teams—i.e., Green Bay and Oakland, Dallas and Pittsburgh, Miami and Minnesota, Kansas City and Minnesota, etc.

In 1978 the opponents would be Dallas, of course, and . . . uh . . . Denver.

Denver?

The Denver Broncos?

Yes, those Denver Broncos, the mediocrity titlists of pro football. Why, the Broncos had never even won a division or been in the playoffs. They had had just three winning seasons in seventeen. This was a team that just two seasons before wasn't playing .500 football. What are they doing here? That's a long story. Simplified, the Broncos had come together incredibly in the 1977 season and brought several hundred thousand diehards with them. They stunned the football world. Orange madness, Broncomania, if you will, had overrun Denver, then Colorado, and, finally, the nation. Orange, an ugly color, had taken on new beauty because of the Denver Broncos.

And here they are, incredibly, playing in football's showcase extravaganza—the Super Bowl.

Some twenty thousand orangemaniacs filed into the Superdome on January 15 to watch their heroes. They had begged, borrowed, and stolen tickets and hocked their wives and secured second mortgages on their houses and called in every favor to reach New Orleans by plane, car, van, train, and even by hitchhiking. Another million would have come if tickets had been available in the Rockies.

In his motel room near the airport, Robert "Red" Miller, the Pied Piper who had led this group to the Gulf Coast by coaching the Denver Broncos, prepared for the last game— much like he would prepare for the Last Supper.

"I don't believe anyone in the world would understand what happened with the Denver Broncos and the state of Colorado if they were not there to watch it themselves. As long as I've been in football I've never seen anything like it, and we'll never see it again, no matter what happens out there today." He pulled out a chaw of tobacco, stuck it in his mouth, and buttoned a white shirt. Gray suit, red tie. He looked in the mirror. Ready to go. Then, with the players, Miller climbed on a bus and headed for downtown New Orleans.

Miller thought about the game. The Broncos couldn't beat Dallas, a conglomeration of a team. But then the Broncos couldn't beat the Pittsburgh Steelers in the first round of the playoffs, and they couldn't beat the Oakland Raiders for the American Conference championship with a lame quarterback. And they couldn't be 14–2. But it had happened. Did the pocketful of miracles have room for one more?

"Everything has happened so fast," Miller thought. "Has it been too fast? Can we handle it today?" He thought of a quote: "Nothing to fear but fear itself."

"I don't want to fail."

In the locker room three players donned vertical socks. When the Broncos were born as a team the uniforms included vertical socks. The players hated them, and they were eventually burned. But general manager Fred Gehrke had several pair specially made for the Super Bowl to remind the players of their roots.

And then Miller gave his final pregame speech. He is not a fiery win-for-the-Gipper type. Very functional. Billy Thompson, a strong safety, thought to himself: "This man talks the same before a game as he does in his office. No hysterics. Not even now, with the biggest game of our lives out there in front of us. If we can just pull it off . . . ," and his attention reverted to Miller.

"Against the flex and that 4–1–6, you keep hunting and pecking, and you'll find a way," Miller was saying.

"Let's not change our approach. I want you to play hard. I want you to play loose. Have some fun. There's just one more game. Go out and enjoy it. Remember that we came a long way to get here, and nobody thought we'd make it. So let's show them that we deserve to be here.

"One more thing. I've never been prouder of a bunch of players."

The Broncos left the locker room, walked out into the light, and waited for the introductions.

It was almost time. Broncomania and Orange Madness had come in the early days of 1978 to New Orleans.

To the Super Bowl.

Ah.

2

ORANGE INSANITY

So (said the doctor). Now vee may perhaps to begin. Yes?
Portnoy's Complaint

Doc, I can't take it anymore. I have to get it off my chest. I have become what you would call your basic berserko. You might as well call for the guys in the white coats. Bring on the straitjacket. I beg of you, take me away. I'll go quietly. The home would be a nice place. A change. Where I can rest. Calm. You've got to help, you understand?

I guess my sickness is Orange Madness. You won't find it in your books there on the wall. There's been nothing like it.

I know. You want me to lie down on the couch, but I have to sit up. I can't sleep at night. It's been months. Look at my eyes. A Rand McNally map. I had this nightmare one night. I was in this orange grove, see, and all the oranges fell off the tree, and they formed one gigantic orange, and I couldn't get out of the way. I was crushed. And Anita Bryant was singing: "A day without Orange Crush is like a day without football." Please, Doctor. It's gotten that serious. Okay, I'll try to calm down, but you don't know what this did to me. It's crazy.

Orange. Orangemania. Broncomania. Broncitis. Whatever it is. It's a disease.

All right. I'll start at the beginning. I think it was when I was five. My Aunt Estelle gave me a pair of orange Argyle socks for my birthday, and every time we went to her house, my mother forced me to wear them. Don't you realize what effect that has on a child? I was scarred for life. Did you ever have to wear orange socks? No, I don't suppose so. Then it was my sister. All she liked to drink was orange Kool-Aid, and she walked around with an orange upper lip. Our first vacation was to Daytona Beach, Florida, and all along the way, my father stopped because they were giving away free juice, orange juice, at roadside stands. One summer, at my grandmother's farm, I had to help preserve orange marmalade.

Let me rest for a moment, will ya? The twitch just developed. I've got a rash on my back. Mind if I smoke? Yes, my hands do shake now, but I have it under control. Did you know, Doctor, that the orange horseshoe bat is a small animal indigenous to Australia and has fur colored bright orange?

Where was I? Oh, yes. The first girl to dump me was Barbara Baggett, and the night she told me she was wearing an orange chiffon dress. They were playing our song, by Hoagy Carmichael, "Orange-Colored Sky."

I should have known better than to go to college. Picked the University of Tennessee, and when I arrived at the airport the sign said: "Welcome to Big Orange Country." Practically everything in that city was orange—whole buildings even. For a year I had to wear an orange beanie. My God, Doc. I was up to here in orange. There was no escape. Across the street from my apartment was the Orange Market.

My sophomore year the Tennessee football team, with its famed orange jerseys, played in the Gator Bowl against the University of Syracuse Orangemen. The next season the team went to the Cotton Bowl and met the University of Texas, whose color was also orange. Whenever Tennessee won, the beacon on a downtown bank would glow orange. Then Tennessee was invited to—you got it—the Orange Bowl. The Tennessee basketball coach had the basketball court painted orange.

I had to get away from that color, Doc. So I went west to Denver, Colorado. That was far enough. You think of Denver, and you picture white snow and gray mountains and blue skies. But no orange.

Wrong.

I showed up at a cocktail party that first day in town, and the bartender asked if I wanted a twist of orange. At a luncheon orange sherbet was served. Liked a house until I saw it had an orange garage door. But none of that prepared me for the worst to come. The Denver Broncos, the local football team. They did me in. It was the final tragedy in a life of orange. Oh, at first, the Broncos really didn't matter, even though their color was orange. The team was pitiful. Wretched mediocrity.

That, however, Doc, was until the season of seventy-seven.

The Denver Broncos became successful, as you've no doubt heard by now. Orange took over my life and everyone else's in Colorado, and then orange began seeping all over the country.

And it's such a dreadful color. Why couldn't it have been navy blue or British racing green? Something mellow. No, not the Broncos and not Denver. Orange it is.

Here, let me tell you. There were orange wastebaskets, orange ashtrays, orange belt buckles, orange commode seats, orange toilet paper, orange telephones, orange hats, orange signs, orange jackets, orange-tinted dogs, orange buttons, orange cakes, orange pizzas, orange omelettes, orange Christmas trees, orange cuff links, orange tennis balls, orange sneakers, orange nightgowns, orange flowers, orange footballs, orange milkshakes, orange pies, orange jokes, orange poems, orange stationery, orange lamps, orange lights, orange ink in the newspapers, orange posters, orange airplanes, orange buses, orange sculptures, orange cars, orange vans, orange bicycles, orange miners' helmets, orange eggs, orange champagne, a Santa Claus in an orange suit, orange candy canes, orange blue jeans (or is it blue orange jeans?), orange rings, orange trucks, orange Jeeps, orange hair, orange faces, orange bagels, orange doughnuts, orange rugs, orange wigs, and, yes, of course, orange socks.

Orange, orange, orange, orange, orange. Eccckkk.

Sorry, Doc, I didn't mean to yell like that. But, even now, I go off the deep end sometimes. That's why I'm here. Did you always have those orange drapes? I would have slit my wrists when all this Orangemania got out of hand, but I was afraid my blood would be orange. I would have jumped in a lake, but I was afraid the water would be orange. I would have taken an overdose, but I was afraid the pills would be orange. I would have stuck my head in an oven, but I was afraid someone would be preparing an orange soufflé. Do they make orange bullets?

I asked to be transferred out of the city, but was given two options: Orange, New Jersey, and Orange, Texas. I drove once to Orange County in California. I thought my hair was turning gray. It was turning orange. Halloween already has been destroyed by orange pumpkins, but can orange Valentines, orange Easter eggs, and an orange Thanksgiving turkey be very far behind?

I mean, Doc, do you know what I'm trying to say here? Orange is, like, everywhere. It used to be Rocky Mountain High. Now it's Rocky Mountain Orange.

I have seen an orange sunset and an orange moon. Wait. It's the truth. They tell me it's because of pollution, but I'm sure something evil is going on. The Oranging of Colorado won't stop. The state has become a cornucopia of the color orange.

It's the doing of the Denver Broncos, I tell you. They have destroyed whole families, ruined lives, changed politics, made sober men drink, put chaste women on the streets, caused babies to scream. We're talking disease here. It's the only answer. I am not the only crazy person. But I'm one of the few, Doctor, who still has the capability to understand the problem.

The people are color-blind to orange. And all because of a football team that emerged from nothingness and went to the Super Bowl. Lazarus rose from the ashes, but Denver rose from the orange. Can you comprehend? I realize my time is up, but don't you want to listen? Orange. A man was trying to move a baseball team to Denver, and a whole bunch suggested that he change the nickname to Denver Orange Sox. Maybe I could wear my orange argyles again. Is there something wrong with me? You can't close the door on me, Doc, or on this orange thing. Remember *The Invasion of the Body Snatchers?* Well, this is the Invasion of the Orange. I warned you.

I am going bananas.

Or am I going oranges?

Doc?

3

AND OTHER ORANGE FANATICS

The Denver Broncos fumbled five times while losing to the Chicago Bears, 33–14, in 1973. That night a Colorado man shot himself in the head and left a suicide note saying, "I have been a Broncos fan since the Broncos were first organized, and I can't stand their fumbling anymore."

Broncos backers are like that.

For seventeen years they had lived and—literally and figuratively—died with their devotion because the Denver Broncos didn't win—enough. They became surly, sour, and downright dissatisfied. But they stuck with the team. Thousands were driven to drink or drugs or despondency. At least one was driven to suicide. Frustration went on.

"If the Broncos ever become successful, you'd better get back out of the way. These people will go crazy," said one astute observer of these goings-on.

Well, it occurred. And the people did go crazy.

Rich Savage and his girl friend walked into the Arabian Bar & Cafe late one Sunday afternoon at the height of Broncomania, with the idea of having a couple of drinks and dancing to Dolly Parton sounds. Savage ordered a beer, slipped a quarter in the jukebox, and got ready to dance. But as soon as the music began, all the drinkers at the bar turned. They were watching the Denver–Baltimore game on television. "Hey, turn that crap off," yelled someone.

Savage replied in form. So a man got up and pulled the jukebox plug. An argument ensued, and a Bronco lover and the music appreciationists retired to the alley outside. Shots were fired. Savage fell dead. His girl was injured. The Broncos fan was arrested and later charged with murder. "They should let him off," another patron of the Arabian said. "Nobody is gonna mess with me when I'm watching the Broncos."

The public transportation system in Denver runs special buses to the Denver Broncos' games each Sunday from outlying areas. Because of peaked interest, enough buses weren't available a particular Sunday, and Helen Harris didn't get a ride and didn't see "her" Broncos in person. She took the bus company to county court, suing for the price of her football ticket and the seasonal bus pass she had purchased—a total of forty-three dollars. After a morning hearing Judge John Sanchez sided with the woman—who testified that "watching the Broncos on television just isn't like being there at the stadium"—and said he would have awarded her more money if she had asked. "That's the money I wanted," she said. "But what I really wanted was to see the Broncos." As the white-haired Mrs. Harris left the courthouse she shouted: "We're number one."

A prisoner held in the county jail, awaiting transfer to the state prison on a robbery charge, asked the court to delay his move two days so he could watch the Broncos' playoff game on TV in his cell.

Andonandonandon.

When the Pittsburgh Steelers reached the playoffs for the first time in that club's long history, fans dressed up in gorilla outfits to salute the team's kicker, Roy Gerela, and formed a Franco-American Army for running back Franco Harris, and wore yellow and black stocking caps and hung from the lightposts downtown when the team returned from a major victory. In Miami the Dolphins' supporters waved white handkerchiefs to celebrate the club's success. When the New York Mets won the pennant in 1969 their followers tore up the turf and acted totally asinine. The examples are endless because this country is insane about sports.

But what transpired in Denver when the football team won far surpassed all previous attempts by other cities for havoc. As one writer penned amid the hoopla of the Broncos: "I've never been a football fan in my life. I've hated sports, to be perfectly honest. But how can you avoid getting caught up in Broncomania? It's everywhere. All around us. I feel like the troops just came home from the war."

In 1977, when the Denver Broncos reached the playoffs, the fallout was incredible. The troops had come home from the war.

At Christmas time a second-grade teacher told her young students to write letters to Santa Claus. The classroom was quiet for a moment. Then one of the students raised his hand. He asked if the class couldn't write to the Broncos instead. A vote was taken. Santa Claus was defeated by a landslide. Yes, Virginia, there are Denver Broncos.

Never had the community rallied around any sport or any project for that matter, like the Broncos. "I like it. It says a lot for the spirit of the city of Denver," spoke the mayor, William H. McNichols, Jr., the elderly self-acknowledged number one sports fan of the area, who had pressed for the expansion of Mile High Stadium from fifty thousand to seventy-five thousand seats so more orange nuts could pile in on Sunday afternoons. "The people want something good to happen for their city, and they want the rest of the country to know that Denver is a big-league city."

Even a Denver psychiatrist believed that the enthusiasm for an athletic team was good for the city and its people. "Broncomania is not only harmless, but it's healthy," said Dr. George Mizner. "For most people Broncomania is a healthy outlet for a whole variety of emotions that need to be channeled in some direction. Commitment, investment, fervor, and interest are always better than apathy, distance, and wanting to be involved. I think probably the most important thing is that anybody in the course of his life suffers disappointments and defeats, and he loves to identify with a powerful winning team that wins national reputation that in a sense symbolizes what we would like to be in terms of power and success."

Success had come, bringing with it all the amazing trappings.

In one Denver hospital the staff decided to start wearing orange frocks. In another, newborn babies were wrapped in orange swaddling clothes. Still another maternity ward put bumper stickers saying "Super Bowl '78" on the sides of baby cribs. A nurse got word to the Broncos through a sportscaster that a man was dying of throat cancer on her floor and had one fond wish. "He wants to live to see the Broncos in the Super Bowl and promises he will not die until it happens." The Broncos sent the elderly gentleman an autographed plaque. Starr Yelland of the CBS affiliate carried it into the room. The man looked up and began to cry. Then he took his pad and pencil and wrote: "Beat the Cowboys."

Midway through the season, the Rev. Terry Paul, pastor of a nondenominational brick church, read that Denver quarterback Craig Morton had praised the Lord after a victory over Oakland. So Rev. Paul, also a paint contractor, got out a bucket and trimmed his church in bright orange. Outside the house of worship he erected a sign: "Broncos No. 1, Morton Says, 'Praise God for all our blessings.' " Inside the church an orange carpet was laid, and the pews were painted dark orange. "I think it's really neat," the Rev. Paul said. Across town, at 1650 Pearl Street, a bottle of Orange Crush soft drink was being used to christen the new Broncos building. A pair of realtors, Mike Moore and Larry Fuller, had chanced upon some Denver players at a restaurant, talked about the possibility of making it to the playoffs, and left impressed. So they took a piece of property they owned with the biggest facade, rolled on orange paint, wrote "Broncos" over the entrance, and put a large "No. 1" on the building's top floor. "The residents love it," Fuller said. "And we've never had so much traffic on the block."

Senior citizens wanted to join in. They held their own pep rally for the Broncos at the Volunteers of America Senior Citizens Center, drank orange punch, and signed a congratulatory card to be sent to the players. Said the center's director: "Senior citizens like football, and this really is a gesture of love."

Broncomania emerged everywhere.

On the western slope of the state, in Grand Junction, a city fireman invited over thirty friends for a "beer-drinking, chili-eating paint party in honor of the Broncos." They didn't know what to expect, but arrived to find the fireman painting his house from top to bottom in orange with a football helmet on the front side.

In a Lakewood, Colorado, school, everyone was asked to wear orange one day, and more than 90 percent of the students and teachers went along with the stunt. Similar demonstrations of support occurred at elementary, junior high, and high schools all around the state. Studies were being turned over to Bronco-mania. Students were asked to write poems and stories about the team. Class projects included studying the team's performances. The Broncos received more than a thousand drawings of the players done in one school. Nobody knew the President's name, but every student could tell you who played free safety for Denver.

As the season wore on, everybody in the state was devising a way to participate. For instance, Cynda Rice added a Broncos touch to her manicuring business. Ms. Rice painted players and team helmets on female football fans' fingernails. "My husband had been after me for weeks to get involved. I did a helmet and the whole shop went crazy, so I guess I have become involved." One fan had every fingernail painted with a different Broncos' player's number, and even Mrs. Norris Weese, wife of one of the club's quarterbacks, had Norris's number painted on a nail.

The Broncos brought out the poet laureate and the show business in Denverites. One newspaper reporter asked for poems about the team and received more than five hundred, and late in the season records about the team were waxed and played on the radio daily.

"The whole thing started as sort of a lark," said Jim Cunningham about a song called "The Modern Battle of New Orleans," a takeoff on the 1959 Johnny Horton hit record. The updated version heralded the Broncos' season and their upcoming trip to New Orleans for the Super Bowl. Cunningham, an attorney and normally a sane man, sang lead on the record, which became, as they say, an overnight hit in Denver. The song was written by another lawyer, Bob Kapelke, and, on the record, a Denver district court referee played banjo and a real estate salesman the drums.

Not all businessmen and companies thrived because of the Broncos, though. On the Sundays when the team played, Denver became a ghost town. Local television ratings revealed that 88 percent of the Denver area TVs were tuned to the football games. Movie theaters, even those showing *Star Wars,* reported tremendous drop-offs in attendance on Sunday afternoons. The quasi-legal massage parlors were affected. "If the Broncos win, business really picks up after the games," said one masseur. At May D & F, one of the city's largest department stores, business "fails to meet expectation every time the Broncos play," said an executive. A real estate developer claimed that on game days "traffic is falling way off. We've gotten nobody out on Sundays, and before, that always has been our best day to sell houses." One shopping center normally open on Sunday was finally forced to close during football season on Sunday because of declining sales. "The only customers we had were in the television department looking at the games," an employee said. Centennial Race Track reported a severe drop in crowds for Sunday. "It had never happened before. Back in the days when the Broncos were losing, we remained stable. But now, well, it shows that when you are winning in football, everything else suffers in Denver." A grocery store chain rearranged its hours, claiming that during games sales fell to nil, "but are strong leading up to game time."

Police reported that the Broncos helped prevent crimes. Once the games began, calls to the police dispatcher dropped to a light trickle. Policemen carried AM radios along to listen to the games because they had nothing else to do. "Either people aren't reporting crimes, or crooks are interested in how the Broncos do," said a police sergeant. Mountain Bell Telephone Co. spokesmen said long-distance calls were at a minimum while the Broncos played. "Sunday is usually our busiest time of the week for long distance, but now it's nothing."

Television repairmen weren't so lucky. "We have been swamped because people wanted their televisions perfect for the games," said one. "We've had to put on extra men because of the emergency calls we get when the Broncos are on TV. People bring the sets in on Saturday and say, 'Either fix it, or I'm taking it someplace else.'" A television salesman said the Broncos "have placed an urgency on buying now rather than later, so sales went up considerably, especially the giant screen sets." Friendly Dan the TV Man, a TV rental service, had to order twenty-five extra sets. "The rental business has picked up 100 percent because of the Broncos."

One high school went into the button-making business and was turning a tidy profit because of the Broncos. John Bucci, a distributive education teacher, sensed a gap in the Broncos market, so as a project for his students, he had them make up "Orange Crush" buttons. They went over much bigger than the ashtrays made the year before. In fact, the school was suddenly in excellent financial shape. But the buttons couldn't match the T-shirt sales. In one week a department store sold sixty-five thousand "Orange Crush" shirts. Others got in line with everything from "I Love You, Denver Broncos" to "Super Bowl or Bust." By year's end, it was estimated that close to a half-million Bronco-related T-shirts had been sold in the Denver area. A new baby was photographed in an orange T-shirt and holding up one finger, and the picture was sent to the newspapers. Another new baby was named after defensive end Lyle Alzado. And a company came out with baby toys in orange with the Broncos' insignia.

According to business analysts, the impact of Broncomania was worth millions of dollars to the Denver economy, with estimates ranging past $35 million, all because of sales of orange T-shirts and coffee mugs and bumper stickers, etc.

A regional airlines, Aspen Airways, repainted one of its planes orange and flew it over the stadium on Sunday. The rapid transit system revealed an orange bus called "Broncos' No. 1." A car dealer promoted his new orange Corvette. Another dealer gave several of the Broncos four-wheel-drive vehicles painted in orange with the players' number on the back spare tire. And more than a few people painted their cars and vans and bikes orange.

The bottlers of Orange Crush soft drink took full advantage of the use of its product's name by the team and turned out every conceivable orange product.

A man showed up at a Denver practice with an orange station wagon. "What's going to happen when you try to sell it?" he was asked.

"I'd rather give up my wife than this car."

And then Christmas arrived, already commercialized, but nothing like what was about to occur in Denver. The bumper stickers read: "I'm Dreaming of an Orange Crushmas." Orange Christmas trees were sold. Orange pizzas—shredded carrots— were big items. What to buy for Christmas was easily solved. Under every Christmas tree was some Bronco-oriented present in orange. "I've never known what to get my husband, but the Broncos took care of it this year," a woman told a department store employee. "I got him the whole mess—a T-shirt, a jacket, a cap, a stadium seat, a coffee mug." A little boy wrote the newspaper and said he wanted to get his mother the players' autographs for Christmas. "She's the biggest Bronco fan ever, and please send the autographs to this address. If I don't get them, we will cancel our subscription to the newspaper."

The newspapers were doing quite well because of the Broncos, too. Not a day went by without full-page ads from companies trying to leap on the Bronco bandwagon with orange specials, and every Monday morning throughout the season circulation rose by thousands. In late November the *Rocky Mountain News* announced that it had the largest circulation in the history of the newspaper—because of a Broncos' story and orange headlines on page one. The Denver *Post* was profiteering too, so both newspapers were printing extra copies and splashing orange ink over their pages. The television stations didn't lag. Each night a new orange product was displayed, and the Broncos became the number one news item— before troubling events of the world. "I thought only assassinations sold newspapers and television time, but I've found something new—the Denver Broncos," said one editor. Mountain Bell marketed an "Orange Crush" telephone, and orange champagne was served to the Broncos at a victory party. At the Denver zoo, keepers began feeding monkeys oranges instead of bananas. A poster with the players' pictures all over it hit the 7-Eleven stores one day, and all thirty thousand copies were gone by the next.

And in one tavern in southeast Denver, the drinkers took out their frustrations on the lack of national attention paid the Broncos in a controlled, volatile manner. The entire city was upset that the Broncos had been snubbed by "Monday Night Football" and weren't even being shown on the halftime highlights. The reasoning behind the network's decision was sound. The last time the Broncos had appeared they were blown out by Washington, and it was a nobody team with slight recognition. But a bar called Sweetwater protested. A drawing was held at halftime each week, and a patron was allowed to throw a brick through the TV screen at Howard Cosell. "It's just our way of letting the networks know how we feel," said one of the owners that first night. "And we might pick up some business with it, too."

The bar was crowded, all right. A young man's name was drawn from a Broncos football helmet, and he grabbed the brick. Cosell appeared, and he threw. Missed. One more time, and the old TV set purchased for the occasion crashed and died. Cosell was later informed of the activity and threatened legal action, but never carried through.

Red Miller, the Denver coach, was hypnotically stunned by the response. "I have been everywhere on every level in football during my life, and I have never seen anything like this. Every time I turn someone is handing me something orange— like a commode seat or a telephone. Wake me up when this is all over. These people are a little bit crazy sometimes, but I wouldn't take anything to not be a part of this."

Unfortunately, the man who had gotten tired of the Broncos' fumbling in 1973 didn't stick around. The Broncos had stopped being so bad, and the people were loving orange—albeit somewhat maddeningly.

4

37,000 FEET OVER AMARILLO

Bob Peck and Dave Frei, the public relations staffers of the Denver Broncos, walked out of the Astrodome, finished off their beer, and squinted into the late-afternoon sun. Even though it was December 4, the weather in Houston was warm and humid. Peck and Frei dashed for their rented car because they had a plane to catch, the one flight in their lives they were definitely not going to miss. They were just about to drive off when a family in a station wagon pulled up. It had come from the direction of the nearby amusement park. The man rolled down his window in the empty parking lot and hollered: "Hey, did something happen here today?"

Peck laughed. "Oh, yeah. Oh, yeah. Something happened."

That something was the clinching of a position in the National Football League playoffs by the Denver Broncos. On that day the Broncos were in the playoffs for the first time in eighteen seasons of play. They had defeated the Houston Oilers, 24–14, to achieve what had been a long, long time coming.

The Broncos flew to Houston the day before with a 10–1 record, the best in the league, and they were truly surprising everyone, themselves included. The coaches and the players refused to talk about what they might be able to accomplish, especially considering their history of traveling to Houston. Denver had played in the Texas city thirteen times, losing eleven. No other NFL team had been so dominant against Denver at home. So while a victory would give the Broncos a spot in the playoffs, they reserved hope. Back in Denver, though, the city was planning for a whirlwind celebration. Authorities at the airport roped off a section of the parking lot, for a major reception area. "Uh," said Red Miller, "I would rather they wait until we accomplish something."

The Broncos landed at the Houston airport in an orange airplane, naturally, provided by Braniff Airlines, which was taking complete advantage of its odd-painted planes. Miller stepped off the plane, jumped on the first bus, and told an assistant coach that he had received a letter just before leaving "asking me why I don't dye my hair orange and change my name to Orange Miller. I've never seen anything like what has been going on in Denver. I didn't realize there was so much orange in the world. I just hope we don't let those people down. All of this has come so suddenly."

Later in the afternoon he said that even though "everyone says there is a jinx when Denver plays here, I don't believe in jinxes. I believe in execution. The Astrodome is 100 yards long, ain't it? To hell with the jinx."

On the long bus ride to the hotel, several players kidded tight end Riley Odoms, a native of Houston. "Hey, homeboy, give us the twenty-five-cent tour." Odoms looked out the window. "Where's the parade? Riley is back. I'm gonna own this town tomorrow."

Most of the players settled in for the evening, but rookie running back Rob Lytle gathered up a dozen teammates and rode off for a restaurant. There was good reason for Lytle's popularity and the caravan. The food was free. The year before, when Lytle was at the University of Michigan, he had finished third in the Heisman Trophy voting, but ended up with what he considered a higher honor. Lytle won the Wiseman Trophy, an alternative award started by the owners of a chain of prime rib restaurants.

"I thought it was a joke when someone called and told me I had won the Wiseman. Never heard of it," Lytle said to a player while awaiting a cab. "Then I found out that it had been going on for several years. The best part is that the player who wins it gets a card entitling him and his friends to go to any Victoria Station anywhere and eat. No matter what happens to me, I'll always be able to eat, and you can't eat the Heisman Trophy. O. J. Simpson told Lynn Swann he'd trade him a Heisman for a Wiseman straight up."

In one of the rooms, quarterback coach Babe Parilli swigged a beer, put his feet up, and said the Broncos "are acting crazy this season. It reminds me of the old Jets who once won the Super Bowl with Parilli as a backup quarterback to Joe Namath. Pass the chips."

Across the hall several players had convened to watch *Hollywood High,* a tame porno movie on the pay TV set. "One of those girls looks like she plays for Houston," said Billy Thompson. As usual, the Broncos were loose.

The next morning the players were up early for the noon game. "The thing about Red is that the longer the season goes on, the sooner he wants us at the stadium. Restless, I guess," said equipment manager Larry Elliott as he awaited the bus. A blistering wind cut across the plains, but the Broncos were safely inside the Astrodome, the dome daddy, the umbrellaed stadium that begat the other domes. In his pregame talk, Miller said little. "We haven't won anything until we win this game," he ended, and the players hit the field.

The Broncos initially looked like they hadn't won anything before and weren't going to win anything this day. After losing the toss, the Broncos sat back on their heels as Houston moved past midfield. Denver stopped the Oilers, but the Broncos weren't doing anything either. At the end of the quarter the Broncos had minus five yards' offense and no first downs. This was the number one team in the NFL?

Houston moved in for a touchdown. Up in the stands a man dressed in orange ranged through the stands waving a sign that stated: "We're No. 1. Ya'll will be crushed." Oilers fans hurled cups at him. A nasty situation was developing when two uniformed policemen escorted the orange fan out of the stadium. But he left waving his sign.

For the moment he was better off than the other several thousand Broncos backers who had come to Texas for the clincher. But they were staring at a deficit. Denver did tie the game when Craig Morton passed beautifully to Riley

Odoms from 13 yards away, and homeboy Odoms had started well. Just before halftime, Denver took the lead on a Morton-Rick Upchurch pass.

However, Morton was popped, and had to limp off to the locker room. He was suffering with hip problems that would bother him the rest of the season. In the second half backup quarterback Craig Penrose guided Denver to a field goal to stretch the advantage to 17–7. But the Oilers made short work of closing the spread via a 29-yard rainbow touchdown from Dan Pastorini to Ken Burrough. Houston threatened again, but Morton returned and flipped a pass to Odoms to set up the final touchdown. Denver had won, 24–14, and the players bounced off the field. At the tunnel, defensive end Lyle Alzado paused, looked at the Denver fans in the upper tier, and waved a number one signal—finger pointed up in the air—at them.

Miller wasted no time in opening the locker-room door.

"I don't want to comment about the game. I want to talk about the playoffs. You hear? *Playoffs!* I want to talk about the playoffs. I want to talk about playoffs. We are number one."

What had happened to this sane man? Well, questioned about the playoffs for so long, Miller had continually replied: "I don't want to talk about that stuff until we do it. Then I'll talk." And now he was talking. "This is the grandest moment in my life. This team wanted it so bad."

Yet the others in the room were rather subdued. The Broncos knew that the Oakland Raiders were just starting a game on the West Coast, at Los Angeles, against the Rams. A Los Angeles victory would hand the Broncos, in addition to the playoff spot, the undisputed championship of the Western Division. The players dressed hurriedly and got on the bus for the airport. They wanted to listen to the Oakland game.

In the other locker room, Houston coach Bum Phillips was saying what others before him had refused to admit. He believed. "They deserve to be 11–1. They will beat Oakland. No way they're not going to win their division. You can't single out any one aspect. That's a great team." Previous coaches who had lost to the Broncos grumbled about bad luck and cruel breaks and untimely injuries, but the Oilers said they were just downright beaten.

Miller was rushing up the excalator in the massive Houston airport. "Goddamn drivers don't even know where we're supposed to go. Will somebody get this straightened out?" Here was the coach of the top team in football for the moment having to play tour guide. The drivers finally found a back road to the runway apron, but the door to the plane was locked. So the Broncos waited. They finally boarded at 5:15 and were informed that the score in Los Angeles was 7-7. Shortly into the air, stewardesses tried to serve meals, but nobody wanted to eat. The Broncos were tying on a drunk as the scratchy broadcast blared through the loudspeaker system. The pilot had passed over an area where he could pick up the Raiders' game.

Los Angeles had scored to go ahead, 20-14. A cheer went up. "I wonder what Al Davis [Oakland's reigning general partner] is doing now. I bet he's crapping in his pants," Denver assistant coach Stan Jones said to Miller. "If Los Angeles ever should win a game, it should be now," replied Miller, calmed down now. A voice wafted from the back: "Will you guys shut the fuck up so I can listen to the game?"

Quiet prevailed suddenly.

Oakland was rallying. "The assholes are holding, I know it," a player said when Ken Stabler completed a pass. The radio gave out. Jones strained his ears. General manager Fred Gehrke said: "They'll figure a way to win. Something will happen."

But the Raiders lost. Whatever was said at the final moment of the game over the radio was also lost to the Broncos. They were throwing seat cushions, drowning each other in beer, and screaming. The Broncos, in one day, had accomplished the two goals they had always sought—the playoffs and the division title.

Offensive line coach Ken Gray, former all-pro lineman and a rookie coach from Texas, looked out the window and said: "We did it over Amarillo."

Thirty-seven thousand feet over Amarillo.

Owner Gerald Phipps wept.

Miller hugged the closest players.

Gehrke rocked back in his seat and laughed.

Equipment manager Elliott raised his index finger.

People acted silly.

The media types on board joined in the frivolity.

And defensive lineman Paul Smith, the only player to make it through ten seasons with Denver, stood in the middle of the aisle, uncorked a champagne bottle that had come out of hiding, and poured the bubbly over his head and down his body. "I have waited so long, and it feels so good."

His roommate, Alzado, claimed he was "in a daze. I do not know what is happening."

Bobby Maples added: "I love it."

But offensive tackle Andy Maurer's voice stabbed through the night with: "I think we should hijack this plane and take it to Los Angeles and wait outside the locker room and thank each of the Rams personally as they come out the door."

Braniff had outfitted the plane with leather seats—a new advertising gimmick. The seats were quickly being destroyed. In the back Billy Thompson said the Raiders "are yesterday's champs. Today belongs to us. Everyone in Denver can appreciate and share with us what we have done. This was great. You go back to those months when the players stood up, and a lot of people thought we were wrong [for demanding the ousting of former coach John Ralston]. But I think we have proven we were right. Red Miller is such a great coach, and this is such a great team."

The word was out in Denver, and the people—ten thousand strong—began to converge on the airport. It was a chilly, windblown night. They waited patiently behind police barricades. "I think this is great," said Angie Bergano, who had sat in the fabled South Stands at Mile High Stadium for years. "I've got a cousin in Houston. When the Oilers scored in the first quarter, my cousin called me long distance. All he said was the score is 7–0, and he hung up. When the Broncos took the lead, I sent him some orange and blue flowers."

Sunny Weingarter had shown up in his wheelchair. "I've missed only two games in thirteen seasons at Mile High Stadium." He watches the road games from an iron lung. "But I'm going to be in Dallas." The public address system kept the crowd advised of the Broncos' arrival. "They'll be here in thirty minutes." A guy turned around and said: "I've waited eighteen years. I can wait another thirty minutes."

On the airplane Miller was hoarse. "This is it." He walked to the front of the plane and said to a couple of front-office types in a low voice: "Who would have ever thought it? Not me. But it proves that we had the right idea. Our philosophy was right. I waited so long to be a head coach, and now I've proven that I deserved the job."

The players lifted champagne glasses and bottles in unison and toasted, first, themselves, then Miller. And linebacker Randy Gradishar said: "This is also for all the guys who were with us over the past few years. They helped us get here. We didn't slide in. We made it to the playoffs by beating the best."

Owner Gerald Phipps walked through the maze crying and congratulating each player. "I'm as happy as I ever thought I would be. It's hard to express myself. We all wanted this for a long time, and right now, I feel like it was well worth all we've been through."

"We are not number two. We are absolutely number one," said linebacker Godwin Turk.

Then the ride developed into a New Year's Eve party. Only a band, a dance floor, and some noisemakers were missing. But the Broncos provided their own entertainment, singing and dancing on the seats. Out of the brouhaha the word "Super Bowl" drifted time and again.

Elliott, who had been taking care of the club's equipment since 1965, said he could remember "when there were rats running around on the floor of the dressing room. Now look where we are."

Kicker Jim Turner, the oldest of the Broncos at thirty-six and among the few Broncos who had been to the Super Bowl with other teams, pointed to a ring on his finger and said: "We're one step closer to that diamond."

Jack Dolbin, a wide receiver, walked around asking for someone to "pinch me. I think I'm dreaming." Someone said: "God bless the Broncos," and linebacker Bob Swenson added: "This sure beats 'Fernwood 2-Night.' "

In the distance, at last, were the lights of Denver. The pilot came on the PA system and asked the players to calm down for a moment, that there was a message.

"Gentlemen, this is the Air Traffic Control Center in Denver, and we want to congratulate you on a great accomplishment. You are the champions. Have a safe landing."

Silence prevailed only momentarily. "We have done it," said Alzado. "Let's all go drink tequila." Most of the players later retired to the Colorado Mine Company, a local restaurant, and drank until the liquor was gone.

The plane landed. The players could see the crowd pinned up against the glass windows. Banners hung everywhere. Lucky Lindy would have been proud of the reception.

Outside, in the cold, Miller circled in front of the police barrier and held up his finger in a number-one salute to everyone in the crowd. The players were asked questions by the TV units broadcasting live from the airport. Fans shouted. Reserve quarterback Norris Weese backed off, looked at the throng, and said: "This sure is a far piece from Oxford, Mississippi." It was a far piece from sanity.

Some time later coach Red Miller had escaped and was downstairs sneaking out a front door. "Can you believe this? I can't." Just then he was spotted again by the throng, signed a few hundred more autographs, and slipped out to the parking garage. He got into his car, turned the key and . . . nothing.

Miller sat there. His battery was dead.

The Broncos' coach got out of his car and was trying to decide what to do. He didn't want to return to the terminal and the crowd.

So he stood. A few moments later a family came along—Broncos fans. "Aren't you the coach?"

"Yeah."

"What's wrong?"

"My battery is dead. Could I hitch a ride?"

And so one Denver family went home with an unexpected hitchhiker.

Miller had gone a long way that day. But the Broncos had gone a long way from their humble beginnings, even if they weren't born in a house their father built.

5

THE BRONCOS ARE BORN OUT OF WEDLOCK

H. L. Hunt had a restless son with a lot of money, so Denver secured a football team.

In the late 1950s, Lamar Hunt, son of the billionaire Texas oilman, sought membership in the National Football League's exclusive, traditionalist club. He wanted his own plaything in Dallas, but the NFL refused. Texans always think big, so Hunt said he was going to form his own damn league, and to hell with the NFL. Hunt called on Barron Hilton, of the Hilton hotels, rich Bud Adams of Houston, and a couple of other money friends and decided to form a rival outfit they named the American Football League. An organizational meeting was held in Chicago on August 14, 1959, and Bob Howsam of Denver happened along. Howsam was more interested in some method of using the new South Stands he had built at Bears Stadium in Denver. Howsam, who owned the minor league baseball team in the city, had been one of the originators of the Continental Baseball League that fell through, so he was left with a hefty mortgage on the stadium. He had to generate funds from some source to pay off the money he owed. Deals for possibly moving in an existing NFL franchise evaporated, so Howsam attended that first AFL get-together. And, suddenly, Denver was a charter member along with New York, Dallas, Los Angeles, Minneapolis, and Houston. Boston and

Buffalo were added later, and the Minneapolis franchise became Oakland.

The news didn't astound Denver. This western city, which sprung up out of the gold rush of the mid–1850s, was still basically a backwoodsy place. Only a few had discovered Colorado a century later, and most of the natives would just as soon leave it that way. The University of Colorado football team in Boulder had attracted some attention and once produced a player named Byron "Whizzer" White, but the University of Denver's football program was dying out—it was, in fact, laid to rest in 1960—and most seemed to get excited only about the annual rodeo and stock show, the city's sole major annual sports event. Minor-league baseball was an up-and-down operation, primarily a way to spend a lazy summer afternoon. AAU basketball held a yearly tournament in Denver, but was a one-week affair for the few basketball crazies. The city had a franchise in the National Basketball Association in 1949, but it won only eleven games and pulled out before the season even ended.

Thus, when it was announced that Denver was obtaining a professional football franchise, no parades were held. The newspapers saluted Howsam's decision with disdain, and Howsam was treated like a fool waiting to go broke. In fact, Howsam was lacking the one tangible asset that the other teams had—money. While most of the AFL organizations hired scouts and put together reports on all the available college football players, Howsam went to a drugstore and bought a copy of *Street and Smith,* a pre-season football magazine. That was his total draft organization. Denver's first draft choice was a young center from Trinity, Roger LeClerc. Where is he now? Where was he then?

Howsam plucked Dean Griffing from the Optimist Bowl as his general manager, and Griffing, in turn, hired Frank Filchock as coach. Both had experience in Canadian pro football and were told by Howsam to give the Broncos their best shot. The team was named Broncos—following a contest among the few fans that existed—after an old baseball team that once existed in Denver, and a ragamuffin outfit gathered for the first camp in 1960 at the Colorado School of Mines. Filchock, a former

NFL quarterback, had just two assistants and considered himself lucky at that. The uniforms were purchased, in a deal, from the defunct Copper Bowl by Griffing and were light gold and what was called at the time "barnyard brown." The team also had incredibly ugly, vertically striped socks, unheard of in football. The players hated them, and most refused to even try on the socks. With and without the vertically striped socks, Denver lost all five exhibition games and entered the season with little hope. Just 2,600 season tickets were purchased. A funeral-home owner bought the first eight, maybe thinking he might get some business out of a quick demise. The Broncos looked in danger of death.

But the Broncos became the first AFL team to win a game—by virtue of playing on a Friday night in Boston, defeating the Patriots, 13–10, led by quarterback Frank Tripucka, who had followed Griffing and Filchock down from Canada. The former Notre Dame quarterback (whose son would become an outstanding basketball player with the team as a freshman in 1977), was also actually an assistant coach, and, on the field, just as in the backyard pickup games, he diagrammed plays in the dirt. The other star on the team was fullback-kicker Gene Mingo, who never attended college, but had come out of the United States navy to head the Broncos' scoring attack.

After compiling a 2–1 record, the Broncos came home for their first regular-season game. They could have been, in reality, 3–0, but Denver was leading New York, 24–21, with fifteen seconds to play when a punt was blocked, and the Titans scored to win. It was typical of things to come in the future for the Broncos. Although today one hundred thousand people will swear on their mother's Bible that they attended the first game, a crowd of 18,372 was announced—mostly curiosity seekers—and that figure was inflated. The Broncos beat Oakland on that day, 31–24, and soon owned a 4–2 record. Interest was increasing. But the Broncos didn't win again the rest of the season—finishing at 4–9–1. The interest just as rapidly declined.

The franchise, on a shoestring, lost four hundred thousand dollars the first season, but it could have been worse. Whenever field goals or extra points were kicked, general manager Griffing stood beyond the end zone and retrieved the balls. In one game he had to fight a youngster for the football and was booed soundly. He didn't realize it was general custom to let customers keep footballs. "We never did it in Canada," he said.

A safety with the unlikely name of Goose Gonsoulin was Denver's representative on the first all-AFL team.

In May 1961, Howsam and his brother, Lee, sold their stock in the team to a syndication headed by Cal Kunz and Gerald Phipps. Howsam moved on to make his name in major-league baseball, after all, as general manager of the Cincinnati Reds. Despite the change in ownership, the Broncos still suffered on the field—going 3–11 and losing their last seven games. Only one team in the entire league, Oakland, was less proficient, with a 2–12 record.

In December Filchock became the first of the Denver coaches to leave. He wouldn't be the last. Jack Faulkner, a former San Diego assistant, took over as both coach and general manager, and his first action was to dispose of the vertical socks, burning them at a public bonfire. And Faulkner set the stage for the mania that developed in 1977—by purchasing orange uniforms.

"I was a Cleveland Browns fan, and I wanted burnt orange uniforms like they wore," Faulkner says now. "But the manufacturer sent us bright orange instead." It would eventually be an excellent mistake. With the fresh start provided by Faulkner, the Broncos won their opener at the University of Denver stadium before a turnaway crowd of twenty-eight thousand and took six of their first seven games. This seemed to be the year. Denver was soon 7–2, and the city had turned on to football. So this was what professional football was all about. But, as quickly as the Broncos had climbed, they fell. There were five straight losses. During the string, Dallas was leading in a game 10–3, and had elected to accept a safety backed up in its own territory. But, on the play, Dallas instead scored, stopping the Broncos' surge. Denver finished 7–7. Despite the collapse, Faulkner was named coach of the year in the league.

Grander results were promised for 1963, but the Broncos absorbed a 59–7 loss to Kansas City (Lamar Hunt had given up in Dallas and moved his team to K.C.), and Tripucka reluctantly retired after two games. The quarterback shuffle was beginning. Denver didn't win once in its final ten games, and ended up 2–11–1. In three seasons the Broncos had finished 0–7–1, 0–7, and 0–9–1, in the latter segments of each year. No fast-closing team here. "Denver is the next best thing to an open date," said a player on another team. The Broncos were the laughingstock of the AFL. They were drafting great players—like Merlin Olsen—but didn't have the money to compete with NFL bidders.

Realizing the need for a shakeup in 1964, Faulkner participated in a massive nine-player trade with the New York Jets. And it came just before the AFL signed a $36 million contract with NBC. The network had opted, after losing the NFL telecasts to another network, to make the struggling AFL a big-time entity in sports. Although the infusion of new money helped the Broncos survive, they were still not a big-time anything on the field. Jacky Lee was obtained from Houston on an odd "lend-lease deal" (he was to return in two years), as the Broncos tried to solve the continuing quarterback problem. But Lee wasn't the answer, and, following a 0–4 start, Faulkner was replaced by Mac Speedie, the former All-Pro with Cleveland. Nevertheless, the record was identical to the previous season, even though Speedie turned to the crowd during an upset over Kansas City (33–27) and led the fans in "Go Broncos." The first combination coach-cheerleader.

Matters weren't fine off the field, either. In a January 1965 league meeting, part-owner Kunz indicated that the team might be sold to interests in another city. There were those in Philadelphia, Atlanta, and Cincinnati who wanted the franchise. So a fight for control of the Broncos developed, with Gerald and Allan Phipps, who had inherited wealth, fighting the ownership bloc led by Kunz. The Phipps brothers were finally able to purchase 52 percent from the other stockholders, giving them almost 100 percent ownership. There was no question that they would keep the team in Denver. "I was more a baseball fan, but I thought if Denver lost its football team, it would be a black eye for the city, and I was more interested that Denver didn't look like a bush-league town," said Gerald Phipps, owner of a construction business. He and his brother, an attorney, have retained ownership of the team ever since, turning a $1.5 million investment into a franchise worth $20 million or more. The takeover by the Phippses may have been just the necessary injection. More than twenty-two thousand season tickets were purchased for 1965, and the Broncos' future was, at last, secure. People who never cared about football were talking about the Broncos. At the same time, Denver was becoming metropolitan.

The city was hurriedly growing because of the infusion of young people from other parts of the country. Colorado was booming as the new California. Local bumper stickers read: "Don't Californicate Colorado." Those coming in had been exposed to professional football in other locales. They wanted to see the game, even if it involved a team that had wallowed in ineptness. Along the downtown skyline a skyscraper was appearing here and there. And the city limits spread along the front range of the Rockies. So the timing was right for the Broncos to emerge as a popular item.

But the team kept failing. Cookie Gilchrist, probably the best-known player in the league at the time, a hard-pouring fullback, was signed by Denver, but not without contract hassles. "He wants a telephone in his Cadillac," moaned a team official. The Broncos had a new, wide-eyed assistant coach, Red Miller, in charge of the offensive line. "We had fun. We weren't any good but we did have fun," Miller says. Denver's second-half slide in 1965 was 1–7, and the team concluded with a 4–10 record. The Broncos opened the 1966 season without Gilchrist, who had been All-AFL the previous year. The team wouldn't give one of his ex-teammates a tryout, and he blasted the front office in return, saying it was not "first class." Denver probably could have used Gilchrist against Houston, but he most likely wouldn't have made the difference in a 45–7 defeat. Denver didn't make a first down the whole game.

Mac Speedie became the latest coach to depart, with Ray Malavasi, an intelligent, cherubic assistant taking over. Denver rallied to beat Houston, 40–38, on a field goal from 46 yards out with twenty-seven seconds left, but it was about the only bright spot in another 4–10 season. The Broncos lost by more than 40 points twice to the Kansas City Chiefs, and in one,

K.C. coach Hank Stram ordered onside kicks with his team well out in front. "I didn't want our guys down in front of those South Standers," a reference to the boisterous group that had become more and more rowdy in the stands originally built for the baseball league that never succeeded. The ticket-holders in the South Stands felt like an inferior, but well-knit group, and bombarded visiting teams with snowballs and bottles and acted insanely when the Broncos came close.

The Broncos, meanwhile, had been lifted by the biggest news in the history of pro football. On June 7 the two leagues, the AFL and the NFL, had agreed to merge. The Broncos had lost all their high draft choices to the other league, which would no longer happen, but, more important, with the amalgamation, they would finally be gaining the recognition of being a part of the number one football league. One day after the season ended, Lou Saban was named coach and general manager, signing a ten-year contract. Saban had been at Buffalo, Boston, and the University of Maryland, and was considered among the elite coaches in the game. The feeling in Denver was that the corner had been turned.

At the time the Broncos were training outside the city stadium on a field that measured just 60 yards, and it was said that that was the major reason the team's drives always ended up 40 yards short in a regular game. A bond issue to expand the football stadium was turned down—there were still a considerable number of non-football types in Denver—but the true fans organized a drive, with pennies and pension checks coming in, and the stadium size was indeed increased. And in 1967 the Broncos finally signed a number one draft choice. Floyd Little, a running back out of the University of Syracuse, would become the city's initial and only true pro sports hero before his career was finished.

The Broncos were scheduled to play an exhibition against the Detroit Lions of the NFL, and Detroit defensive lineman Alex Karras said if his club lost to these upstarts from Denver, "I will walk back to Detroit." He shouldn't have made the declaration. The Broncos became the first AFL team to beat an established NFL club, and Karras wasn't even around for the end. He had been kicked out. A record crowd of thirty-five thousand showed up for the opener on the strength of Saban's arrival and the victory over Detroit, but it wasn't to be—not for a very long time. Denver was 3–11 in 1967. "This is the beginning," Saban said. The beginning of what? It was more of the same. Gilchrist racked up his knee, and his career was ended. In one game Denver punter Bob Scarpitto ran on fourth down and was smothered, and Denver lost a few plays later.

For the 1968 season the stadium was increased to fifty thousand seats and renamed Mile High Stadium, since Denver was located a mile above sea level. Hopes were grandiose. However, Denver lost the first game to an expansion team, Cincinnati, and there were cries at the end: "Wait till next year." Denver's, record for that year: 5–9. Marlin Briscoe became the first black AFL quarterback as the Broncos' revolving door swung at that position. Briscoe, a rookie from the University of Nebraska–Omaha, took over for Steve Tensi, who had started the year at quarterback. And it's not likely Tensi will ever forget his tenure in Denver. By now the fans were rabid—turning out at fifty thousand per game. They had waited too long, they felt, for a winner. So Tensi was selected the target of their frustrations. Garbage was dumped on his lawn; his kids were harassed at school, and he had to change his telephone number constantly because of obscene phone calls. Tensi jokes circulated the city.

"Lou Saban asked Steve Tensi to guess how many footballs he had in a bag over his shoulder. 'If you guess right, I'll give you both of them,' Saban said. And Tensi replied, 'Three.' "

"Steve Tensi tried to commit suicide by firing a bullet into his head. He missed."

Denver played Oakland, which was without starting quarterback Daryle Lamonica. But George Blanda, then forty-one, opened at quarterback for the first time in two years, and the Raiders had 12 points before Denver's offense ever got the ball. Blanda threw four touchdown passes, kicked two field goals, and added five extra points in the blowout.

The next year the Broncos didn't lose as many games, but they didn't win any more, by benefit of a tie, and finished 5–8–1. Steve O'Neal, a punter for the New York Jets, provided the only real excitement in Denver, kicking a ball 98 yards in the rarefied air.

Tensi remained at quarterback in 1970, but the boos continued to haunt him. The Broncos tried to counter public opinion by signing Bobby Anderson, a local hero from the University of Colorado. He teamed with Little to give Denver an explosive backfield, and Little won the AFC rushing title with 901 yards. The Broncos started 4–1 and teased the city again, but then their record became 4–5. At 5–7 late in the year the Broncos had a chance to finish .500 for only the second time in their history. However, with the score 17–17 with just eleven seconds left at San Diego, quarterback Alan Pastrana ran a keeper to San Diego's 35-yard line to set up a possible winning field goal. But Pastrana was knocked cold on the play, and he was the only Denver player authorized to call a timeout. The clock ran out. So much for a .500 season. Tensi retired, although he was only twenty-eight. "Football is not fun anymore." The people of Denver had not made it much fun for him.

Don Horn then arrived as the latest quarterback in 1971. The former All-American had been Bart Starr's backup at Green Bay and was getting his first real chance at starting. "I think I can help this team out of the doldrums," he said then. He says now: "I wasn't in good shape, and it didn't work out." Horn has returned to Denver as president of an emerging pro rodeo team. Most of the Denver players were staying in town once their careers ended. One is a television sportscaster; another owns a bar; another sells used cars, and an ex-Bronco kicker has a chain of laundries.

Early on that season Denver played Miami (who went on to win the Super Bowl), and the score was tied, 10–10. Saban decided on the sidelines to play it conservatively and ran the clock out in the fourth quarter from his own territory. Afterward Saban said: "Half a loaf is better than none at all." That one line was to destroy Saban in Denver. He was forever known as Half-a-Loaf Saban and couldn't live it down. "We had chances. They had chances. We blew them." Saban, currently the coach at the University of Miami, says that the half-a-loaf line was his undoing, "but it was the right strategy in that situation." Horn was inspired against his old teammates, the

Packers, but lost anyway 34–13. On November 17, after a loss to Cincinnati, Saban resigned as coach. "What can I say? Anything I say now people will take as an excuse." Jerry Smith, the offensive line coach, was elevated, but the club had a 4–9–1 mark. Another dismal year. The community was restless. Saban quit as general manager, and the search was on for a head coach.

Up stepped John Ralston, the seventh coach in the club's young history. Ralston had been quite successful at Stanford, taking the Cardinals to a pair of Rose Bowls. He got the job after Bill Petersen, who had agreed to terms, couldn't secure a release from a contract with the Houston Oilers. (Petersen wouldn't last long in pro ball.) Ralston was named both coach and general manager and brought his rah-rah, Dale Carnegie-inspired philosophy with him. "Our goal is to get a team in the Super Bowl, and believe you me, we'll do that," he said in his first speech. The fans liked Ralston's positive attitude; several players didn't. Dave Costa was the first weeded out when he and Ralston couldn't communicate. Ralston was a disciple of Carnegie, preached the words to his staff and encouraged them to take a course in it. Ralston realized, also, that the team needed more than positiveness. It was in desperate need of a quarterback. Wasn't it always? So he traded for Charley Johnson, a journeyman with Houston, and took the team away from home for the first time—to Pomona, California, for a training camp. The Broncos won their opener, and Ralston was making believers out of most. But the team swiftly slid back into old ways and ended 4–9.

The 1973 season seemed, at last, like the one. But Denver had thought the same before. The Broncos played on "Monday Night Football" for the first time. The city council had aided by giving funds to improve the lighting at Mile High Stadium. In the final four seconds against Oakland, Denver's Jim Turner kicked a 35-yard field goal for a 23–23 tie. Rather than make the mistake of his "half-a-loaf" predecessor, Ralston said afterward: "Well, it's better to be the tie-or than the tie-ee." The Broncos beat San Diego, 42–28, to assure the club of its first winning season, and Denver still had a chance to win the division on the strength of a seven-game unbeaten string, heading into the final game at Oakland, with a 7–4–2 record. Denver trailed, 14–10, in the third quarter and had a fourth and ten situation from its own forty-nine. Ralston, noted for his gimmickry, decided on a fake punt. The ball was centered to blocker Joe Dawkins, who was supposed to hand off to rookie running back Otis Armstrong, coming across the backfield. However, Dawkins had trouble getting the ball and kept it. He was buried for a one-yard loss. "We knew it was coming," Oakland coach John Madden said. "We didn't play for a punt." Three plays later Ken Stabler hooked up with Mike Siani for a touchdown. The Broncos still had time, but quarterback Johnson was knocked silly, and Steve Ramsey was called on without warming up. He threw a touchdown in the final moments, but it wasn't enough. Oakland went on to the playoffs, and Denver was left with the satisfaction of its best season. When the players returned home from Oakland, a wild reception awaited. "Gee, if we ever accomplish something, imagine how these people are going to be—if they are like this when we lose," guard Tommy Lyons said to a couple of players as they waded through the mob.

Ralston was ready in 1974. He already had been named coach of the year and had Denver convinced. On the visor in his car, on the mirror in his bathroom, and on the desk at his office the coach had signs that said: "Finish 12–2, go to and win the Super Bowl." To his associates he said: "That's all I want to do. That's my only goal. And we're going to do it." Ralston even wondered aloud to public relations director Bob Peck: "How do you think our players will act when they get to the Super Bowl? We must start training them to be prepared for all the attention they'll get."

Peck looked at him strangely and replied: "Don't you think we should work on getting there first?"

"Oh, it's going to happen, Bob. It'll happen."

Denver won four exhibitions, and the citizenry passed a $25 million bond issue to expand the stadium to seventy-five thousand seats. The fans were recognized as among the most delirious in the National Football League. The fifty thousand season tickets were gobbled up immediately every February, and a waiting list of more than twenty five thousand existed. Thus, the need for an expansion.

In the second game Denver participated in the league's first overtime—against Pittsburgh and young black quarterback Joe Gilliam, who completed thirty-five passes. The game ended in a tie, 35–35. Otis Armstrong had a 1,000-yard season, taking over for the aging statesman Little. But the Broncos weren't destined to be 12–2.

Going into the last game of the season at San Diego, Denver was 7–5–1 and had a chance to improve their previous best. Gerald Phipps walked into the locker room and announced: "Gentlemen, you'll be happy to know that I've just signed John Ralston to a new five-year contract." Only Little clapped. The others looked at each other. Under his breath, one defensive lineman said: "Five more years of this shit." Dissension was setting in. The Broncos went out on the field and were promptly shut out by the Chargers.

Ralston hadn't given up, but 1975 was a return to the bad times. The club had a 6–8 record, saved only by the final appearance of Little, who announced his retirement and exited in style with 56 yards rushing, five receptions for 94 yards, and a pair of touchdowns, including a 66-yard pass, as Denver beat Philadelphia on an Arctic day in Denver. But the remaining players weren't satisfied. Quarterback Johnson decided to retire because of Ralston's continued presence, and the others decided to talk to Phipps. They went to the owner in small groups and said they couldn't handle the Ralston-Carnegie approach. But Phipps demurred. He said Ralston would return. "We pointed out all the things wrong with Ralston's philosophy, but nothing helped," said one player. "We were stuck with him." Ralston told the players he would bring in a quality quarterback, trading for Jim Plunkett, his quarterback at Stanford and a Heisman Trophy winner. He was being offered for trade by New England. The players thought maybe a change was indeed coming from Ralston, but in midsummer, the coach changed only his mind. He announced that Steve Ramsey, a long-time mediocre sub with a sidearm motion, would be his starter. The players were at the breaking point.

The club lost the opener in Cincinnati, 17–7, but then reeled off three impressive victories. Maybe Ralston was right and the players wrong, some were saying. However, the Broncos flew to Houston and ran right into real trouble. Offensive coordinator Max Coley was forced into the hospital because of stomach problems the day before the game, and Ralston had to take over his chores. Ralston had never concerned himself with specific game plans. He wasn't aware of the overall offense. "He didn't know anything," claimed one player. "He came into a defensive backfield meeting and had the assistant explain to him what kind of zone we were using. Talk about jerks." Ralston had an opportunity to prove himself in Houston, but the offensive broke down and Denver lost, 17–3. Defensive end Lyle Alzado was watching the game with friends at his Denver home. He was out for the season with a knee injury. When the Broncos failed to churn out a first down again in the third quarter, Alzado grabbed his crutch and threw it through the television screen. The TV shattered. Everyone else in the room got up and walked out. Lyle sat there and muttered: "We got to get rid of that son of a bitch." The Dirty Dozen, as they were to be named, was born at that moment.

Soon Denver was 3–3, but eventually won three more in a row and was 7–4 going into a game at New England with a respectable shot at the playoffs. Denver came out on the field, and a New England assistant, Red Miller, glanced over at them. "Their assholes are as tight as my fist," Miller told another assistant. "We're loose. We've got this game." It was a rout. New England won, 38–14, and the playoffs were only a continuing elusive dream for Denver. The Broncos had their best record, 9–5, but a cloud hung over the team. So many had believed that, with the easy schedule and the improving team, the Broncos should have been in the playoffs. The players were ready to act. "That record don't mean a thing," said Otis Armstrong. "The worst we could have done with that schedule was 9–5."

Shortly after the season ended Ralston was stripped of his general manager title. Fred Gehrke, a likable sort who handled the players' contracts and still managed to be respected was upgraded from assistant general manager. Ralston was offered the opportunity to remain as coach and took it. "He's come this far with the team," Gehrke told one of the owners, "he should be able to stay."

But Ralston fired Coley—a move that upset Gehrke. Their

relationship strained as Ralston flew off to scout the Blue-Gray All-Star game. But the players tried to help the situation along. On December 20 a dozen of them—Armstrong, Alzado, Billy Thompson, Rick Upchurch, Jon Keyworth, Tom Jackson, Haven Moses, Billy van Heusen, Jim Kiick, Carl Schaukowitch, Tommy Lyons, and John Grant, all of whom lived in Denver during the off season—met at a midtown Holiday Inn. The group was made up of veterans and young players, offensive and defensive players, blacks and whites, starters and hangers-on, so the representation was mixed. After several hours of emotional discussion, the Dirty Dozen, as the bench labeled itself, drafted a statement. "We can't take this anymore," Alzado told the others. Thompson hollered to the others: "We can't let him blow it for us." The players manned the telephones and got a total of thirty-two players of the forty-three-man roster to sign their statement. And the next morning members of the Denver sports media were hastily called to a press conference at the motel.

A friendly sportscaster telephoned the Broncos' offices, but Gehrke had already heard about the event on his radio. So he and Gerald Phipps rushed to the Holiday Inn and asked to speak privately with the players for a moment. "If you will hold off on this statement, we'll try to do something. Give us some time. If you read this, you'll be making a mistake we can't undo," Phipps told them. The players finally agreed; Gehrke and Phipps departed, and the press corps was called in. Thompson, the group's spokesman, read a revised statement saying that the players were "in full support of the ownership and Fred Gehrke and we will try to do everything possible to bring this city a championship." No mention of Ralston was made.

When the brief conference ended, the press left grumbling about the meaninglessness of the statement. One player cornered a writer. "Meet me out back." There he handed a writer a copy of the original statement. "You know what to do with this." In front of the motel two more players sat in a car and called the writer over. "Here. Here's what we were going to say. Just say it was leaked."

The writer peered into the car. "This is no leak. It's a flood."

The original statement said: "We don't believe it is possible to win a championship under the guidance of John Ralston. He has lost the respect of his players and we don't believe he is capable of coaching us to a championship."

Quite defaming. In spite of the attempts to keep it away from the public, the statement appeared the next morning in the *Rocky Mountain News*. Phipps saw it and called Gehrke: "I've never seen anything handled so miserably."

Ralston rushed back to Denver and released a statement of his own, saying he would remain as the Broncos' coach. "Young people are impetuous and make mistakes. I'm not a vindictive person," he said publicly. But privately he was steaming. Van Heusen, the team's punter and a backup wide receiver, was ordered by Phipps to apologize to Ralston, and the coach badgered him for over an hour about the players. "I've never done anything to them," he shouted at van Heusen. Later in the day van Heusen told another player: "I think we made a mistake. He's more determined to keep the job than ever before. That statement has brought management together."

Yet, five weeks later, in a sudden move, it was announced that John Ralston had resigned as coach of the Broncos. Gehrke and Phipps had met and decided that hiring a fresh coach was the only feasible way out of the predicament. So Ralston was called in and informed. They made it easier on Ralston by saying he had resigned. In fact, he was fired. Ralston's statement to the press was terse. "I wish the Broncos all the success in the world," and he left. That night Ralston sat on his bed alone and cried for the first time as a grown man.

Ralston moved into an office at the Dale Carnegie Associates. He was to obtain no other coaching offers, so he stayed in Denver and observed the 1977 season from close-up, yet from afar. He didn't attend the games or practices or even go out to the club's offices. Like Richard Nixon, Ralston became an exiled ex-leader.

"I won't criticize anybody about what happened," Ralston said later. "I don't think in negatives. We made some real progress here. This town accepted losers when I came. Not anymore."

Gehrke reflected the decision: "John wanted to be loved. He used to call people into his office and plead with them to like him. Promise them anything. And when he didn't live up to his promises, they ran to me and complained. Instead of strengthening his position, his approach worked against him. Finally, they were all laughing at him in the end."

As Thompson had said: "Under Ralston our offense was like a ballet—one, two, three, kick." So they were laughing at him when the end came on January 31.

Gehrke had been looking for a new offensive coordinator before the firing and heard nothing but good reports about Red Miller at New England. So he flew in Miller, the former Denver assistant, and discussed the position, but Miller told him: "I'm not prepared to move laterally. The next job I want is as a head man." So when the Ralston firing occurred, Gehrke immediately thought again of Miller. He picked up the phone and called Miller in Boston. "You said your next job will be as a head man. How would you like to be a head man in Denver?"

Miller was quiet a moment, then replied: "You got yourself a coach." Miller became the team's eighth coach. The city of Denver was still searching for one to take them to the playoffs. Could Miller do it? If he couldn't, maybe they could go back to the vertical socks and do a vaudeville show.

6

RED AND ORANGE DON'T ALWAYS CLASH

Red hair on destiny's children should be an influential sign. That particular colored strand of foliage points to and permeates professional coaching. Maybe a kid stuck with the label "Red" feels the greater urge to ascend to a position of power over brown-, black-, and blond-haired types. Besides, red is an indicator of fieriness, burning desire.

Red Hickey coached the San Francisco 49ers; Red Auerbach coached the Boston Celtics; Red Schoendienst managed the St. Louis Cardinals; Red Holzman coached the New York Knicks; Red Kelly coached the Toronto Maple Leafs. Red, red, red.

So when Robert "Red" Miller was born in Macomb, Illinois, maybe his future had already been designed for him. Son of a coal miner and grandson to a muleteer, he saw life early from the bottom up. There were ten children in the Miller house—six boys and four girls—and young Robert shared his bedroom with three brothers. "I automatically got the nickname 'Red.' I had flaming red hair."

The family came together once a day, gathering around a long table for the dinner meal. "The food started in front with the breadwinner. Then it was passed along according to age." Robert was the youngest, "so sometimes there wasn't a lot left by the time it reached me. Maybe that's why I'm hungry."

Hunger turned to sickness when Miller missed a year of elementary school with double pneumonia, "and I had a lot of time to think about where I was going. I didn't want to be in the mines. That's all I knew." So he became a self-acknowl-edged "hell-bent-for-leather" youth whose total existence re-volved around sports.

He studied his high-school coaches and decided that coaching was the route out of the mines. "We had a career day, and a man came to the high school to talk to us about what we were going to be. I didn't even have to think about it. I knew my adult life would be spent in football. I couldn't see myself punching a time clock and going to work in a mine or a factory at four in the morning. College was the answer." He went off to Western Illinois to play football. It was 1946, and veterans from the war were returning to continue their education and football career. A freshman named Miller began the season as the sixteenth left offensive guard. Before the year was over he was on the first team, replacing the team captain. Still, Miller could have won a Howdy Doody lookalike contest—red hair, freckles, broad-based smile. Give him some jeans, tie a string around his arm, and he would be perfect to ask, "Hey, kids, what time is it?"

Miller wanted to be the best. "I was intense, and I still am. When I set out to do something, I generally accomplish it." For three seasons he was selected as Most Valuable Player at Western Illinois, a startling achievement for a guard. Linemen generally receive about as many honors as the team mascot. As good as he was, though, Miller wasn't considered pro-football material at 195 pounds. There were only twelve professional football teams, and a young charger from a small school in Illinois was brushed aside. So he took his degree in physical education—with a minor in journalism ("I studied journalism because it was easy")—and got a job coaching at Astoria (Illinois) High School. Until he joined Denver, it was his only head-coaching experience. The next year he moved to Canton (Ohio) High as an assistant and then joined Carthage College.

"I had pretty much decided I was going to become the best possible high-school coach, and accepting that until I got the call from Art Keller," Miller said. Keller and Miller were a two-man staff at Carthage. "We won games like crazy," Keller says. "I could take from Red's personality, his positiveness, and his enthusiasm that he wasn't going to be with me long. He hasn't changed. I saw him on TV in a Denver game, and he's the same coach."

Miller was good, and Lou Saban, the coach at Western Illinois, noticed, selecting him as an assistant at his alma mater. Miller, more or less, hitched his coaching wagon to Saban's star. In 1960 Saban was picked as coach of the Boston Patriots of the new American Football League, and he asked Miller and another assistant, Joe Collier, to join him. The trio moved to Buffalo in 1962, and a year later Miller parted from Saban, heading to Denver as an offensive line coach. Miller never realized what the three-year stay in Denver would mean. He left in 1966. "I said good-bye to Denver and figured I wouldn't be back. Funny."

Miller was beginning to think his livelihood was destined as an assistant. He had gone on to St. Louis and settled in, when, after the 1970 season, he was fired for the first and only time from a job. "I prefer to say I was released." The 1970 Cardinals finished 8–5–1 and had a chance at the playoffs until a season-ending loss at Washington. The entire staff was dumped, but that didn't keep Miller from applying for the head coaching job. He lost out, but took it philosophically. "It turned out all right. I was hired as an assistant at Baltimore, and it was another step in my learning career. Besides," he laughed, "St. Louis headed down the next year."

Miller's big break occurred in 1973 when Chuck Fairbanks was named head coach of the New England Patriots, and he turned over the offense to Miller. The Patriots became a force in the National Football League while Miller was developing potent offensive linemen like John Hannah and Leon Gray and tight end Russ Francis, but his dream of advancing to a head coaching job wasn't being realized. No one paid much attention to Miller. Some said the reason was that Miller was Goodtime Red, that he loved to straddle a bar and have more than an occasional drink, and he was always up for a party and some good storytelling. He was definitely a late-night jockey. An excellent coach and a super guy, the executives said, but not the ideal man for a head job. In 1974, in fact, he flew into Chicago to talk about the top job with the Chicago Fire of the World Football League, but he was passed over in favor of a former pro quarterback, Babe Parilli.

So it was in 1976 that Miller made a decision. "I'm sure my reputation had something to do with keeping me from getting a head-coaching job, so I quit drinking altogether—cold—and prepared myself to be as serious as I've ever been about football. I was getting close to being fifty years old, and I thought this would be my last push. Either I was going to make it as a head coach now or never."

He had already declined an opportunity to join his two brothers in their cinder-block business. "They talked to me about an executive-type job, but, you know, it was never for me, even if I wasn't going to be a head coach. Football was the thing."

It was a good year to push. New England was a playoff contender and destroyed Oakland in its only regular-season defeat. The Denver Broncos arrived in late November, with both teams concerned about postseason play. New England killed Denver and made the playoffs, but two controversial calls in the game with the Raiders cost the Patriots and Miller their first visit to the Super Bowl.

Meanwhile, across country in Denver, an upheaval had begun. The players wanted John Ralston out as coach. Miller was approached about the offensive coordinator's position, but declined. Then Miller was suddenly thrust into the head-coaching position he had desired for seventeen years as an NFL assistant. "I know Red well, and I know what he has done with the offense in New England. We have to do something about our offense. He's matured the last few years, and reports from around the league indicate he's regarded as one of the top three offensive coaches in the business," Gehrke told the Broncos' owners. "I know he has a strong hand and will run a tight ship, and that's what we need after the Ralston fiasco. Plus, when a team beats you like he did us last season, with material we feel is no better than ours in many respects, you've got to think he knows what he's doing."

On February 1, the new coach was introduced. The night before he had called wife, Nancy, and told her the news. "I had just about figured it wasn't ever going to happen, but my time, I guess, has come," she heard. He was dressed like a pharmaceutical salesman—given to browns and tweeds—and is just as conservative in politics and life-style. He reads all types of books, has never touched a cigarette, and no longer needs whiskey as a crutch. But he claimed not to look with an ill eye on those whose preferences sway in other directions.

At his first press conference he evaded some tough questions, completely ducked others, and talked in generalities. At one point he put his hands together as if in prayer, and the picture moved on the wire services the next day. It was as if he were looking for help from above. At one point he was talking about the team's quarterbacks and said: "I like Craig Penrose. Craig is his first name, isn't it?" He refused to speculate, probably realizing how that had cost his predecessor. "I'm here to do a job, and I'm here to do it right. Predictions? I want to win. Period.

"I'm not on any ego trip. It's a good opportunity for me, and I intend to make the most of it. I think the Denver Broncos are a good football team. I think with the addition of a few players in the right spots we can be an outstanding team. We're not going to fuss about the little things. I'm a coach who wants to get the job done, and who will take whatever steps necessary to do it.

"I'm not bashful. I'm going to win." He was peering through blue eyes—almost directly. He had a ruddy countenance, softening a rugged face. The red hair had all but disappeared over the years. "You will not find one player who has a bad thing to say about Red," New England linebacker Steve Zabel said a few weeks later in Steamboat Springs, Colorado. "He's a player's coach. He'll cut a guy, and the player will walk off loving him. How many guys can you say that about?"

Miller said his coaching philosophy had been derived from several sources. "I took some from Lou Saban—his hard-nosed approach to the game and his ability to deal with players. From Don McCafferty I took his way of handling an individual. Chuck Fairbanks has a great ability to organize and then to delegate work. And he was great with attitude. Morale isn't something you pull on like an overcoat. You build it up day by day by establishing a certain climate with the team."

Mac Speedie, a previous head coach with the Broncos and

now one of the scouts, looked at Miller from the back of the room. "You can't compare him to others, really. Red's his own man. The thing with Red is that quality of extreme knowledge combined with great rapport with players."

And Allan Phipps, one of the owners, said: "Only time will tell us if we have come up with the right answers to the questions being asked. I hope we've found the answer this time."

The cameras were taken out of the room, and the press wandered in the hallway. Miller walked over to Gehrke. "How did I do?"

"You did just fine. But I think you'll do even better on the football field."

Miller didn't have to worry about coal mines. But he did have to worry about an upcoming season.

7

A TALE OF THREE PLAYERS

Shortly after Red Miller took over the Broncos he called the veterans in for a mini-camp. At the first morning meeting the players were somewhat cautious—not knowing what to expect of the new regime. So they filed down the hall in the Broncos' office building, past the old pictures of days gone by, and stopped, as they always had, at the soda pop machine and carried their drinks onto the racquetball court, converted into a meeting room.

"Gentlemen," Miller said. "When we come into this room, we are here to work. Don't bring your Cokes in here. Do you get the point?"

The Broncos got the point. They knew who the coach was. They immediately perked.

By now Miller had looked at the films of last year's Broncos games and knew what had to be done. A quarterback had to be found, and the offensive line had to be improved considerably. So he and Gehrke wrote down a list of possible available quarterbacks, compared it, and saw Craig Morton's name near the top of both. "Let's go after him," Gehrke told Miller, and he made the phone call. At the same time the New York Giants were trying to deal the aging quarterback. He had been booed mercilessly in New York and was the focal point of media criticism. The Giants were willing, and the Broncos said they would give up Steve Ramsey, whose worth ended in Denver when John Ralston was ousted. So a trade was made hurriedly. In

New York a writer said that day: "Denver gave us their shit for our shit. It was an even trade."

Miller began calling the players in one by one. He told them very succinctly: "I'm not here to get my name in lights. I'm here to coach football. You can either help us or get the hell out of the way. I don't know anything about what happened with Ralston. When somebody tries to tell me the names of the players involved, I stop them. We're starting new here. I want you in shape and ready to play football. I didn't come here to lose."

And that word had sifted down to the assistants. Babe Parilli, hired as the quarterback coach, loved to play golf, and April was the time for coaches to catch up on their game. Bob Peck walked in one day and asked Parilli to join him in a round.

"There will be no golf playing this summer."

"What's the problem?"

"Hey, we're under the gun here," Parilli replied. "We're expected to win right away."

"Oh, the people aren't expecting miracles this year."

"Maybe not, but we might just give them one."

In mid-August the candidates began arriving at Fort Collins, Colorado, home of Colorado State University, some 60 miles north of Denver, and the site of the Broncos' training camp. Just before Miller left to drive up, he scanned a bulletin board with the names and vital statistics of all the players. "We are about to find out what this bunch is made of. I know we can't accomplish a lot in terms of record this season, but we sure as hell can get this outfit moving in the right direction."

Checking into his room at Fort Collins, Scott Levenhagen was concerned about his weight. A tight-end possibility, Levenhagen had been told to report at 225 pounds—well up from the weight he played with at Western Illinois. His roommate, Ron Egloff, also would be vying for a tight-end spot on the team. "I really don't know what I weigh," Levenhagen told Egloff. "At home my mother kept changing the scales. She didn't want to know about her own weight. At night I weighed 220, but I was down to 214 the next day." At the weigh-in, though, the rookie was right on the mark at 225. He sighed.

But that was just the first obstacle. Levenhagen recognized the task before him. Denver had four tight ends on the roster, including veteran holdovers Riley Odoms and Boyd Brown. And Levenhagen wasn't a glamorized high-draft choice. He was Denver's twelfth pick, the team's last. Only eleven players were selected lower in the entire draft. But he did have one position angle. The coach, Miller, had also played at Western Illinois.

"Football was just a way to get through school for me," Levenhagen recalls, "but then I had a pretty good year as a junior, and the scouts started coming around. So I got serious my senior year and had a good year. I thought I might be drafted, and when I heard Denver picked me, I was excited. A lot of people come to Denver on vacation, so it's got to be a pretty good place." Levenhagen, 6'5" and long on hair, was no student of the game. "I keep up with the Packers, and that's about it." He was aware that chances were slim as he unpacked, "but I can always say I gave it a try. I enjoy the game, and I came out here to have some fun. Realistically, I'm not in a good position. But I'm not going to be nervous. I'm not going to sit in my room and sweat while wondering if there will be a knock on the door and somebody asking me to bring my playbook. I guess that's the way they do it. It's like that in the movies. I just found out there won't be any cuts made until August 9, so that means I'll get to play in the first preseason game. That's super. At least I'll be able to say I played with Riley Odoms. Who knows? I can play this game pretty good. I may just surprise everyone—me, too—and make this team. If I don't, I'll manage."

Another rookie was much more sure of himself than Levenhagen. But on the first day, on the Colorado State practice field, Bucky Dilts sat on the sidelines, disgusted. "I punt all summer long, and, then, before I can even punt one time in camp, I pull a muscle in the 40-yard dash. Can you beat that shit? If I were the coach of this team I wouldn't make punters run dashes. Too much risk of a pulled muscle. Look at me."

But nobody was looking at Dilts in camp. After all, he was just 5'9" on a 183-pound frame. Chunky. And he was left-footed, of all things. The press guide even called him Pucky

Dilts. "He won't last out the week," said one coach. "Doesn't even look like a punter." But Dilts would beg to disagree. "If this leg will just mend, I'll prove I can punt. I know I'm better than the other guys here. My hang time is great. I just hope they don't cut me before I'm able to get over this injury and show them." However, the Broncos had traded for veteran punter Herman "Thunderfoot" Weaver, giving up two high draft choices to the Detroit Lions, and three other impressive young punters were in camp. Dilts was a lowly free agent with a bum leg. "I know people aren't used to seeing short, squatty punters who are left-footed. Most punters are tall and lean and right-footed. But my size doesn't bother me, and it shouldn't bother anybody else."

This wasn't Dilts's first struggle to impress, though, and maybe his talk had to be big to get the coaches' attention. He had been a walk-on at the University of Georgia, and nobody watched. Then one day he walked directly up to head football coach Vince Dooley and told him: "You should at least take a look at me." According to Dilts, Dooley "acted like he didn't even know who I was, but off that he gave me a chance, and I was the regular punter the rest of my college career." Dilts thought he would be drafted, but a call never came. "I was disturbed, but then, after the draft, I got calls from four NFL teams, and I decided on Denver because of the climate and since the club needed a punter."

Dilts pointed to the rest of the players. "Look at them. They all think punters are a bunch of whimps who can't do anything else. That's all right. A punter is valuable. I can be a help to this team, and if they don't want me, I'll find another team that can use me. They're gonna have to run me out of football."

Billy Thompson didn't have to show the Broncos' coaching staff. He was a solid eight-year veteran at strong safety. Some said he was among the best in the league, but had never been picked to any of the all-teams. By now he had accepted his fate. "I used to think honors were important, but I got over it. Now I just want to play well and hope the team does well."

Thompson sat behind the dormitory under a shade tree, wearing a straw hat and cutoff jeans, with a blade of grass in his teeth. A cane pole, a can of worms, and a small pond and he would be right at home. It was summertime, and the livin' wasn't easy in Fort Collins. "Red is working our butts off. But I can see a difference—a good one. It's hard on us, but it's gonna make us better. Ralston was too easy." Thompson almost spit out the last sentence. "We're so far ahead of last year.

"Red Miller is organized, and he knows the game. Red Miller isn't trying to prove anything to us about himself. He knows he can coach pros, and he knows we know." Thompson, who had just turned thirty, was a realist. "We aren't there yet. I was hoping some more trades would be made. We have shaky areas on offense, and I'm not going to kid myself. A few things could fall into place, and we could shake some things up. But we're not going to be great. But this year we aren't going to lose games because we are out-coached."

Thompson hadn't always been a defensive back. He played some quarterback around Greenville, South Carolina, as an army brat at a Catholic high school, and was about to go off to Grambling College, where all the good young black players in the South went, when Emerson Boozer and Art Shell, who would become standouts in pro football themselves, "kidnapped" him after an all-star game and carried him to Maryland State.

"But they don't have any scholarships," Thompson told his elders.

"We'll take care of you, kid," Boozer said. And Thompson had a scholarship a few weeks later. He became a defensive back at Maryland State and was drafted by the Broncos. But they had selected six defensive backs that year. "I was able to outlast all of them. I'm still here, aren't I? Nobody around the rest of the world knows I'm here, but I'm here."

Three days into camp Scott Levenhagen quit the squad, packed up his belongings, and went home. "This is not for me," he said on the way out.

That same day Bucky Dilts got his chance to punt. The leg had mended sufficiently. "Hey, that kid may be mouthing off a lot, but he's pretty good," said special teams coach Marv Braden. Dilts made the team, beat out Weaver, and was named to the NFL All-Rookie team.

And Thompson was selected All-Pro in 1977.

8

RAGTIME RED

The first day of training camp Red Miller drove his golf cart and his players hard. The head man had ordered a golf cart so he could get from one end of the field to the other without wasting a moment. "There's so much to do," he said as he pulled the cart to a stop. "I am pleased with the conditioning but not with the results. But at least we got it going. I can shuffle papers only so long."

When the veterans joined the camp during the second week, the squad included twenty-nine holdovers, twenty-two free agents, and nine draft choices. Miller had cut down considerably the number invited to camp. In past years Ralston had brought in as many as one hundred, hoping to find a pearl among the oysters. "We can't spend a lot of time with guys we know can't make this team," Miller said. "Everyone of these guys has a legitimate chance." A young man named Mike Dunafon had been cut the year before, went on a strict weight-training program, got himself up to 223, and appeared at camp for another try at running back. He brought with him an orange Corvette, apparently searching for any edge. But the coaches had the form on Dunafon right away. While the other players walked the half mile to the training table every day, Dunafon got in his Vet, drove around a cement barrier, up on the sidewalk, and to his lunch. Dunafon was among the first group to go.

The Broncos brought to camp four quarterbacks—returnees Craig Penrose and Norris Weese and newcomers Craig Morton and Steve Spurrier, who brought reputations, both bad and good, with them. Otis Armstrong was coming off a 1,000-yard season, and Jon Keyworth was returning at fullback, with a fight on his hands against Lonnie Perrin, in his second year. The receiving and tight-end positions were fairly set, and the defense was almost intact from the previous season. Defensive end Lyle Alzado was returning from a knee injury, sound, and veteran Bernard Jackson had been obtained from Cincinnati to play free safety, replacing John Rowser, who had been released. Quarterback and the offensive line were still the concerns. Out of the Dirty Dozen, Billy van Heusen, the punter, Tommy Lyons, a starting guard a year ago, and Carl Schaukowitch, a reserve offensive lineman, were gone. Van Heusen had been told he couldn't do the job anymore; Lyons was too small, and Schaukowitch was informed a knee injury hadn't sufficiently healed. But the undercurrent of their insurrection had meaning to the other players involved. They knew they had to do the work, or they would join the trio cast out.

The horn blared for the first break of the day. The players wandered over to the tower and were surprised to see Allen Hurst, the trainer, pull open an ice chest and hand out Popsicles. "You guys keep up the good work, and we'll try to get you banana Popsicles for Saturday," Miller said. Popsicles. "It beats the hell out of Gatorade," said linebacker Tom Jackson to one of his teammates. "But I hope Oakland doesn't see us here eating these things. They'll think we're a bunch of pussies."

Over to the side, tackle Bill Bain was drinking a gallon of water. He had ballooned to 290 pounds during the off season, and the Broncos were trying to force him down to 270. "I'm working at it," he told Hurst. "I haven't had anything more than a salad the last two days, and it's killing me." On the corner of the practice field sat Bain's wife, the only player's wife at Fort Collins. "She likes to watch me." She was sketching.

Linebacker Godwin Turk was the first to fall. He grabbed his knee. So an assistant trainer carried him off to a Denver hospital. "Wait a second, will ya?" Turk said. "Hey, get someone to take care of my dogs. They're in the back of the van over at the dorm. Tell them I'll be back. If you're gonna be hurt, now is the time. I'll be well before the season starts." As Turk limped off, Myrel Moore, the assistant in charge of linebackers, said: "Well, that's too bad. He might have been a starter. We're gonna have to get used to that. There'll be others."

Larry Elliott, the team's equipment manager, walked around muttering. "Dammit, if they'd water this place, something like that might not happen. This damn field is like cement." A few writers and sportscasters sat on the blocking dummies in the middle of the field, trying to get out of the heat. "They still ain't shit," said a sportscaster who once played the game. "A coaching change isn't going to make enough difference. Who's going to quarterback?"

A writer chipped in. "Morton throws like an old man, and they're pinning their hopes on him." But Joe Sanchez of the Denver *Post* looked out at the players and said: "I have a funny feeling about this team. I think they're going to be better than you give them credit for. Look at the way they're going at it." Practice ended, and the players started shuffling off to lunch. Near the practice field students were playing tennis and not paying attention to the football.

"Look at those fools playing tennis in this hot sun," one rookie said.

"Yeah, but they could be saying the same thing about us. Look at those fools practicing football in the hot sun."

"But we're getting paid to do it."

"You call two hundred dollars a week for two practices a day out there getting paid."

"I guess you're right. We are fools."

Within a week both were gone.

Miller fell onto a sofa in the dormitory a few days later. He looked like a tired man. "Some awful late nights. I've got to get used to it. The players have, at least, accepted us as coaches. We've got our hands full, though. We've got to smooth it out. The attitude is good. Now if we can just bring up the ability."

One of the interested spectators at practice that day had been Mike Montler, a veteran center with the Buffalo Bills. He had told the Bills to trade him or else he was retiring. Montler had been a member of O. J. Simpson's famed Electric

Company line, but he was tired of losing and wanted to be close to his home in Boulder, Colorado. He had asked for a trade to Denver and, to show the Broncos that he was in shape, had biked down 44 miles from Boulder to the Denver camp. The Broncos' coaches avoided talking to him because it might be considered tampering, but general manager Fred Gehrke looked over from a distance. "Maybe I'd better get back on the phone. Mike looks like he can play."

The next day Montler belonged to the Broncos.

"It's like being out of prison," he told a couple of players who greeted him at the dorm. "The bike trick worked pretty good, didn't it?"

That evening Richard "Doc" Urich sat in the bar at a restaurant called the Prime Minister. He felt like a man on the outside looking in. A year ago Urich had been the offensive line coach of the Broncos, but in the Miller shuffle, he had been pushed to the side. The Broncos had created a job for him as director of pro scouting. He dealt with computers that spewed out information about players on other teams. "I wanted to be back in coaching, but I wanted to stay in Denver, and this job has its positive aspects." But Urich never felt a part of the Broncos and, at year's end, he resigned to return to coaching with the Washington Redskins. "I think it's probably good that there was a change. Maybe Red can take this team farther than we did," he said that night.

Back at the dormitory several coaches were playing bridge. A slight breeze came through the window. Miller walked through. "There's work to be done, guys." The bridge table emptied. But soon enough the attitude and the ability in camp picked up, so Miller decided it was time for a breather. He scheduled the traditional rookie show for Saturday night and put running back Rob Lytle in charge.

"But, coach, you're a rookie head coach. Shouldn't you do something, too?"

"Get a piano," Miller barked in reply.

And at the rookie show Miller astounded the players with ragtime, a la Scott Joplin. "The guy never ceases to amaze me," said Alzado at a back table. "A piano player, too. I get the impression that if we would let him put on a uniform, he'd be out there practicing with us."

Signs were surfacing that the Broncos were coming together. But it was too early for hysteria.

9

A DAY IN THE LIFE

Silence. Then two long, reverberating bursts from an airhorn. An unpleasant noise; but an effective noise. The Denver Broncos woke up. Seven in the morning, and the sun should have been rising to spotlight the nearby mountains. Only it wasn't, and the mountains had to be remembered and imagined. The sky looked like the inside of a used sweat sock—gray and damp and musty. A day for lying about. But the Broncos couldn't. They had to work.

Broncos assistant coach Stan Jones peered out the window. "Hey, in Buffalo this would be a great day. People would be getting ready to go to the beach." Head coach Red Miller gave no thought to calling off practice. We'll see how good they are in the elements."

Coffee was on and the coaches began to ease out of first-floor rooms into the alcove at Corbett Hall, a nondescript dormitory with an architectural form that could be termed early penitentiary. Plopped down about 350 paces from the hub of the Colorado State University campus in Fort Collins, the dorm would soon be home for two hundred students. Two to a room, two beds, two closets, two desks, one sink, one shower, one commode, one telephone, and two football players and no air-conditioning. And shy about two coats of paint. The Broncos requested the nicer, modern, air-conditioned apartmentlike tower, but, as one member of the team said, the school didn't want "a bunch of animals running around tearing up that building."

While the coaching staff pulled out the sports section from a stack of newspapers, the players staggered out of third- and fourth-floor rooms and out the back door. Breakfast, served at 7:20 promptly, was mandatory.

One coach looked at the front-page headline "just in case a war starts. I guess we should know about it." But the major interest was the National Football League transactions and reported injuries around the league. "Look at this guy signing with Green Bay. Told me he had a bonus with Detroit. We could have used him," said director of player personnel Carroll Hardy to no one in particular.

Meanwhile, Jones had discovered a picture promoting the movie *The Island of Dr. Moreau*. Several of the humanoid animals were carrying one of their own in the photograph. Jones took out a pen and captioned it: "Bronco veterans show up for weigh-in bringing a reluctant Bill Bain," and put it on the bulletin board.

"Well, mens," said coach Red Miller. "Mens" is his favorite word to start a conversation. "Time to get started."

At the Faculty Club, a quarter of a mile away from the dorm, the players were eating, generally without conversation. The ranks had been depleted by two that morning. A pair of tryouts had been asked to report with their playbooks—a subtle but sure sign of the finish of camp for them.

Omelettes, ham, hash browns, toast, juices, and a radio in the background spouting a sports segment. "Willie McGee of the San Francisco 49ers injured his knee yesterday and probably will be out for the season," the radio said. Haven Moses— like McGee, a wide receiver—paused for a moment, looked up, and went back to eating.

At 8:00 the players filtered into the training room at Moby Gym. Just beyond the wall, in the basketball arena, an early-morning religious service was being held. Crusaders for Christ, a youth organization, had swarmed onto the campus. "The Lord will find a way . . ." the evangelist was saying.

In the next room Bill Bain, the offensive tackle with the weight problem, was trying to find a way by himself. If he wasn't down to 275 today, he would be fined twenty-five dollars a pound for overage. Into the whirlpool. "You look like Moby

Dick in there," fullback Jon Keyworth said. Other players were being taped, reading the newspapers, and relaxing during the lull before the storm.

The coaches arrived. Players lined up at the scales in shorts, jocks, nothing. Keyworth told Bain: "Your hair is wet. Dry it. That'll take off a few more ounces." Bain grabs a bed towel, ran it through his hair, dropped his shorts, and stepped on the scale.

"Two-seventy-five."

The place erupted. "All right, Bill. Way to go, baby." Bain had a smile from here to Cheyenne, Wyoming. The taping went on. Before the day was out, trainer Allen Hurst wrapped 3,700 feet of the stuff around players' ankles. More than two miles' worth every three days.

The players dressed. Shoulder pads, leggings, jerseys, helmets, Rob Lytle was first out the door.

A girl bicycled by. "Same girl comes by every day at this time. Wears the same clothes. Either she washes every night or sleeps in her dress," Lytle said.

By 9:10 the quarterbacks, centers, punters, and kicker Jim Turner were on the practice field for specialty teamwork. The Broncos had several acres to themselves, but a rope surrounded the field. Equipment manager Larry Elliott was disturbed that morning because someone kept cutting the rope down. "That is not funny," he said to a player, who immediately laughed.

At 9:25 all the players were on the field and in position for group exercises. "Reach for Wyoming. Get that leg back." On the platform tower where the movie camera sat, the focus was on Turner, the oldest member of the team, a veteran of fifteen training camps. At night, when the films were played, Turner was shown waving at the camera while the other players were deep-knee-bending. "Which way is Wyoming?" a rookie asked.

After the loosening up, the players broke down into their own concentrated areas—defensive linemen over here, defensive backs by the baseball field, quarterbacks to the far corner, and punters to a section called Marvin Gardens in honor of special teams coach Marv Braden.

Miller's practices were divided up into nine periods—10 to

15 minutes each. A huge number hung from the tower to indicate the period, and that airhorn signaled the end of each. As linemen ran the roped structure developing football coordination, the defensive backs went into their early-morning routine that was the envy of the camp.

"Last one over doesn't get a milk bath after practice," assistant Bob Gambold hollered. The backs stepped up and down on small boxes, but to break the routine, they did it to soul hand-clapping and a group version of the song "Car Wash." "Working at the car wash, oh, baby, working at the car wash." One of the black backs said to white back Steve Foley: "You just don't have it, kid. You just mouth the words."

"Bunch of ballet artists," a lineman grumbled. "That's all they are." When the defensive backs returned to the other side of the field, the linebackers said: "Get out of our way. Some of us are here to work, not to dance."

But there was a togetherness on the practice field. Maybe it was the honeymoon relationship with the new head coach, or possibly it was a genuine feeling that the team could go somewhere in 1977. "For once we're not linebackers or running backs or tackles. We're all Broncos," linebacker Randy Gradishar said.

Each period lasted just long enough to prevent boredom, and they built from individual tests to one-on-one work against another group, then to five-on-five and finally seven-on-seven. "The concept is to begin with stressing the player and eventually reaching the whole team," Miller said.

In the trenches Bain was going head-on against Lyle Alzado. Alzado was winning. Miller drove his golf cart over, checking in briefly with each group. Suddenly a lineman went down in pain, clutched his knee, and shouted out: "Goddamn it. Not again." Other players cringed. "Hang in there, bro," a mate shouted. Trainers rushed in. No one said a word. They had seen it happen too many times to too many players. The knee was meant to move front to back, not sideways. The workout moved down a few yards, and the player was put on a small truck and taken from the field. Miller whispered to him: "You'll be back." He wouldn't though. It was his second knee injury in two years, and this was the finisher.

A small crowd gathered on the edge of the field. Retired men, young women in halters, students, men up from Denver for the day. The Colorado State coaching staff wandered in, and Monte Clark, the 49ers' coach in 1976, showed up. He was in the area for some fishing, and with the opening of a camp, it was just too hard for him to stay away. "Looks like these guys got it going," he said almost jealously. Clark would soon be doing B.A.R.T. commercials in San Francisco.

The blocking sleds and blocking dummies were due for punishment. Linebackers pushed around a heavy beachball. Shortly before 11:00 it was break time. Popsicles. Trainer Hurst used the moment to repair ankles and cover cuts and check eyes. The sun had finally appeared, and the temperature was rapidly headed to 90. When the break was over, the players were involved in a short, scrimmagelike session—concentrating on the running game. The afternoon workouts groomed the passing offense and defense. And the coaches' personalities emerged.

Gambold tended to soft-speak his defensive backs. After a fouled-up play, "Carl, that was interesting. Not good, but interesting." Myrel Moore, who coached the linebackers, rah-rahed them. "Get on that bunch like a bad smell. Way to get on him, Lyle. Right, Tommy. Yeah." Stan Jones was more of a friend to his defensive line troops, pointing out a mistake in low tones. The defensive coordinator, Joe Collier, a former head coach at Buffalo, walked around and surveyed the situation. Someone said he last uttered a word in 1968. Quiet man.

The offensive coaches were loudest. Fran Polsfoot, the receivers' coach, was a scolder, but comes right back with praise. Paul Roach, with the offensive backs, made repeaters out of those who erred. A player screwed up and tried it again. Ken Gray, the rookie coach with the offensive line, has a Texas marmalade accent and pours it all over his men. And Babe Parilli witnessed his quarterbacks' moves with a nod and a frown. He was waiting. "You point out mistakes out here, and it really isn't that effective," Gambold said. "It means more when you're watching the films, and they can see for themselves."

Miller was a man of many moods that day. "That's good,

O[offense]. Where were you, D? Come on, mens. Let's get it going. Having fun. Get the job done." Then he called receiver Rick Upchurch off to the side, pointed out a small maneuver in a pass route, and he was off in the cart to another section of the field.

A team huddle was called at 11:25, and Miller had a few parting words. "It's looking better. But we've still got to improve. When we're out here, let's think that we're the best, and maybe you'll show it." With that, the players chanted, "Cool down, cool down." The cool-off period is a winding down from the practice. "You don't take a thoroughbred and throw him in the show after a workout. You've got to bring him down gradually," Miller told them.

Lunch—BLT's, vegetable soup, french fries, banana splits. On and on. "Best food in years," a player said. "I think I'll go take a nap, and I may never wake up again." But he would. Team meetings are at 1:00 P.M.

Shortly after 2:00, the morning routines began all over again. Training room, taping, pads, on to the field. Exercises, flexing, special teams, practice together, long passes, short runs. The players seemed to enjoy the passing drills the most. No hitting. Working on interceptions. Coming down with feet in bounds with short, choppy steps. The crowd was larger in late afternoon. Several hundred. Turner walked the fringes. As the only kicker in camp, he had no competition. "That doesn't mean a thing. Got to make the team. You're never secure."

"One more," Miller said. Craig Morton tossed a lengthy pass. Upchurch missed. That was the end. But Lonnie Perrin, fighting for the fullback job, stayed on to practice his kickoffs. Steve Spurrier, a quarterback, convinced a tryout receiver to catch a few more. Norris Weese, another quarterback, met his wife and daughter who had come in from Jackson, Mississippi. Players signed autographs. Others limped into the gymnasium. Two-a-days showed mostly in the legs. Two-hundred-pound men acted like shredded wheat.

Back in the dorm Miller met with the press. "Hi, mens. I liked the intensity out there. We're still trying to get the tempo down. The quarterbacks threw well at times. We're putting a little more in each day . . ."

The players were heading for the dining hall, the third trip.

Country-fried steak, potatoes, salad, vegetables, pudding, apple juice, vitamin pills. The imprint of the day's activities was apparent on their faces.

Outside the dormitory a girl sunbathed in the courtyard. The wind, whatever there was of it, refused to come in the window. The sun didn't refuse.

On the hallway walls, hurriedly lettered sheets hung. "The Phantom will strike, but when?" A ballboy asked one of the coaches: "Who do you think the Phantom is?" "I don't know, but it's gotta be one of those defensive linemen." The players and the coaches went off in groups again in meeting rooms to study films. The Broncos filmed practically everything that moved at practice. In color. Expensive film. Great quality. Two cameras. One for offense, one for defense. Revealing the drops and missed tackles and timing of quarterbacks in the pocket. Then the camera zoomed in on a pretty girl in the crowd. "That was to break up the action. You get tired of looking at football players," said Bill Goldie, assistant general manager and cameraman.

The coaches reviewed the day's pluses and minuses and discussed the plan for the next day. No days off. "I don't believe in them," Miller said. "You come to camp, and you go straight through. Not enough time for days off."

By 8:00 P.M. the meetings concluded, and the players with playbooks filed up the stairs to temporary homes. Alzado and Paul Smith shared a room and came prepared. Color TV, bags of potato chips, an easy chair, soft drinks in the refrigerator, a fan. They are the only two on the team who have crossed the color barrier as roommates. Once close friends, they have somewhat drifted apart. Alzado was an emerging star. Smith was trying to hang on to a job. "I like what I'm seeing," Alzado said over the roar of the TV. "I like it. I'm not going to make any predictions, but we're going to surprise some people." His attention went back to the police show. Smith was on the phone getting the message from home.

Down the hall players were dividing up for card games and backgammon and studying the playbook. Running back Jim Kiick had gathered up three other players and drove off for a pizza. Some had already fallen asleep.

A cherry bomb exploded in the hall. There were no witnesses

or suspects. The coaches checked it out and returned to their own floor. Two have been selected as bed checkers for the night. A few others have gone off to the Safari Club, a local hangout with one of the few live bands in town, after the final check of the waiver wire.

At 11:00 P.M. all the doors were closed. The halls were empty. Lighting was sparse.

A day in camp was over.

Silence.

10

AT LAST, A GAME

Everyone was getting excited about the Denver Broncos' first exhibition game. Everyone except Tim Ellis. The Broncos, in addition to debuting a new coach, a new quarterback, and a new cheerleading squad, were bringing out a miniature horse, TD, as the new mascot. And Ellis somehow had been talked into . . . well, following the horse around with a shovel. "I'm glad I don't do this for a living."

But the Broncos were anxiously anticipating the game. "We've seen each other long enough. We need to look at somebody else," Miller told the squad. So the players assembled their belongings at Fort Collins and headed to Denver. The rest of the workouts would be held at the club's own headquarters. "We've spent enough time up here," Miller said. And he wanted to see the team in action. Miller is against scrimmaging, so the Broncos had only shadowboxed for a month. It was time to find out if the training had accomplished anything.

Morton told the four quarterbacks in camp that they would be splitting time in the first four exhibitions—two per game, a half each. It was a foregone conclusion, though, that Morton would have to lose the job during the exhibition season in order to lose the starting status.

The four quarterbacks were totally different types—Morton, who had been to the top with the Dallas Cowboys and to the depths with the New York Giants; Craig Penrose, the young warrior with the great arm; Norris Weese, the scrambling, overlooked quarterback fighting for a job, and Steve Spurrier, the

Heisman Trophy winner who had never lived up to his credentials in professional football.

Craig Morton . . . 6'2", 212 pounds . . . bird legs . . . thinning hair . . . fourteenth year in professional football . . . born in Flint, Michigan . . . age thirty-four . . . All-American at California first-round draft choice of the Dallas Cowboys in 1965 . . . played behind Don Meredith until Meredith retired to the broadcast booth . . . eventually bumped by Roger Staubach . . . played in four NFL championship games . . . traded to Giants in 1974 . . . came to Denver for Steve Ramsey . . . was a three-sport star in high school . . . likes to ski in Aspen . . . did a magazine underwear ad . . . great arm, no mobility . . . experience to burn.

Craig Penrose . . . 6'3", 203 pounds . . . mustache . . . likes ice cream . . . four-handicapper in golf . . . second year in professional football . . . born in Woodland, California, son of a sporting-goods owner . . . age twenty-four . . . honorable mention All-American at San Diego State . . . NCAA passing champion in 1975 . . . drafted in the fourth round by Denver . . . started one game, a victory, against Kansas City in 1976 . . . played all sports in high school . . . strong arm . . . lacks experience . . . team leadership abilities questioned.

Steve Spurrier . . . 6'1", 196 pounds . . . southern drawl . . . All-American looks . . . eleventh year in professional football . . . born in Miami Beach, age thirty-two, but grew up in Johnson City, Tennessee . . . All-State in three sports . . . All-American and Heisman Trophy winner in 1966 at the University of Florida . . . set eight Southeastern Conference passing records . . . drafted number one by San Francisco . . . generally played behind John Brodie and was the team punter . . . in 1972, while Brodie was hurt, led San Francisco to NFC West title . . . was starter in 1974 before getting hurt . . . then traded to expansion team, Tampa Bay . . . started all 1976 for a team that didn't win a game . . . disagreements with John McKay led to waivers being asked on Spurrier . . . signed with Denver during summer of 1977 . . . all-around qualities, but not overwhelming at any phase . . . excellent golfer.

Norris Weese . . . 6'0", 194 pounds . . . Mr. Friendship . . . a certified public accountant . . . third year in professional football . . . born in Baton Rouge, Louisiana, age twenty-six . . . followed in Archie Manning's footsteps at University of Mississippi and led the SEC in total offense as a junior, but never recognized as quality player because of poor team around him . . . National Football Foundation Hall of Fame scholar athlete . . . outstanding college baseball player . . . Hula Bowl MVP . . . drafted fourth by Los Angeles Rams, but played in World Football League in 1974 with Hawaii . . . tried out with and cut by Rams in 1975 . . . signed by Denver in 1976 and made the club off strength of exhibition showings . . . never started a game, but came off bench early in final regular-season contest of 1976 and took Denver to victory over Chicago . . . great scrambler, but lacking skill to throw long . . . field general . . . has smarts.

QB IV. One would be number one when the battle was over. One would be gone.

Morton shared a corner room with Penrose on the top floor during camp. They had become very close. On a night just before leaving for Denver, Morton was passing along information about being an NFL quarterback, but he also was convincing Penrose that the young man wasn't ready. Penrose's feelings had changed. A few months earlier at a golf tournament in Steamboat Springs he had felt that "this year is when I take over. I'm ready. I had a year of sitting, and I can lead this club." He had been impatient, but now he seemed settled.

Miller and Penrose had not hit it off extemely well in the early days of camp. Their personalities clashed. Penrose took everything in stride. Miller wanted him to be a take-charge guy. "That's not my personality. I think the players want me to lead by example. I'm no rah-rah guy," Penrose said. "I think if I go out and say, 'Okay, guys, let's get it going' and I don't prove myself, they're gonna wonder who the hell this kid thinks he is. I can't be everything the coach wants me to be."

But Penrose thought he was "improving every day. I really feel good. I just want to get better and better, and everything else will take care of itself." Morton had gotten to him.

Penrose liked the possibilities of the offense. "Miller brought it with him from New England. There are a lot of complexities, but it should be easy enough to learn.

Penrose asked Morton if he wanted something to eat, but the older Craig shook his head no. Penrose was fretting over a one-pound gain, but went off for a snack anyway. "I'm sure two-a-days will take care of it."

Morton was left in the room. He pointed to the door. "Someday Craig is going to be an outstanding quarterback. He needs some seasoning." Morton felt certain he had the quarterback position. "I didn't come out here to be number two. I've got the best arm out there. I've never had any problems with it. It's feeling good. And this is a good offensive system to be in. There are a lot of different things for a lot of different people. They didn't have imagination in New York and not that many good players to do much with. I took a lot of abuse, but you get that if you play the game. I'd just as soon not even think about the Giants anymore.

"I have confidence in my ability. I had good seasons in New York, although the overall team's results weren't. Denver is a new start for me. Of course, all of us think we should be number one. That's good. I know records are being kept, but I have no idea how it's going. You don't worry about those things. You think about the team. Once this team gets the feel of winning, it comes easier. In Dallas they used to say we couldn't win the big game, but we sure won a lot of big games to get to the big game. And once we developed that winning attitude, we kept coming back. If Denver can only get in the playoffs once, then the second time will be that much easier. I don't know if it will come this year. We've got to overcome Oakland. You're not supposed to point at one team, but if we can beat the best, and Oakland is the best right now, then we should be able to beat the rest."

Long after everyone else had departed from the practice field, Steve Spurrier was working on his 20-yard sideline passes. Like Morton, he was a starter in 1976 and was beginning anew in a strange city. But Spurrier knew this could be the end unless he stuck. This day he was upset by a conversation he had with a writer who had called from Florida. "He tells me he understands I'm running fourth. That's not true, darn it. I think it's unsettled, and I think I'm getting a chance to prove myself. I hope that guy doesn't know something I don't know. Just because I'm the fourth guy to take a snap in practice doesn't mean I'm fourth. I'm beginning to feel more comfortable. But I need the work whenever I can get it. When four quarterbacks are sharing the load, you don't get as much as you normally would. So I use my free time to practice. Every pass counts out here because they're keeping that damn chart. You look up and that kid [assistant coach Joe Collier's son] is writing down something about you. To be honest, and I'm not copping out, I've never been a good practice quarterback. But you have to have something to go by, and statistics are probably one good way.

"You look around at these three other guys, and you can't worry about them. You have to go out and think about your own play. The way I got it figured, they'll probably keep Penrose as a backup, and then it depends on how Morton and I do. If we both do well, Weese will go. And if one of us screws up, that's it. I'm just concerned that I could have an off-night in a preseason game, and I could be gone. But I'm sure when it's all over the guy who deserves to be starting will."

Later Spurrier played backgammon with Norris Weese. The two, as longshots, had gravitated to one another. After losing to Spurrier, Weese went down to the dormitory lounge on the third floor and chewed on a candy bar. He had taken a new approach this year. "I'm no longer going to berate myself. I've talked too much in the past about what I can't do. But I proved to myself in the Chicago game last year that I can play in this league as long as I don't do the things I can't do. Everyone knows I don't have the arm of Craig Penrose, so I concentrate on short passes. And my running abilities and leadership on the field are strengths.

"That's why I like this new offense. It's a lot like New England's, with play-action passes and options and rollouts and pitches available to the quarterback. Steve Grogan ran a lot for New England, so it suits my style. Last year when I scrambled it was on my own. Another thing I like is that we're competing like hell out there, but when it's over we come in and sit around and talk about it. We're all getting along. It was tough last year for Steve [Ramsey] to get close to me or Craig [Penrose] because he was feeling a lot of pressure. The pressure exists this year, but we're accepting it. But we know that one of us isn't going to be here in a few weeks."

Weese may have been the strangest of the quartet. He worked during the off-season for a CPA firm in Jackson, Mississippi, and actually made more money at it than football. "I keep asking myself why I come back, but I can't get football out of my blood yet. Maybe I don't want to escape from a kid's game. I don't know."

Morton and Penrose had been selected to split the duties against Baltimore in the opening preseason contest. The interest in Denver was starting to peak again, but it was higher than normal this year because of the presence of another new coach. A new era, as it were. The Broncos' staff had picked out twenty-six new cheerleaders and were trying to emulate the Dallas Cowboys' cheerleaders with swank uniforms, a bit on the alluring side. The designer of Las Vegas showgirl uniforms had been brought in, and he had them showing a lot of the three B's (bosoms, buttocks, and bellybuttons).

The stadium staff was getting ready with twenty-five thousand hotdogs, twelve thousand five hundred gallons of Pepsi, and enough beer for seventy thousand 12-ounce cups. But Clarence Lowe, who lived a block from the stadium, wasn't happy to see the football season starting again—Red Miller or not. "Those fans are just like cattle. They come urinate in your yard. You got to clean up beer bottles and junk. I won't put up with it this year. If they park in my driveway, I'll just push the car out in the street."

But forty thousand others—abnormally high for an exhibition—were streaming into Mile High Stadium on a nice summer evening in Denver.

The cheerleaders danced as if they had been chosen that afternoon. And neither team looked much better.

Bert Jones, NFL Player of the Year in 1976, quickly guided Baltimore into Denver territory, but the Broncos' defense held, and a wounded duck of a field goal by Toni Linhart gave the Colts a 3–0 lead. A moan went up in the stands. Oh, no. The

Broncos were once more starting badly. Both teams missed field goals. Then Denver punting candidate Larry Steele sealed his fate. He kicked the ball almost directly sideways into the crowd. An assistant coach cursed on the sidelines. "I wonder if he can still get a flight out of town tonight." Upstairs in the press box someone asked: "Hey, Bob, has any Bronco ever been cut at halftime?" Following the punt, Baltimore had the ball at Denver's 30-yard line. Jones hooked up with Ron Lee on a quick gainer and then completed another toss to the one-yard line. With only four seconds remaining, Linhart was brought on for a field goal attempt that was good and gave Baltimore the 6–0 edge at intermission.

The Broncos, who had been inefficient and lifeless the first half, broke out in the third quarter. Lonnie Perrin sneaked out of the backfield and was waiting for a crosstown bus, it seemed, at Baltimore's 25-yard line. He took the pass from Morton and was all alone, running for a touchdown. But he tripped—someone joked that it was over a yard line—and ended up doing a double jackknife dive into the end zone. Denver was ahead, 7–6, after Jim Turner's conversion.

Bert Jones had retired for the evening, and the Baltimore offensive subs weren't up to the task. However, the defense did trap Morton in his own end zone for a safety, and Baltimore regained the lead. "Well, I guess we'll start hearing Craig Morton jokes," said one spectator. "They'd better find somebody else."

Penrose took over for the fourth quarter and started Denver at its own 45. Seven plays later, from Baltimore's 15, the young quarterback hit receiver Rick Upchurch in the right corner of the end zone, and Denver possessed its first victory under Miller—even if it didn't count. The players walked slowly into the locker room. They still weren't in shape to play a full game in sultry conditions. "It's a start," Miller told them. "It was a good victory. We're not there, but it's a start."

An hour later, relaxing in his office, Miller said it was a "great thing for me in my first game. We were very spotty on some things. I said to the players I wanted to do two things. Number one, win. Number two, take a look at a lot of new players. We did both things." But Miller was concerned privately about

Morton, who had looked spotty. Penrose was so-so. Thus, the battle for the quarterback job went on.

General manager Gehrke reported his findings to the owners. "Red kept his cool. He didn't get carried away. He didn't let the crowd affect him. He did what he wanted. I think we made a good choice."

Well, it was a start.

And Tim Ellis had done a good job with his shovel following the horse.

11

FIVE PRESEASON
WINS, AND SO WHAT?

The Denver Broncos had arrived in Seattle about two hours before, and, as was becoming his custom, general manager Fred Gehrke opened his room for a cocktail party. The assistant coaches were mingling with the traveling press when Allen Hurst, the trainer, walked over and turned on the TV set. Pictured was a man familiar to everyone in the room. John Ralston smiled and spoke as the people gathered around. "I have mixed emotions about the game. I still pull for Denver, but now I'm working with Seattle. I would like to see them do well." A year before Ralston would have been standing in this room himself, but he was no longer associated with the Broncos. Instead, he was a commentator on the preseason telecasts for the Seahawks, and was appearing on a Seattle TV talk show.

In the back of the room a film cameraman for Red Miller's own weekly show sneered. "Can you believe this shit? This whole bunch wanted to see John gone and didn't care if they ever heard him again, and here they're hanging on every word he says." But it was worth listening to. Ralston said his ultimate goal was still the Super Bowl, and he wouldn't stop until he got there. "When I win the Super Bowl, I'm going to walk off the field and quit coaching."

"Hey, John," someone said into the TV. "Don't you realize how tough it's going to be to go to the Super Bowl when you're not coaching?"

Ralston didn't hear the question. He was busy saying he

"holds no grudges against Denver." The interview concluded. The set was turned off.

Assistant coach Bob Gambold lifted his glass. "I'll drink to that." And everyone returned to their conversation and their drinking. The mood was very free that night, with good reason. The Broncos had won three of their first four exhibitions, and had come close in the other, and a triumph over the second-year Seahawks the next night at the Kingdome was all but assured.

After the opening win over Baltimore, the Broncos had settled in at the team's practice field north of downtown, just off the city's main expressway artery, Interstate 25. The players checked into a motel a block from the team's office, and the routine continued. Miller allowed everyone to relax for a couple of days while he walked about in a daze, silenting celebrating his first victory as a head coach. Then, by Tuesday, normality returned.

In the city the routine greeting of "Hello, how are you?" had changed to "Hello, what do you think of the Broncos?" Two businessmen were talking over lunch at the Denver Athletic Club. "My barber cuts one of the Broncos' player's hair, and since they've just come back from camp, he had a chance to talk to him. He says they are going to be tough this year."

His friend looked up from a salad. "Who says they are going to be tough? The barber or the Bronco?"

The Broncos were approaching their next game much more seriously than St. Louis coach Don Coryell, who said he wanted to "get some experience for our younger people. I really don't like to play a team I'm going to have to play again in the regular season. I'd rather be surprised. How does Red feel about it?" Miller loved it, since St. Louis was the club that once fired him, and he sought personal revenge. Denver and St. Louis would be meeting once more in the regular-season opener.

Jeff Severson, a St. Louis defensive back, had a particular anxiety about the contest, though. He had been dealt away by the Broncos and laid claim to being the only player to have appeared in the playoffs in a Denver uniform. What? During the summer he had a bit role as a football player in a movie called *Semi-Tough,* about a football team going to the playoffs. Severson had played for the Denver Broncos in the movie, but the Miami Dolphins beat them. Figures. "The game was supposed to be in Denver during the dead of winter, but we filmed in California, and it was hot. They had to keep wiping the sweat off us. But at least I can say I'm the only Bronco in the playoffs."

Miller told the players at the midweek meeting that he wanted to show St. Louis a little "bit of everything. I want the whole league to wonder what we're going to be doing." So Miller unleashed a trick bag that included the shotgun offense with Weese at the trigger. Denver also tried a tight-end reverse, a split-end reverse, naked bootlegs by the quarterback, five-player shifts, a quarterback shift, a halfback pass. St. Louis showed almost nothing. Quarterback Jim Hart watched the game from the press box, and running backs Terry Metcalf and Jim Otis also didn't play. As a result, Denver won easily, 15–7, behind five field goals by Jim Turner. The Broncos played enough people to attack a well-secured fort, and the defense was dynamite, giving up only a meaningless 68-yard run for a touchdown late in the evening. Weese and Spurrier had indecisive performances, but Otis Armstrong flashed signs of brilliance, picking up 42 yards on nine carries before sitting down. An audience of forty-four thousand went home satisfied.

"We won. I'll take it," Miller said afterward. "We're still looking for improvement, but it's another step." He was beginning to sound like a broken record with his "another-step" dialogue. But it was difficult for anyone to knock a winner. The home part of the preseason was over for Denver. The Broncos were facing four consecutive games on the road. Early the next week Miller told the players: "These games will be indicators. This club has a history of not winning away from Denver. Let's end it."

The first stop on the month-long excursion was to Atlanta, and the Falcons were in the midst of rebuilding. In the first two exhibitions Atlanta had averaged a grand total of two and one-half points. The weather was humid and muggy when the Broncos arrived, and most of the players wandered up and down the street outside the motel. "I wish this were a swim meet instead of a football game," said one. Several players examined the menu in the restaurant motel and ordered the local favorite—barbecue ribs, hamhocks, red-eyed gravy, and cornbread. "No wonder Atlanta is a bad team. They have to eat this stuff all the time," said linebacker Tom Jackson.

The game itself had all the earmarks of an eyesore. "If you're looking for artistic success," Miller said on the plane ride back, "that wasn't it. We may have been rag-tag, but we're winners, and it's beautiful to win." A crowd of twenty-one thousand sat on its hands until it finally had something to applaud, when the Falcons picked up a first down, which didn't come often in a 10–2 victory by Denver. However, the outcome wasn't decided until late. The Broncos were leading by a baseball score, 3–2, when Craig Penrose stepped in for Craig Morton and threw a touchdown pass to tight end Odoms. In the locker room Penrose grabbed Weese. "If this is the kind of weather they have down here, I'll never let them trade me here."

"This makes a man out of you. That's why there are so many good players in the South. It's just a little humidity," Weese said.

A writer from *Sports Illustrated,* traveling around for the magazine's pro football issue, watched and then decided. "You can write off these two teams." And most of the other national publications had written them off, too, already. In many of the prognostications the Broncos had been picked third in the American Conference's West Division—behind Oakland, naturally, and San Diego, an emerging force. One magazine said the only thing "terrorizing about the offense is the fear it throws into the Bronco defense. Red Miller and Craig Morton are not two of a kind." Another magazine said the "only way Denver can win the division is if Oakland transfers to another division."

Despite Denver's 3–0 record, it didn't seem to do much for Miller's reputation. A national story was asking the question: "Who's Red Miller?" Then he arrived in Philadelphia for exhibition game number four to read a story that referred to him as "Red Phillips." Miller laughed as he was telling Gehrke, "That's all right. I used to wonder how solid my position was in Baltimore when I was an assistant. The owner's wife kept calling me Red Smith."

In Philadelphia Bobby Anderson, once a starter with the Broncos, was along to provide commentary on the telecast back to Denver. He had finally given up the year before, after being waived by the Broncos. "I really could still play, I believe." He was selling cancer insurance, but none of the players were buying. "Whenever you mention cancer insurance, it seems to turn them off." But he had faith in the team. "This is the best I've seen the team play. They're short some, but it will be a pretty good season. Maybe we'll get to the playoffs in a couple of years."

The players found rides to a downtown disco that catered to visiting football players. At the door they were told they couldn't get in because they were wearing jeans.

"Hey, we're with the Broncos, you know, 3–0."

"Okay," the guy said. "If you promise not to beat the Eagles."

But that's what Red Miller was preparing for in his motel room. "We have not dominated anyone yet. I want to overwhelm Philadelphia."

Morton wasn't preparing too much. He was walking down a Philly street that night watching all the people go by.

The Broncos didn't dominate. The offense, behind Spurrier and Weese, picked up, but the defense cracked, and the Eagles won, 28–24. The Broncos almost pulled off a finishing rally, scoring 14 points in the final quarter and threatening to win in the final minute. But Weese was sacked on fourth down. He had misunderstood the play brought in from the bench.

A decision was supposed to be made on a quarterback the next week, but both Spurrier and Weese had been impressive enough to make the choice difficult. Spurrier completed seven out of ten, with two dropped, and Weese was twelve of twenty-two. Spurrier did hurt his leg slightly in the game, and rubbed it constantly on the plane, but said there were no problems. He asked for a beer and pulled out his backgammon set. "I think I've proven myself. I don't see how they can cut me. Hell, I've done everything they've asked. What the hell. I can't worry about it."

Four days later Spurrier was gone, and Morton was the Broncos' number one quarterback. "Miller tried to be nice, and there's not much to say about it," Spurrier said, and then went out to play golf. Spurrier had the best statistics of the four during the four games, but Morton always had the inside track.

When Morton was selected, Weese took it harder than Penrose. "I don't guess it was so really wide open after all," he said. "I'm not ashamed. I gave it a shot." Penrose thought he "would be able to help the team if called on," and Morton added that his "ego is not going to be shattered if I get taken out of a game. The object is to win. I'm happy, and I think the important thing now is to get the team together." But he was inwardly concerned that he had missed some valuable time on the field while the quarterback charade had gone on. Outwardly he asked for the number seven for his uniform, disregarding the sixteen he had worn previously. "Let's start over."

The squad had been sliced to fifty-two players—seven above the limit—but there was another major concern. Bill Bain, a starting offensive tackle, had been felled with a knee injury against Philadelphia, and the Broncos had absolutely nobody to replace him. Gehrke was on the phone the next day, but teams weren't trading offensive linemen. Real trouble, since the offensive line was already porous—even with Bain.

The Broncos went off to Seattle trying to find a lineman. Even though the Seahawks had beaten three established NFL teams during the exhibition season, the Broncos took them lightly. "It'll be a walk," Armstrong said in the hotel lobby while one of his single teammates chased after the hotel's group sales director.

Denver won, 27–10, with ex-coach Ralston looking on from upstairs. Although the doubt still existed about Morton, he erased some of the negatives by completing thirteen out of nineteen passes for 101 yards and a touchdown. On the night plane ride Miller lit up. "Did you see Craig? Right at home in there. We got it going. Every week more confidence."

The city wasn't so sure yet. The fans had been led astray so many times before with early successes. In a downtown bar's lavatory a graffiti lover had penned:

The years may come,
The years may go,
Don't matter 'cause
The Broncos always go
Nowhere.

Against the 49ers, though, the Broncos looked like they were going somewhere—to a 20–0 victory. But not before trying moments in the motel. The Broncos had shifted to a Berkeley motel, next to the Bay's marina, and the motel was also the headquarters for the annual speedboat regatta. On the Saturday morning the Broncos were in for a rude awakening when the boats started up noisily at dawn.

"Can't you do something about that?" a Bronco official asked the manager.

"They were here before your team, and what they do is their business."

The motel didn't think much of the Broncos to begin with. In the lobby were insignias from every team in the American Conference but Denver.

Since they were up early, by force, the Broncos whiled the day away by shooting pool and playing the pinball machine. Armstrong knocked in a eight-ball and then questioned the coach's philosophy about running backs. He had always carried the ball twenty times a game, at the minimum, and played all four quarters. This year, according to the dictates of Miller, Armstrong would be rested, and alternated with rookie Rob Lytle.

"I'll give it a chance, but I might have to talk to the man about it if it doesn't go so good. Maybe I'll be stronger in the fourth quarter if I rest some, but I need my yards. I want another 1,000-yarder."

Denver had finally picked up an offensive lineman from, ironically enough, San Francisco—the opponent that night. Andy Maurer, a Paul Bunyan of a man, had come from the 49ers for a future draft choice. Maurer had a bad reputation around the league, so he had played for four different teams. But the Broncos needed any form of help. "Andy, we're all starting new here. You work hard and do your job, and we won't have any troubles," Miller told Maurer, who had been a guard recently, but was being switched to tackle to take Bain's place.

Miller established his own reputation that night. In the closing seconds at Candlestick Park, Denver tacked on a needless touchdown, and Ken Meyer—the San Francisco coach replacing the popular Monte Clark—reacted threateningly. He already was under fire because the 49ers had been miserable so far, and he rushed at Miller when the game ended. "That was a low-life thing you did, and I'll get you," Meyer shouted at Miller and pointed his finger menacingly. "Screw you," replied Miller. Players stepped in and broke up the verbal warfare. Miller smiled about the incident later. "We don't have to play them again. Besides, the idea of football is to score, isn't it?" Meyer was gone at season's end.

It was early Sunday morning when the Broncos arrived in Denver. They had concluded the exhibition season with a 5–1 record, but good preseason marks had been achieved before. Nobody greeted the plane. But Miller was pleased, he told an impromptu press conference. "To be 5–1 while accomplishing the goals we set for ourselves, to get everyone an equal chance and to put in our offense and try to smooth out our system was very good. I'm not saying we'll go to the Super Bowl, but this is going to be a better team than last year."

The cast of characters had been all but decided. Morton would be at quarterback, with Weese and Penrose filling in, and Armstrong would be at one running-back spot with Jon Keyworth and Lonnie Perrin alternating at the fullback position. Jim Jensen had been picked up late from the Dallas Cowboys and would be the fifth running back. Rick Upchurch, Jack Dolbin, Haven Moses, and John Schultz were the four receivers—as they had been a year ago. Schultz held off the bid of several young players because of special teams play, but he still didn't look like much of a football player—with long, sweeping hair and a beard. He would seem more at home in a Denver singles bar. Riley Odoms was established at tight end, but veteran backup Boyd Brown had been displaced by rookie Ron Egloff, whom Miller wanted to hang on to and transform into a tackle. Maurer was stepping immediately into one of the tackle spots, and Claudie Minor, a big, strapping black man who loved to carve in wood and hold defensive ends, would be at the other tackle. Second-year-men Tom Glassic and Paul Howard, a veteran coming off a knee injury, would be the guards, and Mike Montler had passed Bobby Maples, the returning starter, at center. Maples, a fun-loving Texan, went along with the demotion cordially. Besides, he was trying to start his own business. "I want to get the rights in Dallas to the telephone-booth washing. I know a guy who has twenty-five thousand booths. You contract with the phone company to keep them clean. The way I look at it you go in with a crew of three, and it takes a minute and a half to wash the windows, get the puke off the floors, and clean the phones. I can make a fortune."

Offensively, Miller had also decided to keep rookie Rob Lytle; number one draft choice Steve Schindler, a guard; wild man Glenn Hyde, an offensive lineman who had played in the World Football League and would pay his own room and board, given the chance. Punter Bucky Dilts also stuck, and Jim Turner would do the kicking, as always.

There had been very few questionable spots on defense. Lyle Alzado and Barney Chavous would start at ends, although Brison Manor, a rookie in effect because he had sat out the previous year with a knee injury, had pushed both. In fact, before the San Francisco game Miller had said Manor might beat out one of the starters. At the airport Alzado read the information in the newspaper. "What's this? It ain't gonna happen." Rubin Carter would be back again at nose guard. And the four linebackers were Randy Gradishar, Tom Jackson, Joe Rizzo, and Bob Swenson, all veterans. Godwin Turk was still recuperating from an early camp knee injury, and another player said: "His knee will be well as soon as the season starts. He don't like camp." Turk led the team in wardrobes, wearing a black suit, black shirt, white tie and black hat, with feathers, on the last exhibition trip. Bernard Jackson, the pickup from Cincinnati who wanted to own a Baskin-Robbins ice cream franchise, had moved in at free safety alongside Billy Thompson, and Steve Foley and Louis Wright returned as cornerbacks. The Broncos had also decided to keep John Grant, the silent middle guard, and veteran Paul Smith, becoming the first player to make it into a tenth season with Denver, and defensive backs Randy Poltl and Chris Pane and linebackers Rick Baska, Larry Evans, and Rob Nairne, a rookie who had been awful the first few days of camp, but came on and got a chance when another rookie, Charles Jackson, saw his season end because of a knee injury.

It wasn't a powerhouse outfit, by the standards of, say, Oakland, but the group appeared respectable. The Broncos would find out soon enough. The first regular-season game was upcoming. Everything until now had been meaningless.

12

IT'S NOT IN THE CARDS

" 'Sports Talk,' you're on the air."

"Bob, do you think the Broncos can make it this year?"

It was a question Bob Martin—voice of the Denver Broncos and host of a nightly sports talk show on a Denver radio station—heard on a constant basis during the week leading up to the opening regular-season game. Mid-September, and thoughts in Denver annually turn to the Broncos. Football takes over the city, even in a bad year. And with a new coach, renewed hope burst forth. The metropolitan area had grown to 1.5 million, and the new people joined the old in wanting a winner.

As usual, Howard and Patti Witkin, like thousands of others, sat down to plan their Sundays. Weekends revolved around the Broncos' games. When Denver was at home, the Witkins would join their friends Sunday mornings at The Plank House, a midtown restaurant. For seven dollars a person, the restaurant supplied a steak-and-eggs breakfast, a bloody Mary, and a bus ride to and from the game. When the Broncos were out of town, the Witkins would gather with a group at one of the houses for a buffet and then watch the game on TV. It was an annual ritual. "I'm not that big a sports fan, but you have to be behind the Broncos if you live in this city. We've all been waiting and waiting. It's that elusive goal, and everyone keeps hanging on with the team because they know some day it's going to happen, and they want to be a part of it. Until then, we'll go out there and sit and accept whatever happens."

The callers to Martin's show were forecasting records from 0–14 to 14–0, depending on the strength of their beliefs. Martin took a middle-of-the-road stance, claiming the Broncos' success would be based on a number of factors—injuries, play of Craig Morton, improvement of the offensive line, et al. A nightly news show on the ABC affiliate took a poll in the streets, and the largest majority was predicting an 8–6 record. In Las Vegas, however, nobody was betting on the Broncos. They were listed at 20–1 to make it to the Super Bowl on the big board in the Stardust Hotel's sports lounge. "I couldn't get a bet down, so I moved it up to 30–1, and we ended up with $220 worth of action. That's nothing. We got $20,000 from one guy on the Cowboys," said Joey Boston, the oddsmaker at the legal bookie operation.

But Red Miller wasn't concerned about odds or phone calls or polls. "We haven't proven anything. I have no idea how we'll do."

The St. Louis Cardinals were somewhat concerned. They came in a week early and trained for the game in high altitude at Laramie, home of the University of Wyoming. As the team pulled up to the practice field in a school bus, a player looked out the window and said: "Are we preparing for a trip to the moon?"

"No, don't you know this is where the deer and the antelope play," another said.

The Cardinals were having problems, though, and coach Don Coryell wanted to escape the increasing criticism in St. Louis. "We're very uncertain about what we'll do this season. We didn't accomplish what we wanted in the preseason. We're not panicking, though." Well, the shift to Laramie had panic written on it.

"They can go practice wherever they want to," Miller said. "But I don't understand their reasoning."

In midweek Denver's Fred Gehrke stood on the sidelines at practice and scuffed at the grass with his cowboy boots. "They look pretty damn good to me." Gehrke had painted his way into the Football Hall of Fame, putting a logo on the side of a helmet for the Los Angeles Rams in the 1950s. Gehrke was the first to do it. Now he was on the spot, in his first year of running the Broncos. He had just finished signing all the players—with wide receiver Haven Moses the last to agree. "Haven wanted a long-term contract, and we weren't in a position to give it to him. But we settled it. We should have happy players. Everyone's signed. I think we've improved ourselves overall without sacrificing our own talent. We traded draft picks for players, and the only one that didn't work out was Herman Weaver, and, hell, he could have been punting for this team if Bucky hadn't come along. We're still interested in some others, but I don't think we'll make any changes." Miller sought New England's John Hannah, an all-pro guard, and had talked long and hard to Gehrke and the Patriots about it. Hannah had left the New England camp and wanted to be traded—to Denver, preferably, to rejoin his old coach, Miller. "But I don't want to give up a number one draft choice—not unless it's a guy who can really make a difference," Gehrke said. The Broncos never did get Hannah. He rejoined the Patriots and wore a Broncos cap to practice everyday.

Linebacker Randy Gradishar came off the field and pronounced the defense ready. "I don't think we've ever been more prepared going into a game. For the first time since I've been a pro, I feel like I know everything that can happen in a game. I really believe the defense will be improved on last year. St. Louis can score. We know that. And it will be a different team from the one we faced in preseason. But we're going to try to shut them out."

Gradishar proved to be a prophet.

Craig Morton said he had "no reason to believe we can't win the game. We've accomplished a lot in the last two weeks with the offense."

It was 70 degrees outside and not a cloud was in the sky on September 18. At 9:00 A.M. the first of the camper trailers pulled into the parking lot at Mile High Stadium. Within two hours this area would look like a recreational vehicle convention. Some two thousand camper trailers. A couple pulled a grill out from the back of one and started cooking brunch over a fire. Another camper pulled alongside. "Joe, how are you and the missus doing this year?" Broncos games have developed into social affairs. The same people sit and park next to each other year after year, and it was a fall reunion at the first game.

Bill Sheffield parked his car a few hundred feet away and headed for the South Stands. Sheffield is the founder of the South Stands Superfans Club. "It began in 1966 when somebody up here hit Hank Stram with a can of beer—a full can. We didn't want that kind of action going on. We don't want people hurt. We just want to be rowdy and raise hell." So, with the cooperation of the Broncos, Sheffield started his club of twelve hundred members, whose main duty was to police those South Stands.

Sheffield drifted into becoming a Broncos fan in the midsixties, even though he worked for the sheriff's department on Sunday afternoons. "I didn't get off till 2:30, but I had this lovable old sergeant who would let me sneak out early on game days." Eventually he was hooked. "I'm not even sure how it happened. It just got to the point where, hell, the Broncos were my whole life." Sheffield even has a "Broncos Enemies List," and if any of the coaches or players would come into that area, the South Standers would go wild.

Red Miller walked up to the players' entrance. He'd had a sleepless night. He had waited so long to be a head coach. "There are only two kinds of coaches—those who have been fired and those who are going to be fired," he had told himself. He walked through the freshly painted orange door, past the television interview room now piled with equipment, into the laundry room, and out toward the spacious locker room with blue carpet and orange lockers. All the players' equipment was laid out in front of each locker. Nobody was around. Miller picked up a blue helmet momentarily, remembered the first time he had put one on, and then walked into his small office with the tattered sofa and brown mahogany desk. The daydreams were over. He went to work.

Outside, the first-arriving fans were talking football. The kickoff was still several hours away, but "we're getting psyched up," one said. Police were placing barriers along Federal Boulevard, and the fast-food restaurant, Daniel Boone's, was overrun.

By 1:30 a record crowd for a sports event in the state, some 75,002, was in the stands. The expansion project, at a cost of $25 million, was complete. The stadium rose three decks on three sides of the field, and at the end were those fabled South Stands. Earlier in the week the East Stands had been architecturally brought in to hook up with the rest. The stands floated on water, some architectural marvel copied from ship factories on the West Coast. No other stadium in the United States had that type of movable stands. With the hope of major-league baseball on the horizon, the city wanted to be able to adjust the stadium to fit both sports, unlike the round stadiums in other cities that were not really suitable for multiple sports.

Denver linebacker Bob Swenson, who was loosening up on the field, looked up at the crowd and thought: "If we can just get out of this one, I think we'll go four and oh." And then the announcement of the teams. In the press box a writer mused. "Well, there's no stopping it now. The Broncos are here again, and the crazies are ready."

The stamping began. It was traditional for the fans in the upper decks on the West Side to stomp on the steel flooring, reverberating throughout the stadium. It was as if the whole construction would tumble down at any moment. Twenty thousand feet in unison. And then seventy-five thousand bodies were up. Denver was readying to kick off. Lonnie Perrin raised his hand. The referee blew his whistle.

The season was here.

St. Louis, following a 48-yard pass play from Jim Hart to Mel Gray, lined up at Denver's four-yard line. "Well, wait till next year," said a guy sitting next to the Witkins in the second tier. "First quarter, and we're already out of the playoffs." But Gradishar, who had predicted a shutout, stacked up Jim Otis for a loss of one, and the Broncos took over. St. Louis came right back, but Jim Bakken, a dependable kicker, missed a field goal. Then another Bakken field-goal attempt was blocked. An interception by Billy Thompson stopped another St. Louis drive, and the half ended the same way it began.

The Cardinals threatened in the third quarter, but Lyle Alzado reached up and knocked away a Bakken field-goal attempt.

St. Louis finally had to punt, and Steve Jones, normally a running back, filled in on the long snap because of an injury to a regular. His snap to punter James Joyce was high, and the ball scooted around on the ground for a moment. Joyce grabbed the ball and fired a pass, but it wasn't long enough, and the Cardinals also had an ineligible receiver downfield. Denver owned the ball at the St. Louis 34, in strong position for the first time of the day. Otis Armstrong snaked for four yards. Then Morton hit Jack Dolbin for six, and another 15 was tacked on when St. Louis knocked down the quarterback late. Jon Keyworth punched out two yards to the St. Louis 10, and Armstrong finished it off when he slid along the right side of the line, found an opening, and jetted in for the touchdown. Jim Turner kicked the extra point, and Denver had a lead.

That was it for the Broncos' offense, but the Cardinals were not lying down. They reached the Denver 11 in the closing minutes. First down. Hart swung a pass left, but Thompson came up to stick the receiver for a loss of two. Second down and 12 at the two-minute warning. Hart threw in the right flat to Terry Metcalf, who was wrestled out by Thompson at the seven. Third and six. Cardinals tight end J. V. Cain sprinted to the left corner of the end zone and awaited a Hart pass. But Steve Foley and Bob Swenson were there to tip the ball away. Fourth down. Hart tossed over the middle at the goal, intending for Metcalf. But the Cardinals' running back was tangled up in a shuffle and fell. The ball hit Denver's Joe Rizzo smack in the chest and dropped to the ground.

Denver had held, but still wasn't safe with 1:44 to go. Craig Morton trotted onto the field. He had received less than a vote of confidence during the game from the crowd and was met by a round of boos again. The Broncos wanted to eat up the clock, but two plays produced nothing. St. Louis called time. Morton talked with Miller. "Give it to Armstrong," Miller said. "No, I've got an idea," Morton offered and went back to the huddle.

On third down, with the flow of the offense left, Morton, never noted for his running ability, rolled right on a naked bootleg, catching everyone—including Miller—by surprise and picked up the first down that enabled Denver to run out the clock. Later in the season Morton pointed back to that one play. "Denver always had a history of not being able to hang on, and there was always doubt that the offense could come up with something when it was needed. That bootleg, I think, showed the defense we could help them and gave the offense some confidence."

When Miller came off the field, he got a standing ovation. With one play he had won them over.

As darkness settled over the stadium Red Miller reflected: "Well, it was a good start."

Meanwhile, Joe Rizzo was smiling about the last pass of the Cardinals. "Maybe it was pass interference," he told a teammate. "I don't know. But we've never gotten those kind of breaks since I've been here. Maybe this is our year."

At least it was a grand opening.

13

FOR GOD,
FOR COUNTRY,
FOUR AND ZERO

Kay Dalton sat in the Buffalo Bills' offices, looked at the films of the Denver Broncos' defense, and moaned. "It looks better now than a year ago. And that's what I've got to try and beat." Dalton should have been aware of the Broncos. A year before he had been Denver's wide-receiver coach, but in the Ralston shakeup, he was let go and joined the Buffalo Bills in a similar capacity. So he knew what to expect.

"Jim Ringo [Buffalo's head coach] asked me what we should try and do against Denver, and there was no specific thing I could tell him. Those four linebackers are about as talented a bunch as anywhere in football. It was a good defense when I left, and it's improved."

In Denver that defense was concerned about stopping Buffalo's fabled O. J. Simpson. "He cuts back better than anybody. You can't stop him with one man," Miller told his defense. The Denver coach was still peeved about a statement made by St. Louis coach Don Coryell following the opening game. Miller was trying to maintain a low profile for his team, but Coryell announced for the world: "Denver is a playoff contender." When a sportscaster shoved a microphone into Miller's face he replied: "Coryell is blowing smoke. We've won exactly one game."

Miller was trying to improve his offensive line and was getting down in the trenches with them every day at practice. He was showing Claudie Minor an arm-blocking technique when the big tackle popped the coach in the eye. Blood spurted. "Don't worry, Claudie. It was a clean blow."

Stan Jones, the defensive line coach, wanted a name for his troops. "Dave, see what you can do—something like Baltimore's Sack Pack or the Purple People Eaters."

"How about 'Orange Crush'?" said David Frei, the assistant PR director. The name had been used briefly the previous year in a newspaper column and had later been coined by a sportscaster. Frei didn't know what he had brought on the world by that one line.

O. J. Simpson had more things on his mind than "Orange Crush." He had injured an ankle against Miami the Sunday before, and his wife was due to have a baby any minute. Before the game in Denver Simpson limped onto the field, tested the ankle, told Ringo: "I'll try it," and started the game. It was an exercise in futility. The Broncos had keyed on Simpson, knowing he was hurting. They wanted to force the Bills to throw. But neither Simpson—who was held to 43 yards—or the passing game—which accounted for 66 yards—succeeded for Buffalo. The final score: Denver 26, Buffalo 6. The "Orange Crush" defense would have recorded another shutout, but Denver fullback Lonnie Perrin fumbled deep in his own territory and Buffalo's Bo Cantrell picked the ball up on the run and scored. Denver led only 10–6 at halftime and heard from Miller.

"The offense has got to do something, dammit. I'm tired of the defense carrying this team," he told the players just before intermission ended. "We've got to make up our minds to go out in the second half and move the football. I mean it, goddammit. If the offense quits on us, we're through."

His tirade produced sixteen points and an easy triumph. Miller never yelled again the rest of the season at halftime.

Tom Jackson hadn't helped the Bills' cause, either. With the Bills lined up for a 52-yard field-goal attempt, Jackson hollered: "Ref, they've got twelve men on the field. Hold everything."

The Bills stopped to count their personnel, and the thirty-second clock ran out. They were penalized five yards, taken out of field-goal range, and never threatened again. Actually, only eleven men were on the field. "You do what you can do," Jackson smiled afterward.

Miller brought the players in early the next week. "We have to go to Seattle and kick their butts. That's all there is to it. Don't let up on me this week." That night the assistant coaches gathered around the conference table in Miller's office. He had few mementos on the wall. It was a functional room with a blackboard and a bulletin board, a desk and a table. None of the trappings of a successful businessman. "I want to go over every conceivable situation that could occur late in a game with you, and let's come up with the answers. I don't want to be searching for one when we come to that situation." An assistant coach slumped. It was midnight, and they had been going all day.

"Suppose we've got the ball and we're trailing with forty seconds to play at midfield. Any suggestions?"

An assistant coach spoke up. They were going to be in that room for a while.

In practice Thursday there was a brief scare. Rick Upchurch, the premier punt returner in the league and one of the team's messenger wide receivers, was spiked on the Achilles tendon. He hobbled off. The players paused, but Upchurch looked back out at them. "Shit. Ain't nothing." They laughed and went back to what they were doing.

Steve Myer was having his own problems in Seattle. He had just been informed he would start his first National Football League game at quarterback—against a defense that had not given up a point in two games. "I can think of better teams to start my career against," he said. Myer had been a reserve quarterback in his rookie season and was in the same position until a week before when Jim Zorn had been knocked silly during the last offensive series by Seattle. "This might work to my advantage. Denver's got such a super defense that if I do well, maybe I'll get to stay out there for a few games. But I don't know about the Broncos. You can't pick on any one area."

Myer was more proficient than the two previous quarter-backs, but not enough. Denver won, 24–13. However, it was a struggling, functional victory. The Broncos were in control throughout, but they didn't look like a 3–0 team playing a young NFL franchise. Miller, upset about his team's play, snapped at a reporter afterward: "You talk as if we lost the game. We're undefeated. You do what's necessary to win. We won."

The next day Miller called his secretary in. "There's something strange about this city. We've won three games, and the people are beginning to go crazy. It's too early. How can I convince them of that?" She didn't have a solution for him. There already was talk of running Miller for mayor. This was the best start the club ever had. Tacking on the two straight victories at the end of the previous season, this was the first five-game winning streak in the team's history.

The next opponents were the Kansas City Chiefs in Denver. Kansas City, Denver's nemesis for years, had battled Oakland closely the previous Monday night before falling.

Just before game time, Larry Elliott discovered that the special shoe Lonnie Perrin used for kickoffs had been left at the practice headquarters. He rushed outside, grabbed two police-men, and, with siren wailing, fought the oncoming traffic. At kickoff Perrin had his shoe, and nobody in the crowd was wise to the mistake.

But the Kansas City Chiefs weren't so fortunate. Early on, Chiefs owner Lamar Hunt, ever the stickler for detail, spotted only ten men on the field during a punt. He leaped up, rushed into the press box, and picked up a telephone to call his coach-ing staff. Only he reached the Broncos' bench instead.

"Hello, Lamar, how are you doing," Miller said.

Hunt promptly hung up and returned to his seat in silence.

It didn't matter much how many players Kansas City had on the field because it was a losing struggle. The Chiefs didn't score in the first three quarters, and, by that time, the victory was certain for Denver. The Broncos' defense had four inter-ceptions and two fumble recoveries while thoroughly dominat-ing Kansas City.

"This is the first time in a long while, maybe forever, that a Denver team has gone out and overwhelmed Kansas City," Miller said. His grin told the story. "Our defense was a dominant force."

So Denver was 4–0. But Oakland owned the same record, and the Raiders were on the schedule the following Sunday.

14

THE YANKTON FLASH

A massive, hairy human being sat in darkness in a film room at the Broncos' office complex. He was taking notes and studying the moves on the screen. He was suffering from eye strain. "I know him like he was my brother."

The man doing the talking was Lyle Alzado, and he was talking about Matt Herkenhoff, a tackle for the Kansas City Chiefs. "When he moves, I want to know why and what he's thinking. But once the game is over, I forget it all. I don't remember the guy's name from Seattle I played across from."

Against Herkenhoff Alzado planned to use his outside speed "because, look there [pointing to the film]—he doesn't get back that quick. He's a powerful hitter, so I don't want to give him a straight-ahead shot. I'm going to put a new maneuver on him—the halo spinner. You run upfield, fake outside, slap him in the direction his momentum is carrying him, and then spin around toward the inside. Once I've got him thinking about that, he'll protect his inside, and I can beat him outside. It's a game going on between the two of us. I'll never beat him all the time, but if I can some of the time, then I've succeeded.

"I know I'm not always going to get to the quarterback before he releases. If I can get one sack a game, that's about all I can hope for. But I can remind him. I might hit him just after the ball has been released. I won't hurt him—I'll pull back a little. But I'll nudge him, and the next time he might release the ball sooner because he knows I'm coming. If he throws an incompletion, I've done my job without getting to him."

In the Denver victory over Kansas City, Alzado, the hulking 6'3", 250-pound defensive end, was held in check most of the first half. His "halo spinner" wasn't working against Herkenhoff. Late in the second period, the Chiefs' quarterback, Mike Livingston, threw an incomplete pass and was smothered by Alzado. Roughing the passer was called. Kansas City had to start the second half with a new quarterback; Livingston was nursing a sore shoulder from Alzado's blow. Meanwhile, Alzado's play did pick up. He stopped Ed Podolak for no gain. Later, Herkenhoff became frustrated with Alzado's outside move and was called for holding. Alzado then broke free and sacked quarterback Tony Adams for an eight-yard loss. Shortly after, Alzado knocked Adams out of the game. Livingston had to return. But, by then, the Broncos were safely in control, and Alzado sat down. He had three tackles and two sacks for the game. As Alzado walked off the field at the end, he thought that the Chiefs were a lot like what the Broncos used to be. They were mixed up. "I feel sorry for them," he told Paul Smith.

But Alzado didn't feel sorry for himself. After the first play of the opening game against St. Louis, Alzado got up off the ground and went around shaking the hands of his teammates. He had made it. A year prior, in the opening game at Cincinnati, Alzado lined up at middle guard. It was a running play, and Alzado moved left. A tackle fell on his knee, and the leg twisted. Alzado got up and returned to the defensive huddle.

"Lyle, what's wrong with you? You're flushed," Billy Thompson said.

"I'll be all right."

But during the next play Alzado collapsed. He was carried off the field, and doctors announced he was through for the season. The knee was operated on, and Alzado boiled up inside for months. He didn't know if he could come back, and he wanted so badly to be the number one defensive lineman in the game. He also wanted a new coach and helped form the Dirty Dozen that led to Ralston's ousting. Now, however, Alzado was back, and the knee was fine.

So he set his sights on the Super Bowl. "I'm not going to rest until I get there. I want that ring. They'll have to cut the finger off to get the ring off when it happens. And I think when I win the Super Bowl, I'll just pull off my uniform and call it quits right there. That's got to be my goal because I'm never going to be recognized as a great defensive end. The media in New York control the voting for the all-star teams, and they don't even know Denver exists."

While growing up, Alzado didn't know Denver existed, either. Son of a Spanish-Italian father and a Jewish mother, Alzado was born in the Spanish Harlem district of New York City. Tough district. It made Alzado tough early on, especially when his father decided to push on and leave the family. Alzado's best outfit was a torn pair of jeans, and he had to wait in line for food behind two brothers and two sisters. He knew the only way out was to fight his way out.

So Alzado was in and out of jail on a regular basis as a kid on assault-and-battery charges. By age fifteen, he was a bar bouncer—at 6'2" and 190 pounds. He once knifed two guys and got cut up himself. One night he and a friend, Marc Lyons, beat up four adults and threw one through a glass door. He and Lyons were tossed in jail—again. "There were a bunch of winos lying around in the cell, and Marc and I decided we had to do something with our lives." (Lyons became a high-school teacher, eventually.) So Alzado turned to football and organized boxing—Golden Gloves. "Up until then I used my bare fists, and I was color-blind. I beat up everybody—blacks, whites, greens. And I had told the football coach where to stick his football." But the new Alzado won twenty-seven consecutive Golden Gloves fights—twenty-one by knockouts—and advanced to the national semifinals before losing. On the football field he became an all-star, even though his methods were somewhat unorthodox. He was ejected from several games for punching, but there was hope. Several colleges became interested until they saw his grades, barely passing.

A school in Texas did offer a scholarship, but after three days, Alzado had returned home when a coach found out about Alzado's police record. So he decided to join the service, but his high-school coach suggested they go through the letters Alzado had received and pick the smallest, out-of-the-way place.

That was Yankton, South Dakota, and Yankton College.

Alzado hopped on a bus, even though the fall semester had begun, and headed to South Dakota. The bus pulled into town, and Alzado thought how nice the campus looked. Only it was the University of South Dakota. A few hours later the bus arrived at deserted Yankton. But the football coach showed up, bought Alzado two hamburgers, and a young, troubled man decided he would never leave the school. Nobody had ever bought him anything.

With Yankton, Alzado was a terror at several positions before settling in at defensive end. He also had changed his major to special education after the athletic director's wife opened a new world to him. "I walked into a class one day, and there were a lot of kids just sitting there. I asked one if she wanted to play ball, and she paid no attention to me. I was told then that the kids were retarded. I didn't even know what a retarded child was, but I figured it must be bad, and maybe I could do something about it."

Alzado wanted to play professional football, but not many scouts were interested in players from Yankton College. Then one day, Denver assistant Stan Jones was motoring through Montana on a recruiting trip when his car broke down. The mechanic told Jones that repairs would take all day, so the coach asked if there was a college around. He ended up at Montana Tech, looking at films of the previous season, and his eye kept coming back to a defensive player on Yankton, which had played Montana Tech in the Copper Bowl. The college coach told Jones: "That's Lyle Alzado. Some player. He was the MVP in the game." So Jones returned to Denver, told the other coaches about Alzado, and he was drafted, to the surprise of the NFL, in the fourth round.

When Alzado heard the news at Yankton, he knocked a projector down to the floor in his haste to get out of the room and celebrate. The Broncos brought Alzado to Denver for contract negotiations, and Jones decided to take him out to a country club. They sat down in the bar, and the waitress asked if they wanted anything. Jones ordered a drink; Alzado ordered a steak. "Uh, Lyle, we'd better go in the restaurant if you want to eat." Later Jones would say: "Lyle knew nothing about the world. Here he was in a cocktail lounge trying to order a steak. All he knew was he wanted to play football."

Alzado had never owned a coat or a tie, but he soon had a nice, lucrative contract, and he asked his sweetheart at school, Sharon Pike, to marry him.

That first season, Alzado was a reserve on the bench when Pete Duranko, a starting lineman, went down with a knee injury. Alzado was called on and never missed a game until his own knee injury. Meanwhile, he returned to children's work. In Denver he became involved with countless youth organizations, and then, last year, because of his off-time passion, he was selected as the winner of the Byron "Whizzer" White Award, given by the NFL Players Association, for community support. In Chicago, at the dinner in his honor, Alzado sat on the podium with Muhammad Ali. "This is the grandest night of my life," he said. And tears streamed down his face.

Alzado had become the most popular player in Denver. He couldn't go anywhere without attracting a following. A fan club was started early in the 1977 season for Alzado, and he was the most sought-after speaker. But not all his fellow players loved him. "If you watch a game closely, you'll see Lyle screw up a lot. All he thinks about is getting to the quarterback. Because of that, he gets burned," said one defensive mate. "All that background stuff of his makes him a media person, I know. But you look at Barney Chavous down at the other end, and he does exactly what he's supposed to every play and never gets the recognition."

So the Broncos weren't as close as it might have seemed.

"Hey, I know people on this team don't like me. I just want their respect," said Alzado. "I can't be what everybody wants me to be. I'm my own man. I keep to myself, and I do my job."

Red Miller called Alzado "a catalyst—somebody you can build on. You have to like him, the way he jumps around and gets everyone going. He's moody, though. He'll be sitting in a corner sulking, and the next minute he'll be hollering. I just let him do what he wants because he makes so many things happen. We have a lot of holes in the wall around here that Alzado caused."

Jones, who is a father figure to Alzado, believes he is a "throwback to the old-timers who played the game. He's not in it for money or personal glory. Coming out of Brooklyn as a no-count kid, he just wants to make sure he doesn't go back to that kind of life. That's why I don't have to get him up. I have to temper him. He was having problems in the preseason. He wanted to know what he could do. I told him to take his wife out to dinner and forget about football. He just doesn't want to take his mind off the game."

Alzado said his main purpose in dealing with young groups "is to keep them from going through what I had to grow up with. And if I can keep a couple off the streets, then I've accomplished that. So I'm able to use my football career to get me through to them."

After the Kansas City game, Alzado had to get psyched up for Oakland and his favorite player, Art Shell. "If, when I quit, Shell says I was a good player, then that will be good enough for me. He's the toughest man I've had to face, but I'm looking forward to this match-up in Oakland. I want to beat Shell. That's all I'm thinking about."

Alzado was sick. He had been throwing up all week when he went to visit a former teammate, Ray May, who sold used cars at a Cadillac dealership. Alzado went into his office and greeted May, who had played with the Baltimore Colts and the Broncos. "Got the flu, Ray. Better stay away from me."

"I'm going to turn on the air conditioner. It might smell in here."

"Ray, I had the locker next to yours for two years. I'm used to your smell."

"Good luck against Oakland. I wish I was still with you guys," said May, who had been cut loose a year earlier under mysterious circumstances.

"We're 3–0. If we beat them, then we're going somewhere, buddy. If we can just beat them," added Alzado, who had only one thing on his mind this night.

And that's all the Broncos were thinking about—beating the Raiders.

1. Dean Griffing was the Broncos' first general manager. He fought the kids in the stands for footballs after field goals and drafted from a football magazine.

2. Typical of the club's early standouts was a player appropriately named Wahoo McDaniel.

3. In 1960 the Denver Broncos were the laughingstock of the American Football League, to begin with, because of their play, and the lack of fans proved it. The now infamous vertically striped socks, which were later burned in a public ceremony, only heightened the comedy effect.

4-7. (*Clockwise from top left*) Kicker Jim Turner, Defensive lineman Lyle Alzado, quarterback Craig Morton, punter Bucky Dilts.

8. Buffalo's O. J. Simpson had dancing partners all afternoon.

9. Kicker Jim Turner (15) and his holder, Norris Weese, yuk it up at practice with general manager Fred Gehrke. Weese and Turner surprised the entire football world and, especially, the Oakland Raiders by combining on a fake field goal that ended up with Weese throwing a touchdown pass to Turner, of all people.

10–11. Orange Crush. Denver's front three: Barney Chavous (79), Rubin Carter (68), and Lyle Alzado (77). And linebackers four: Randy Gradishar (53), Tom Jackson (57), Bob Swenson (52), and Joe Rizzo (59). Together with the cornerbacks and safeties, this unit formed the fiercest defense in the NFL in 1977.

12. Franco Harris discovers just what Orange Crush means.

13. Rick Upchurch is off and running against Baltimore and finds a friend, Haven Moses, waiting for him with congratulations in the end zone.

14. Red Miller exhorting Craig Morton and the other Broncos as the AFC championship game against Oakland approached.

15. It was an upside down day for the Oakland Raiders and particularly for wide receiver Fred Biletnikoff, who was upended by Randy Gradishar and Joe Rizzo and had to leave with a shoulder separation.

16–17. The newly enlarged 75,000-seat Mile High Stadium was sold out even before Denver's meteoric climb, but now the Broncomaniacs have a lot to cheer about.

15

D DAY IN THE BAY AREA

The week leading up to the Denver-Oakland game must have been proclaimed "Salute to Duane Thomas." In the grand tradition of the National Football League running back who kept his mouth shut, nobody on either team was talking.

"We're not going to say anything that might land on a bulletin board somewhere in Oakland," linebacker Tom Jackson said. "It's so close, something like that might make a difference."

Art Shell, the usually vocal offensive tackle from Oakland, said he was doing no speaking. Denver quarterback Craig Morton was not giving interviews.

In the Broncos' locker room the players were going about their business when each was handed on Friday a sheet as a joke, asking them in twenty-five words or less to give their immediate thoughts about the Oakland game.

A number of players replied: "No comment," or didn't answer the query at all.

However, several of the other players were loosening up:

Louis Wright, cornerback: "My mother told me there would be games like this."

Glenn Hyde: "My individual thoughts are that we are ready, very ready. The team is intense but relaxed, and somehow we will be on top."

Norris Weese: "The Broncos believe we can win against Oakland, which I don't believe was true when we played them both times last year."

Tom Jackson: "The game is usually the biggest of the year up to now. I think defensively we need to have a good day. Offensively, we must control the ball. Mojo go to Oakland and walk on hot coals."

Randy Gradishar: "I'm not saying anything. I'm keepin' it in my heart."

Godwin Turk: "It's just another game."

Bob Swenson: Bring back 'Fernwood 2-Night.' "

Joe Rizzo: "I'm pulling for the Yankees."

Larry Evans: "I just want to win. The Dodgers in six."

Rick Baska: "What game?"

Rob Nairne: "If we win, I think we'll be 5–0."

Jim Turner: "Nobody wants to know what I think. Go ask the boys."

Bobby Maples: "They were champs in 1976; the outcome made us all sick. Here we are in '77, the Broncos are ready to meet their level."

Billy Thompson: "Orange and black, pumpkins and cats, at two o'clock Sunday everyone will know where it's at."

Claudie Minor: "Apples, peaches, pumpkin pie. Denver will not be denied. Then we're going to take home a victory for the Broncos to own."

Jon Keyworth: "Rope the dopes and dash their hopes."

Otis Armstrong: "We're gonna hit 'em and stick 'em and knock 'em down. We're gonna smack 'em, crack 'em; we're gonna beat those clowns."

Craig Penrose: "The Oakland Raiders are a great football team but time has come to stop their machine. To beat Oakland you must play like them—tough and very aggressive."

Paul Smith: "This will be the biggest game of my ten-year career."

Off to the side Lyle Alzado said: "Hey, this is no week to be talking. A lot of pressure is being put on one game. It's only the fifth game of the year. I hope we don't psyche ourselves out."

But there was importance. Oakland and Denver were 4–0. The winner would lead the American Conference's Western Division alone. The Broncos wanted to be just like the Oakland Raiders. For the first time in two seasons the Broncos would be seen on national television. And *Sports Illustrated* had put middle guard Rubin Carter on the magazine's cover and talked at length about Denver's 3–4 defensive front.

On Friday Miller hurried from practice to the Denver Quarterback Club meeting. "He hates those meetings," someone with the team said. "Asked that they be cut back, but then he shows up at the meeting and tells everyone how great the meetings are, that there should be more of them." Miller hated public speaking. "I'm here to coach, not to talk," he said. But he was improving as a speaker. Some of the clichés were disappearing.

At the meeting he looked at the one hundred and fifty gathered and said: "We want to go out there and beat Oakland, and that's what we're going to do."

But the next afternoon in the parking lot at the Berkeley, California, hotel where the team was staying, Miller stood in the wind and said: "I really think we have a better chance of beating them two weeks from now [in the rematch]. I just don't think we can win out here."

Over in Oakland, John Madden, the Oakland Raiders coach, wasn't so sure. "The Broncos look very good to me. There's a lot of evidence that they are playing well. I think they're getting great coaching now, and that has made a difference." It had not come out, but Madden was interested in shifting to Denver in 1977 as coach. It would have been a way to get out from under Al Davis, the managing general partner and the man most people thought was responsible for the Raiders' success—culminating in a Super Bowl trophy the year before. But the Broncos had immediately gone to Miller as coach, and Madden's thoughts of a move never materialized. But he knew Denver was improved. A year before in a Chicago hotel he had said that any time Oakland set foot on a field against Denver, "there's no doubt we'll beat them." He wasn't so sure this time.

The upcoming four-game stretch would be the key for the Broncos—Oakland, Cincinnati, Oakland again, and, finally, at home against Pittsburgh. Some month of Sundays. "I would take a split right now and be happy," Miller said to an assistant privately.

The hallways were quiet that night before the Oakland game. Nobody ventured out. In the motel disco a girl said: "I thought the Broncos were staying here." A groupie looking for a home, but no takers.

The sky over Oakland that Sunday was like the Raiders' colors, gray and black. Outside the Oakland–Alameda Coliseum, a man was dispensing buttons that said: "Welcome, Denver," and had a picture of a hand with the middle finger raised. "It's nothing against Denver. We have the same buttons for everybody. Fuck the other NFL teams. The Raiders can't be beat," he said.

And it was beginning to look so. Oakland had won seventeen games in a row, but Denver owned a six-game winning streak. "Hey, guys," Miller said to the players before hand. "Oakland isn't supermen. We can beat them. Be cool on the field. Don't panic if it doesn't start off good."

The Oakland press box is the most crowded in the world, and the team's management couldn't care less. No effort was made to make life easy for the media. And the Raiders didn't like to make life easy for visiting teams. Broncos owner Gerald Phipps settled in a seat upstairs with a frown on his face.

And the frown didn't leave when Oakland took the opening kickoff and moved quickly down the field for an easy touchdown. Quarterback Ken Stabler was throwing on first down, a maneuver that surprised the Broncos. They were expecting the Raiders to try and shove it down their faces. "As soon as I saw them passing, I loved it," said linebacker coach Myrel Moore later. "We had to adjust somewhat, but we knew they were thinking they had to beat us with the pass."

The Broncos couldn't move after the touchdown, and Oakland came right back. They were at the Denver 41 and seemed to be in position to score again. But Denver's Joe Rizzo, who was wearing a shoulder harness because of a lingering arm injury, stepped in front of a receiver and stole the ball. The interception run ended up at Oakland's 29, and soon Denver scored to tie the contest. Instead of a 14–0 deficit, the Broncos were in the game at 7–7.

"It definitely gave us some confidence," Rizzo said. "All of a sudden we're thinking, 'Hey, we *can* beat these yo-yos.' "

After an exchange of punts Denver drove down for its second touchdown. Then Stabler became shaky. Under heavy pressure, he fired toward Rizzo again. The Broncos didn't get any points, but they got the ball again when Stabler's pass was tipped and fell into, that's right, Rizzo's hands again. His third interception in one half. A field-goal attempt by Jim Turner was short, though.

But Stabler still wasn't gun-shy. He went back to the air, and this time Randy Gradishar stepped into the passing lane and presented Denver the ball at Oakland's 32. Three plays were shy of a first down, and in came Turner with only a minute remaining before halftime. The ball was snapped to holder Norris Weese, and Turner's leg swung through. But the ball wasn't there; Weese had pulled it up and faded back and to his right. It was a fake field goal, and Oakland wasn't prepared for what was coming. While the attention was focused on the Broncos' receivers, Turner sneaked out and headed for the left flat. All alone. Weese lofted the ball, thinking: "I hope I don't overthrow him." He didn't. Turner tucked the ball in at the 10-yard line and loped into the end zone. Denver was ahead, 21–7, and the crowd of 53,616 couldn't believe what it had just witnessed. The Oakland Raiders, world champions, had just been made fools of. A field-goal kicker wearing high-top shoes catching a touchdown pass. Turner runs the 100-yard dash in about three days. He had never caught a pass in his long football career. But Oakland went into the dressing room wondering what had just hit them. "It's all over," Alzado said as he walked to the locker room. "We've got them demoralized."

Assistant coach Marv Braden had suggested to Miller the fake field goal. "Marv, you know we only practice that for fun." "It'll work, coach," Braden pleaded. "It better," Miller said, and called it.

The Broncos came out in the second half as cautious and conservative as they could possibly be. As a result, they picked up only two first downs. But the defense was holding on, and Tom Jackson was having fun at the expense of Raiders head coach Madden.

"Hey, fat man. Take this," and Jackson gave Madden the

internationally recognized obscene sign. "We got you, fat man. We got you." Stabler did move his team to the Broncos' 21, but Pete Banaszak was tackled on a sweep and fumbled. Alzado recovered. The Broncos moved across the 50, but were forced to punt deep.

From his own end zone, Stabler looked to throw back across the field. But Louis Wright came up from cornerback, grabbed the ball on the rush, and went in for the score. Oakland still had time for one of its patented miracles. "Hey, I don't want any celebrating," Miller told the players on the sidelines. "We're not out of here yet," The Raiders moved rapidly down the field, but on fourth down, Banaszak, having a rough afternoon, was stacked up short.

On another series Stabler's pass over the goal was intercepted by Thompson. Stabler, becoming a glutton for punishment, tried to pass again a few minutes later, but hit defensive end Paul Smith in the chest. The ball "stuck," and Denver had possession at the Oakland 15. Jim Turner kicked a field goal, and with 7:07 left, the Broncos had it wrapped up, 30–7.

"Now you can celebrate," Miller said.

The seven interceptions were a record against Stabler, a beaten man who retired to the side and put on his jacket.

The Broncos went up the tunnel delirious. "We beat those fools," one said. "We are for real." In the locker room it was D Day all over again. But Red Miller wasn't about to let loose. "It was a big victory, another step."

But Tom Jackson was saying: "The world champions. We beat the world champions. Mojo came to Oakland and walked on hot coals." Defensive back Bernard Jackson added: "This week a lot of people are going to have good things to say about us."

The Oakland dressing room was a wake. "They beat the crap out of us. What can I say?" offered Stabler. "Denver must be recognized now. Maybe they will believe me when I say this is a tough division. They beat the hell out of us."

Madden talked briefly about "mistakes" and "respect for Denver," but his face was more revealing. He couldn't comprehend what had occurred. In a small corner office Al Davis paced around the room with a cigarette in his hand, as if someone had just told him a relative died. One of his peons walked into the room. "Don't bother me, damnit," he said.

It was the biggest triumph in the history of the Denver franchise. Always before, when the Broncos entered an important contest, they folded. Not this time, though. That's what Thompson was thinking as he flew home to Denver that night. He told his girl friend later: "We are going to the playoffs. This is our year. That victory today was all we ever needed." Thompson began a scrapbook that night. "This will be worth savoring later on," he thought.

The Broncos could have made it home without a plane. There was no champagne on the flight, but enough beer to float a submarine, and the Broncos drank it all. "Can you get the pilot to stop somewhere and get us some more beer?" center Mike Montler asked a stew.

In Denver a crowd of ten thousand waited impatiently. They had spilled from the terminal out into the corridors. There was nothing the police could do. The Broncos finally came in, and a narrow path was formed. "I want you guys to go through there," Gehrke said. "These people deserve to join you." So the Broncos snaked through the crowd. "It's hotter than hell," assistant coach Ken Gray said to Myrel Moore. "There are so many bodies in one small place, and the heat can't escape. When I was playing with St. Louis, we won a big game, and there were thirty people waiting for us. This is something the rest of the country wouldn't believe."

As the players passed through everyone tried to lay a hand on them. "I think my shoulder is broken," hollered one player. Several people fell down the escalator trying to get through to the Broncos. The hysteria went on, and most of the Broncos were trapped for more than an hour. "Let them enjoy it. They have been waiting," Miller said. "For seventeen years they have been waiting."

Another group interested in the Broncos' success was back at the Oakland airport as midnight approached. A loyal band had followed the team out and had a late return trip. In the waiting area about every ten seconds someone stood up: "Let's hear it for the Broncos."

"Broncos."

Pause.

"Let's hear it for the Broncos."

Only the plane's arrival stopped the madness. On the flight the stewardess quickly ran out of booze. A card dealer sat in his seat and mumbled: "Is it possible? Could this be the year?"

One young man, though, had another thought. "I see by your orange shirt that you're a Bronco lover," he said to a young lady. "Me, too. Want to go in the bathroom and talk about it?"

"Not on your life," she replied. "Miss this? Not for anything."

The plane rocked back to Denver. The fans were "mile high," just like the city and the football team.

16

THE FOUR HORSEMEN

It had been said of the four Denver Broncos linebackers that if one is scratched, the other three bleed. The four were almost one in 1977. They were more concerned about the unit. Off the field they acted like the Marx Brothers. A laugh a minute. Their performances should have been called: "A Day at the Football Game." In the tradition of John, Paul, George, and Ringo, the Beatles, the Broncos had Tom, Joe, Bob, and Randy.

"I like to think of them as our bunch of savages," their coach, Red Miller, said. "I don't mean that in the wrong way. I've never been around a more intelligent group of guys, but they love to get after people. They're headhunters, and that's what I like."

The quartet had come together fully in 1976, when injuries reduced the number of available defensive linemen. So the Broncos' coaching staff elected to go to a 3–4 alignment, with four linebackers. And because the quartet clicked so well, the defensive scheme carried over.

Randy Gradishar is the Mid-Western All-American lad. Joe Rizzo is the serious, shy sort with the New York accent. Bob Swenson is the long-haired, single California beach boy. And Tom Jackson is a down-in-the-ghetto, fast-jiving scuffler.

Before the season was out each would be a major influence in a victory, and other teams were beginning to refer to them as the best linebacking unit in football. Rizzo had intercepted three passes against Oakland to set up the victory. Gradishar had been in on all the major stops, and Jackson and Swenson's turns were coming.

These were four different young men. Rizzo was the oldest (by a few months) at twenty-six, Jackson, twenty-six, Gradishar, twenty-five, and Swenson, twenty-four. Gradishar, the heftiest at 233, grew up in Champion, Ohio, and became an All-American at Ohio State. Then he was a celebrated number one draft choice of the Broncos in 1974. Rizzo, the worldliest, with the mustache and the kinky hair, came out of Long Island, went to the Merchant Marine Academy, failed a physical with the Buffalo Bills, worked in a shipyard in San Diego, and joined Denver during the players' strike of 1974. Swenson, the quickest with a 40-yard-dash time of 4.6, was born in Stockton, California, played collegiately at the University of California at Berkeley, and stuck with the Broncos as a free agent in 1975. Jackson, the shortest at 5′ 11″, survived a tough youth in Cleveland—he was hit on three separate occasions by automobiles—and attended the University of Louisville. He was a number four draft choice of the Broncos in 1973.

After a soggy practice in midseason, the four linebackers gathered in the players' lounge of the Broncos' locker room, ate four orange Popsicles, and stripped to their socks and jocks.

Jackson: "These guys are a pain."

Gradishar: "As you can tell, we don't take each other seriously."

Jackson: "Except Joe. He's too serious."

Rizzo: "These guys are full of shit."

Jackson: "Look out, Joe. This is being taped, and you don't want to say anything bad. If I may speak for the group, I think we have a lot more fun playing this game than most people. We get serious when it's time to get serious. We get our work done. When we're off the field, we have our fun and just sort of hang out, you know."

Swenson: "Jack got a letter from a guy awarding him the honor of saying the most 'you knows' in the history of one interview."

Jackson: "Ron Lyle [a local heavyweight boxer] used to have the title, you know."

Swenson: "We get together except for the married one

[pointing at Gradishar]. He can't get out of the house much."

Gradishar: "I'll get out of the house the day Jackson buys. Most linebackers have to beg him to pick up the check."

Has this group matured?

Gradishar: "We've played together for a year, and it would be hard if one of us wasn't with the team now. You need to play together to become good. That's what championship teams have. We've gotten to know each other, and I think that's why we've improved."

Swenson: "Sometimes that's bull, but if you know who you're playing with it really helps make you a better player. You know what to expect. Like the three of us are a little bit faster than Randy."

Gradishar: "There you go picking on me again."

Swenson: "And if Randy is matched up against Cliff Branch, we know we should be looking to help him out. It's the same with all of us. If we have a tough assignment, we know we'll get help."

Jackson: "I've been playing linebacker since the ninth grade, and this is the best group I've ever been around. Not only in the way we feel for each other, but in ability, too. We've learned a lot of things together, a lot of extra things. We're growing as pro players together because we're about the same ages. When we're on the field, we're always talking to each other to keep ourselves aware. When we first started playing together, we made a lot of mistakes. A couple of games we were really messing up, but we have it down now. We have that extra communication. In a game, we might be in a tight situation, but we keep each other loose. That's what it's going to be—a gut check—when a team's on our one-yard line, and it's fourth down. You've got to survive that pressure, and these guys can do it."

Rizzo: "I think we ought to mention the linebacker coach, Myrel Moore, who prepares us. Ever since I became a starter, I've been very confident going into every game. I might blow a coverage, make a physical mistake, but I've always been prepared mentally. I believe the linebackers are the best-drilled players on the field."

Jackson: "The longer we're together the better we get. We've been a unit for just the two seasons—it seems like a long time—but we can see ourselves getting better, you know."

Gradishar: "Our whole defense could stick together for a long time, if we can avoid injuries, and we could really have something going. We've just got to be patient for the offense, and it will continue to come. Red has done a lot of good things with the offense already."

What about linebacking?

Swenson: "It's the greatest position. It's very physical, but worthwhile. A lineman is down there in the pits against those big guys, and if a defensive back gets beat, that's all there is. A linebacker doesn't have all the problems of those guys, but he has a little of both."

Jackson: "You're involved all the time."

Swenson: "The mental aspect makes linebacking what it is. You can do so many things, like blitzing. You can play with a quarterback's mind because he doesn't know what to expect from you."

Jackson: "And linebackers are supposed to be your leaders. The defensive backs and the defensive linemen don't communicate with each other, truthfully. They have their own things to worry about. The linebackers have to be the media. Both the backs and the linemen look at the linebackers to do their jobs—to give support in both places. And that makes us work that much harder because we don't want to blow it for those guys."

Ever get mad at each other?

Gradishar: "No, we all make mistakes. If we do get mad, we'll say something constructive. It's kind of high schoolish to be running around, jumping on people for a mistake when you might make the same one on the next play."

Swenson: "We're not rah-rah, yelling at people. We try to lead by example. If we do our job, then maybe the others will do their job."

Jackson: "The one thing we need to improve on as a unit is hitting receivers. We're not physical as much as we are finesse players. I'm not going to overpower people, but if two of us get them, well. We need to start breaking patterns and hitting people. Randy has gotten the idea. He has been knocking down people everywhere. I don't know if it was accidental. And when you see that happening, you kinda start doing it yourself. Leadership by example is right. It doesn't matter how rah-rah you are if you're not getting the job done."

Swenson: "Take Joe."

Jackson: "Yeah, take him."

Swenson: "He's quiet."

Jackson: "He might not say anything for a couple of weeks, but if it's on his mind, he'll bring it up. Talk about guys getting mad. Joe will get into an argument with the coach over a point."

Rizzo: "I'm not arguing for the sake of an argument. I want to make sure we all understand so it will be easier."

Jackson: "Joe keeps us on our toes. He's the intellectual. He does everything different, even the exercises."

Do you really know each other?

Gradishar: "We played Bob's team in my sophomore year, and Woody [Hayes, the Ohio State coach] was upset at halftime because we were leading only 9–7. We won, 42–7. That tells you the kind of football they play at Berkeley. And King's Point [Merchant Marine Academy] plays that semi-Triple-A high-school ball. Joe doesn't talk about football. He talks about his boxing experience. And Louisville is noted not for football but horse racing."

Jackson: "I thought about going to Ohio State."

Gradishar: "Too tough for you?"

Jackson: "No, they had nineteen starters coming back, and I would have had to beat out Jack Tatum. No thank you."

Rizzo: "I didn't think about going to Ohio State. I didn't get a scholarship from anybody. Well, I did get an offer from Vermont if I studied agricultural mining, and that was out. I played in a high school all-star game and got a letter from King's Point saying, 'Dear Footballer.'"

Jackson: "Real personal, like 'To Whom It May Concern.'"

Rizzo: "It was a great school. It's rated in the top twenty academically."

Swenson: "Could we have some background music?"

Rizzo: "Football is relative. There is just as much pressure when King's Point plays Hofstra as there is when Ohio State plays Michigan. It's playing against guys your own size of your own ability. You get the same nervousness as we do when we played Oakland. It's the thrill of victory, the agony of defeat."

Jackson: "That's an original line."

Rizzo: "It doesn't matter. I used to think I wasn't as good as guys like Randy because they played at big schools. But he's no Bionic man. I wouldn't back off anybody—like Archie Griffin. I hit him twice last year, and his Heisman Trophy didn't keep him from falling any different from anybody else. But I don't feel jilted. I feel lucky to be here. After I failed the Buffalo physical, I worked in a shipyard in San Diego and went up to Pomona to try out with the Broncos. I told my boss to keep my job open, that I would be back in two weeks. I matured late. I played everywhere in college. I was ninth in the nation in punting. Finally, I became a linebacker. And here I am."

Swenson: "I matured late, too."

Jackson: "Your brain matured late."

Swenson: "But I found out I could play."

Jackson: "I realized early at Louisville that, no matter what I did, I wouldn't be a number one draft choice, that it might be better, even if those players aren't better, to go to a big school and get one of those multimillion-dollar contracts like some linebackers we know in this room. Last year I was upset for a while that I didn't get to the Pro Bowl, but I got over it. Nobody knows about Denver. When I was drafted by the Broncos, I didn't know the players or even where the city really was."

Swenson: "I'd heard of Floyd Little, and I thought he retired five years ago."

Rizzo: "That's it. The recognition won't happen until we get into the playoffs and the Super Bowl. Then we'll start getting the recognition."

Jackson: "You're going to tell me Pittsburgh has the best three linebackers in the NFL? That's crazy, but they've been to the top. I think we pull for each other to get honors. Myrel Moore says we'll make it big when all four of us are All-Pro. If we get a championship, you can have the rest."

Gradishar: "You have to watch, Jack, though. I never knew any blacks growing up. He's all right, but he's all the time tap dancing and singing. We've learned a lot about each other."

Jackson: "Yeah, I've told him about knife fights in Cleveland."

What about this season?

Gradishar: "I'm not getting into the predicting business, but if we can keep beating the playoff teams, like Oakland, then we'll be considered a playoff team. We're proving ourselves more and more this season, but we have to continue. This is the roughest schedule Denver has ever had, and this will be the year to see if we can do it."

Jackson: "To win our division, we have to be consistent. If we can improve, we can win ten or eleven games, and that will put us right in there. There's a lot—a lot—of talent here now. We've got to do something with it. We can't go messin' it up."

Rizzo: "Randy and Tom said just about all of it, but in terms of what the linebackers want to accomplish, we've got to improve in every phase of the game. And I know we can."

Swenson: "I'm looking forward to the rest of the season. We've got the coaches to get things done. Like I've never seen offensive adjustments at halftime, and we're doing it all the time. We come into the locker room at halftime and on the blackboard . . . well, maybe I shouldn't talk about it."

Jackson: "Oh, you mean the way we bug the visiting team's dressing room?"

Swenson: "Well, just say that improvements have been made, and I think all the linebackers are excited about what's going to happen."

Jackson: "Will this be on TV?"

Swenson: "See, guys, I told you we were going somewhere."

Rizzo: "You people are crazy. Why do I have to put up with this?"

Gradishar: "On behalf of the four linebackers we appreciate this opportunity to talk. Now, let's go have lunch."

17

BRONCOMANIA ERUPTS

Joe Iacino, the distributor for Hires root beer in Colorado, had not missed a Denver game in ten years. But he was just another fan until the whirlwind excitement developed over the Denver defense, nicknamed "Orange Crush." Iacino loved the nickname. In addition to root beer, Iacino bottled a soft drink called Orange Crush, a generally weak seller in Colorado and around the rest of the country. "Why don't we give in on this?" Iacino told his son-in-law, who immediately searched for marketing ideas. After the Oakland game, two players were presented with six cases of the soda. "This is a lifetime supply," said Bob Swenson. "Anybody want any of this stuff? I'm not gonna drink it."

Iacino, sixty-two, has been supplying soft drinks to supermarkets for thirty years, but business had never boomed like this before. "It's like the Fourth of July," he said. "Sales increased by 100 percent. "I can't keep the shelves full. We're working night and day to come up with enough Orange Crush. I am very enthused. We've been waiting for something like this to happen in Denver for a long time, not just because it's helping our company, but because Broncos fans deserve it."

From the nickname came the "Orange Crush" T-shirts, and within forty-eight hours after they reached the department stores, 65,000 were sold. The phenomenon was beginning— spurred by the Broncos' victory over Oakland. The support had always been there, bubbling. And now it was overflowing. The marketplace was very quickly filled with orange- and

Bronco-related products. Orange Crush, the company, came out with sweaters and jackets. The mayor sported one.

An editorial cartoon by Ed Stein, usually reserved for presidential matters and Mideast war problems, suddenly turned up with the devil reading a newspaper with the headline that the Broncos had beaten the Raiders. All around the devil snow fell. A cold day in hell, so to speak.

Broncoitis became a legitimate disease with these symptoms. Stiffness of the index finger—caused by repeatedly signaling number one; compulsion to purchase anything orange—it was estimated that by now fifty new items with orange as the theme were going on sale each week; sprained knee joint—caused by constant jumping up and down at Broncos games; irrational behavior—as evidenced by Denverites' reactions to exclusion from ABC's "Monday Night Football" highlights; glassy eyes— a look commonly associated with those dreaming about a weekend in New Orleans; unbearable foot irritation—known as the Super Bowl itch.

The Orange Crush people were quick to jump on the bandwagon, coming up with an Orange Crush punch: five 10-ounce bottles of Orange Crush, two quarts of Vernor's ginger ale; two pints of orange sherbet, one cup limeade concentrate; one fifth gin or vodka; and two trays of ice cubes. Put the sherbet in a punch bowl. Pour chilled vodka over the top and then add Orange Crush and ginger ale. Garnish with orange slices, strawberries, and mint leaves. Serves forty. It had not been reported if anyone had tried the concoction.

A poem was sent to a Denver newspaper about the Broncos, so the writer, in a good mood, asked for more poet types to step forward. In the next two weeks he received five hundred, on the order of:

THE WAY IT IS

We are the Denver Broncos,
We're from the Mile High City.
Just try and defeat us,
We'll put you at our feet.
We're the Denver Broncos,
The team to defeat.

We take the ball from goal to goal,
Every time we play,
This is the Denver Broncos,
The team of today.
Now you know how we stand,
We are the Denver Broncos,
The Team of this Land.

ORANGE CRUSH

There is a warm, sunny day
When the Snake will come to town,
To deliver his worst.
He'll bring Freddie and Casper
And the fleet-footed Cliff.
But the Orange Crush will be ready
To lay them out stiff.
After the game Snake
Will march off the field
And yell at coach Madden
The Broncos are for real.

They weren't good, but they were plentiful. And the letters started pouring into the Broncos' offices from everywhere.

Dear Broncos: Congratulations. The way you are playing you might make the playoffs. I'll be watching you. M. D., Aurora, Colorado

Dear Broncos: Last year the kids in our school had a favorite team except nobody liked the Broncos that I know of except myself, and you are still my favorite team. J. C., Aurora

Dear Rick [Upchurch]: I am a fan of yours. I am a ten-year-old girl. I'll bet you don't get a lot of girl fans. B. A. A., Aurora

Dear Broncos: Something really strange happened while I was writing this letter. I forgot what Penrose's first name was. While I was downstairs my dad said that Louis Wright will be living right down the street from us. Well, I don't know if this is true, but I can trust my mom and dad. S. C., Aurora

Denver Broncos: I think you guys have a good chance to go to the Super Bowl and a very good chance to go to the playoffs. One of the plays I would try is the Upchurch reverse, and also pass on second and two and stuff like that. M. T., Aurora

Dear Mr. Miller: I would like to know where the best seats are in Mile High Stadium. I have only been there once to watch a Denver Bears game. Thanks a million. J. H., Aurora

Dear Broncos: I hope Craig Morton will do better in Denver than he did in Bronxville, N.Y. Against Houston try to run weak side. C. S., New York

Denver Broncos: I know you're going to win the Super Bowl, because if you don't, well, I lose some money to other fellas. L. N., Tarrytown, New York

Dear Denver Broncos: I wait for Sunday to come. You play well on the field. Trust me. When you lost a game I got really mad and broke the stool. I have not seen Craig Morton lately. I can't because we live in Vermont. T. S., Ripton, Vermont

Dear Sirs: I would like it if you would send me as many of your stickers as you can so I can give them to my friends and put them on my Dad's car. D. Q., Houston, Texas

Red Miller left the studio after his post–Oakland Monday night replay show, the highest-rated program in Denver, and found an eighty-five-year-old grandmother waiting outside in a wheelchair. She had an orange afghan for him. "I've been making this for you, coach. I hope you can use it."

"Thank you, ma'am."

"Now win the rest of the games."

Miller went home and showed the gift to his wife. "I knew this town was crazy about football, but this is extending over the whole region. It's up and down the mountains."

In fact, for the next home game, two busloads were coming in the 560 miles from Gallup, New Mexico, and a group had rented a plane in Billings, Montana, to make the trek to Denver. (Later Miller would speak at a banquet in Billings before 550, and more than half of them would show up in orange.)

An entire class at a Denver school came up with poems, and grown men were sitting around office buildings trying to think of things that rhymed with Bronco.

"Just think what would happen if we win the championship," said Jon Keyworth at practice one day, "after what's happened this week—just beating Oakland."

But as far as the people were concerned, nothing better

could have happened. They had been waiting so long to beat the Raiders, and, finally, it was a reality.

But it was a costly victory. Red Miller, in a moment of fervor, had awarded a game ball to everyone on the team. Cost: $1,350. "My paycheck may be a little less next time around, but it was worth it.

A few minutes later a huge sculpture arrived with the index finger raised high, indicating what the artist thought of the Broncos. A secretary looked at the four-foot object and said: "Last year that thing would have come here with the middle finger raised. What a difference five victories make!"

"I've never seen a town become so excited so early about a football team, and I've been everywhere and seen everything. At least I thought so," said Miller, sitting in his car and scrutinizing an orange commode top someone had just brought to him.

The city was taking much of its ire, though, out on ABC for not showing the Broncos on "Monday Night Football" and, for the most part, not on the halftime highlights. Denver felt slighted, and Howard Cosell was the recipient of most of the curses, even though Cosell had nothing to do with the selections. But he was the most well known, and he took the brunt. People wanted to kill Cosell if he ever came to town. The letters by the hundreds were mailed off to ABC. But ABC tried to explain that the films of each Sunday's game had to be flown to Philadelphia for editing, and there were no available flights out of Denver. The excuse didn't help matters.

The Broncos had been criticized in the past for lease negotiations by the morning *Rocky Mountain News,* but the *News* took time out following the Oakland game to set aside the prime spot on its editorial page for:

Even if the Denver Broncos' season ended today, it would be enough. In neighborhoods throughout this state, whoops and hollers could be heard through the open windows on a warm Sunday afternoon as the Broncos intercepted one pass after another and went on to defeat what has been called the strongest team in professional football, the Oakland Raiders. Thousands of fans jammed into Stapleton International Airport to welcome the players home.

All that emotion may seem strange. But this is perhaps the best sports city in the nation. And this was a game in which all the dreams of 17 years of frustration came true. We have, from time to time, criticized the operations of Allan and Gerald Phipps, the owners, in some of their sweetheart deals with Mayor Bill McNichols of Mile High Stadium and city subsidies. But for today, let's call them the soundest, best and most thoughtful owners in the National Football League. We'll regain our senses when the glow wears off . . .

Even if the season is so-so for the Broncos the rest of the way, we hope that every player and all the coaches and the owners know that they gave us something special on Oct. 16, 1977. And we thank them all.

So even the staunchest critics were coming around.

But unlike what the editorial said, the season wasn't over. In fact, there were nine games left. Nine. Could the city remain stable for more than two months?

As Miller said to the players in a Monday meeting after the Oakland game: "Mens, we've got Cincinnati Sunday." Don't forget." That night Miller and several of the coaches settled back and watched Cincinnati on the Monday night game. They didn't take notes, but watched more out of pleasure. "You can't pick much up on the television. We'll get our report tomorrow from Doc [Urich, the team's scout]."

The next day the Broncos examined their wounded and moved on. Actually, one of the major positive factors for Denver was the fact that few had been injured over the first five weeks. Bill Bain, the offensive tackle, a starter, had been lost for the season during an exhibition, but nobody else had gone down severely. "Let's knock on wood," Miller said, searching for wood. "But I think it's because of our conditioning. We started a stretching and exercise program with the players last winter—sent it out to all of them—and I think it's making a difference."

But Cincinnati coach Bill Johnson wasn't knocking on wood. His team had lost that Monday night to Pittsburgh, "and we're suffering. We've had so many players hurt I may have to suit up." No less than seven Bengals were bothered by injuries.

However, the Broncos weren't going into Cincinnati over-confident. "We've still got to play our best every week," Miller said. "But I've seen a change in attitude. Our players no longer go into a game hoping they can win. They expect to win. We didn't come to Cincinnati to lose."

The Broncos arrived to find Billy Graham ahead of them. The evangelist was in town for a revival at the Cincinnati Coliseum, across the street from Riverfront Stadium, where the Broncos were playing. As usual, the Denver team arrived late Saturday afternoon after a good meal on the plane. Miller preferred to get into town as late as possible, hoping the players would eat a leisurely dinner and retire. "You get into a city too early, and the player have all day to fool around and think about the game too much." The players lounged around the hotel lobby. Otis Armstrong was about to take an elevator up to his room. "Dead town. We'll liven it up tomorrow."

The Broncos' hangers-on headed out to a disco while Merlin Olsen, the former All-Pro and now a star on "Little House on the Prairie" and a TV commentator, talked to several of the assistants about the team. "Is it this good, Babe [Parilli], or are you just fooling me?"

"You can answer that after tomorrow," Parilli said and sipped from his drink.

The day was cloudy in Cincy. As the players waited outside their hotel for the bus, one said: "It could affect us playing this early. It will only be 11:00 back home at kickoff." Miller turned, heard the comment, and said: "You've got to be ready to play at 2:00 A.M." Miller looked up: "You know. We've had nothing but good weather so far. I wonder if that's an omen. I'll take anything as an omen."

The players piled in the buses and were silent on the trip over. Except for Jack Dolbin, the wide receiver. "They need to start a new statistic, for 'receptions called back.' I'd lead the league." He had had a touchdown and another long pass called back because of penalties earlier in the season.

But it wasn't to happen against Cincy. Late in the first half Dolbin took an 81-yard pass play from Craig Morton and raced for a touchdown at midfield—and Denver was ahead to stay, 17–10. The assistant coaches in the press box—Fran Polsfoot, Bob Gambold, and Paul Roach didn't even get to see it. They were headed down to the field in an elevator. "The radio the elevator operator had didn't work when it was moving. We

could hear a roar, but didn't know what happened," said Polsfoot, "until we walked out onto the field. I'd like to take credit
for calling that play, but had no idea it was happening."

The Cincinnati field is among the hardest in the league. The
Cincinnati Reds also play there, so there's not a give cushion
underneath. A few of the players who were accustomed to it
tested it out before the game, and rookie Rob Lytle said: "This
is like a marble floor." Across the way a high-school band practiced the themes from *Star Wars* and *Rocky*, two songs the
Broncos heard over and over wherever they went.

The hard rug in Riverfront proved disastrous for the Broncos,
but may have helped them toward the end. Jon Keyworth
went down with a knee injury; quarterback Craig Morton had
to leave; Otis Armstrong pulled up lame; linebacker Tom Jackson had to retire from the game; tackle Andy Maurer went
down. "What's going on out here?" Miller hollered. "My God,
we're losing everybody."

The Broncos nursed a 17–13 lead going into the final eight
minutes and had to depend on young Craig Penrose at quarterback and Jim Jensen and Lytle in the backfield. None had
played very much, especially Penrose. Denver had possession
at its own 37 and had to accomplish something if it wanted
to hold off the Bengals. Three running plays picked up a first
down, and then Penrose took a cue from Morton, going on a
misdirection bootleg for 17 yards and a first down close to
midfield. Jensen, who lines up in the backfield in the unorthodox manner of a frog (and picked up that nickname from the
players), churned out nine more yards, and Penrose dove for
a first down. Then Penrose spotted Lytle free over the middle,
and Lytle ran to the two-yard line. Two running plays earned
a yard, and third down arrived. Jensen took a handoff and
went in for a score behind tackle Glenn Hyde and tight end
Ron Egloff, both also backups forced in because of injuries.
So Denver led, 24–13, with 2:45 showing, and it ended up
that way.

Earlier Cincy could have made it rough, when it reached
the Denver six early in the fourth quarter. It was third and
one. Fullback Pete Johnson, who had popped for a long gain
earlier, went left with the ball, seemed clear for a moment,

and then tripped—over the seam of the baseball mound. So the artificial turf, Cincy's own, had stopped the Bengals.

In the dressing room Miller said the "young players have come through for us. That's what we've been hoping for, and it happened. Penrose, Jensen, Lytle. Hey, this is another step."

Outside the locker room Miller met some friends and talked briefly. Along came Rich Upchurch. "Hey, you better go get on the bus, Rick. I'd hate to fine you for missing it," the coach said.

Miller then walked off in the direction of the buses.

They were gone.

He had to fine himself.

Miller found a carload of Bengals fans heading toward the airport and hitched a ride.

But he was feeling fine. The Broncos were 6–0 and getting ready for Oakland again.

18

ORANGE SUNDAY

The city had exploded over the upcoming Broncos' return match with Oakland, but one man was trying to retain his calmness. Gerald Phipps, the owner of the team, didn't want to become too excited. "We had a team in 1962 that won six of the first seven games. We ended up seven and seven. This is a tough business. You can't relax for a moment."

So he was holding on to his emotions. In his mid-sixties (Phipps doesn't give away his age), the club owner never actually had shown much emotion in good times and bad. At the conclusion of the previous Denver victory over Oakland, he had stood at the end and clapped politely for his team. But otherwise, he remained low keyed. He is a fan, but he does not want to be carried beyond the point of rationale. He's no Charlie Finley on an ego trip. But he admits it burns inside. "I get worked up at the games. It's a helluva nervous strain. It takes me twenty-four hours to wind down afterward."

Phipps is head of his own construction business, but gets out to practices about twice a week. But mostly, he leaves the running of the team to the executives he has hired. In the past Phipps has been considered both a hero and a miser for the successes and failures of the team, but he tends to ride out the era. "When you get into something like this you expect the notoriety. The Denver Broncos are not a construction company. If we make a mistake in the construction business no one knows about it but us. You go ahead and take your loss, but in silence. Here, if you make a mistake, everyone knows about it, and they tell you about it. It's as if the public owns this team, and maybe they do. It has been terribly, terribly frustrating at times, but it's been nice most of the time."

Phipps was concerned about depth as the Oakland game approached. "We don't have that much depth. And our offense is not there. I'll tell you what it takes to win a Super Bowl. You have to have a helluva good squad and a lot of luck."

Someone walked into the outer office and said in a loud voice: "I don't guess there's anyway to get a ticket to the Oakland game."

Not really.

There were at least six reasons for the importance of the Oakland–Denver contest:

1. Oakland had not lost a game at Mile High Stadium since 1962.
2. The Broncos had won both games from Oakland in just one season, 1962.
3. Oakland led the series by a whopping 26–7–2 margin.
4. The Raiders had not trailed the leader in the American Conference West of the National Football League by two games since 1966, and a Denver victory would force that, since the Broncos were 6–0 and the Raiders 5–1.
5. Denver had beaten Oakland two weeks before, 30–7, and the Raiders were seeking revenge.
6. These two teams always wanted to beat each other bad.

Oakland's Monte Johnson had said after the first meeting: "They beat us today, but we're the better team. If we play them ten times, we'll win the next nine." The Broncos had the quote circled and on the bulletin board in their dressing quarters.

The focus of the entire NFL was on the upstarts from Denver, who were quickly becoming a true Cinderella team, and the perennial great Raiders. So media types from over the world—including Australia—were converging on Denver for the game. Over here was Curt Gowdy, while Phyllis George was over there interviewing a player, and Larry Merchant was back there talking to a player. Out of necessity, Red Miller finally had to close practice. "I hate to do it, but every time any of us turns on the practice field, someone has a camera pointed in our faces. It's kind of difficult to concentrate."

The Broncos had an armed policeman outside their practice field, but it was like hiring a lap dog. He was a Fuller Brush man to everyone that came along.

"Hey, how ya doing? The Broncos really don't want you to watch, but if you'll move across the street, I'm sure they won't mind." One of the players looked out the fence at the guard and said that if "Al Davis himself walked up, the guy would be nice to him and say it's all right to watch."

Bob Peck, the public relations director, wasn't having such an easy time. The phone never stopped ringing in his office. "I just don't have room for you. I'm sorry." It was *Playboy* magazine. Dave Frei, his assistant, hollered in: "At least you could have found out who they were sending. It might have been one of the girls."

"Dave, can you believe this? We've got fifteen publications in Colorado I've never heard of wanting tickets. I wonder what could possibly happen next?"

A man walked into Peck's office and said he wanted to leave a sample.

"Of what?"

"Orange Astroturf. It would be great for your football field."

"Orange turf. You got to be kidding."

"No, we'll make you a deal. Imagine a whole field orange, like in 'Orange Crush.'"

"I'll try not to imagine it. I don't think we're interested."

"You don't have any tickets, do you?"

Everyone was looking for one. A bellhop at the Regency claimed tickets were being scalped for two hundred dollars. "I wish I had five thousand [tickets]. I could retire for life."

But two hundred dollars may have been top price. In the classified section of the two Denver newspapers tickets were being offered for less. One ad offered a ticket for $9.90, the going price. But the woman on the phone said: "Yeah, I've got six for ten dollars each, but there's a fifty dollar finder's fee on each." Others were being pushed for more. "I've got one left," a man said over the telephone. "Make you a deal. Seventy-five bucks since it's in the end zone."

Meanwhile, the mayor and the governor had proclaimed "Orange Sunday" in honor of the Denver–Oakland contest.

It had become an annual affair, with a radio station giving out orange placards to everyone who attended.

The orange epidemic began, actually, in 1971. The Broncos were losing, for a change, and Charlie Goldberg, a Denver businessman and long-time faithful Quarterback Club member, tried his best to brighten up a dismal season. He purchased every piece of orange cloth he could find and convinced a friend to cut them into manageable sizes. "We had enough to give maybe thirty-five thousand fans in the crowd a piece of orange cloth to display that day. Denver beat the Chargers, 20–16, and Floyd Little made it a point to say how much the support had meant. So we've kept it up."

As one New York writer wrote for the folks back home, "This is Denver's first Super Bowl." And the air around the city was taking on that aroma. More than three hundred, a record, turned out for the weekly Quarterback Club meeting, and heard a representative of the Raiders' front office talk about how much Oakland respected Denver and heard Red Miller talk about how much the Broncos respected Oakland. But the Raiders had gone into hiding again. None of their players wanted to discuss the game, and the Broncos were once again holding back their own thoughts. Publicly. Privately they felt it would be close. "Final two minutes will decide," Lyle Alzado said as he climbed into his four-wheel drive. "They know," said defensive back Louis Wright, "that we can beat them. We proved it. But they don't know if they can beat us. So that should help us."

Miller was concerned, though. Tackle Andy Maurer definitely would not play because of a knee injury, and Red was announcing that journeyman Glenn Hyde would step in. But privately Miller was preparing rookie Steve Schindler for his first start. Miller didn't want Oakland to know the alteration, so they wouldn't pick on the first-year man. Hyde was upset, though, and showed it openly. He felt he deserved to start. Tom Jackson was standing on the sidelines at practice. "I'd give anything to play, but I don't think I can. In the Cincinnati game I was going so well when I had to pull up. The hamstring. I'll figure out something."

The Broncos' ticket office got in a shipment of "Orange

Crush" T-shirts on Thursday and went through thirty-one dozen in one day.

"For the first time in Denver's history, Oakland is chasing us. We're not chasing them. I'd rather be in this position," Miller said at the press conference later that day.

But out in Oakland, some things were finally being said.

George Buehler: "I think football is a game of ups and downs. We had one of those down days against Denver. Some days you'll be driving a car and do stupid things like pull out in traffic and get in somebody's way. You have those days no matter how hard you try not to. I don't know why they're caused. I don't believe in biorhythms, but maybe it's true. But there are just days when the team doesn't click. We knew what Denver was going to do, but we couldn't do anything about it. Like when you're playing golf, you might just go out one day and slice or hook everything. Then, on the other hand, you might go to Las Vegas and beat impossible odds by hitting every slot machine. That's the way it is in football. I'm not criticizing Denver. They can play. But it doesn't take much to change things. We reduced our odds by playing poorly, and they improved their chances by playing well. That's the way it is in football. If several players have bad days, it can even up in a hurry."

When told what Buehler said, Denver's Billy Thompson replied: "What?"

But the Broncos had an understanding of what the Raiders were going to do this time. The passing attack hadn't worked before, so "smashball," Miller's reference to a running game, was expected. "They're gonna come at us," said linebacker coach Myrel Moore, lying on a bench after practice ended. "Nothing cute. I think they'll run and run and run. And that's what we're preparing for." And it scared the Broncos, although the 3–4 defense was the strongest against the strong-side running.

The Broncos were relatively small. "The way to beat us," said linebacker Bob Swenson, "is to come right at us. We can't go up against a 250-pound guard. We're a lot better when we have the angle. If Oakland comes straight at us, we'll have some problems." But Swenson was also having problems with the washing machine in his house. Rather than washing his sneakers, the machine had coughed them up and bounced them three feet across the room. Swenson led a typical bachelor life—living in suburbia with teammates John Schultz and Chris Pane, just down the street from the Craig Penroses. All his dinners were eaten out, and Swenson was still trying to figure out a way to hire a maid.

The people were gearing up.

Abe Shur, a bar owner, was sipping a drink. "This town will go berserk if we win." Tom Nelson, an investigator for a supermarket chain, said: "Any time you have national coverage you like to stand up and shout, 'Hey, we're a great city—eat your heart out, New York.' "

Christeen Johnson, a sixty-four-year-old teacher, had gotten in the mood. "In a way, this is like the Super Bowl. Denver hasn't received the recognition it deserved. People back East always thought this was a one-horse town. They have the feeling that this town is still the heart of cowboy country. But it's not. It's changed."

The crowd came early on Sunday. They had brought their flasks of whiskey and were settling in their seats as Swenson turned in the locker room and said for all to hear: "I was nine years old the last time Denver beat Oakland here." Nobody replied.

As the crowd entered, each person was handed one of the orange placards. At the first kickoff, they held them up. It was a real sea of orange, especially considering that everyone in the stands was also wearing an orange T-shirt or jacket or sweater. "Will you look at that," rookie Rob Lytle said on the field. Later: "I didn't think I was going to be able to concentrate on the kick. It was such an awesome sight."

And it was. The cards waved while the Broncos kicked off. "I didn't think there was that much orange in the world," said a writer from Chicago in the press box. "You think orange is ugly until you see it like that."

But orange wasn't the color of the day.

It was Orange Crash.

The Oakland Raiders ran over and through and around the Broncos and ended up with a 24–14 victory. Just as suspected, the Raiders ran right over the left side—behind linemen Gene Upshaw and Art Shell—and destroyed the Broncos. Defensively, the Raiders ganged up on the rookie, Schindler, and poured through like a sieve to constantly tackle Craig Morton. Denver trailed, 24–0, before finally putting up a couple of fourth-quarter touchdowns. It was never really a contest, and the orange placards were scattered on the cement steps. "Tomorrow will be a blue Monday," said the supermarket employee.

Typical of the afternoon was a 48-yard drive that developed thusly:

—Clarence Davis to the left side for 19 yards.
—Mark van Eeghen to the right side for four.
—Davis to the left side for two yards.
—Ken Stabler passes for 13.
—Van Eeghen to the left side for nine.
—Carl Garrett to the left side for four.
—Garrett to the left side for two.
—Davis to the left side for six.
—Van Eeghen to the left side for minus one.
—42-yard field goal.

In taking advantage of Denver turnovers, the Raiders coasted to a 24–0 lead and became as conservative as Ronald Reagan. And Ray Guy, the Oakland punter, backed Denver up all day. His first punt was 74 yards, a career high. In six first-half possessions, Denver started at its 20 four times, the seven, and the 22. The second-half possessions began at the 20-, 20-, 18-, 20-, 30-, 30-, and 25-yard lines. On the sidelines Denver assistant Myrel Moore looked at another punt and whispered in his earphones to defensive backfield coach Bob Gambold upstairs in the press box: "Send me down a shotgun, and I'll stop that."

In the coach's box Gambold, Fran Polsfoot, and Paul Roach had little to say. "It's days like these where you just want to go hide somewhere," Gambold said. The others wouldn't disagree. The Raiders intercepted a pass, recovered two fumbles, and sacked Morton eight times. "If there was ever a 180-degree turn from the first game, this was it," Morton told Penrose afterward.

So the Broncos and the Raiders were tied again for the division lead. Nothing comes easy.

"I wonder how tight their assholes get now," said Monte Johnson over in the Raiders' locker room. Guy sat in a corner and said it would be nice to work in Denver. "If I played here it would add three to four yards on my punting average." Stabler smoked a cigarette as do most of the Raiders, and said it was "too early in the season to be a 'must' game. We won. We're 6–1. Denver's 6–1. That's it."

And that was about it for the Broncos, whose locker room was so quiet you could hear a quarterback drop. Morton disappeared into a crevice and avoided the New York writers, who had seen him play ineptly for the Giants the year before and had come to see a new Morton. But they saw the same old Morton.

"Now we know how they felt two weeks ago," said Otis Armstrong. "After they lost to us, they wanted to play us again bad. That's how I feel. I hope we can play them in the playoffs."

Billy Thompson agreed as he left the stadium under a cover of darkness. "I figure we'll get another shot at them somewhere along the line in the playoffs."

The Broncos were talking playoffs, nevertheless.

Swenson said: "Well, last year that would have been 45–0. We got down, but we didn't let them blow us out. It's a loss, and we've just got to go on."

Miller said the Broncos "lost to a fine team." But he was thinking about the loss of Andy Maurer, who had been replaced by Schindler. Miller had reverted later in the game to Hyde, but by then the mistake was done. He couldn't bring it back. "A lot of the sacks came through Schindler, but hell, he's a rookie starting his first game and shifting from guard to tackle. My fault, not his."

Silence hung over the city now because of the loss, but earlier because of the attention riveted on the contest. Shortly after 1:00 P.M., the police found themselves alone on the streets. Everyone was indoors watching television. The bars, with the six-foot TV screens, were full.

There could have been a war out on Colfax Avenue. Not a soul was around.

The Colorado Mine Company, a local restaurant, was packed.

"The Snake can go to hell," a guy hollered after a good play. Every good play by the Broncos brought a roar and another round of drinks.

But later that night, a bartender at the Four Mile Houston counted her money and said the day had been good, "But if they had just won, they'd still be buying drinks."

Red Miller added: "Hey, the sun will rise tomorrow morning, anyway."

Several hundred thousand moaners might not have believed it. The first six games had been a fairy tale, but once again Oakland put a damper on the Broncos, as always before. "It was all a pipe dream," a man said over his beer at the Mine Company. "I don't know why I got so excited. The Broncos aren't any better than before. They had some easy teams, and then got lucky against Oakland. But now they'll fall. They'll lose to Pittsburgh next week, and downhill from there. Want to buy an 'Orange Crush' T-shirt?"

Miller was wondering about the team as he drove home that night. Could it come back against Pittsburgh? That game would be the indicator. Lose to the Steelers, and the playoffs would be out. Win, and the team would be in. "We'll find out," he told himself.

And the sun rose promptly at 6:12 A.M., Monday morning. Miller said it would.

Some of the newspapers around the country were curious about the Broncos, according to their reports of the game.

Chicago *Sun-Times:* "Cancel the hearse. Send back the flowers. Tear up the obituaries. The Oakland Raiders live. Pro football's super team, which had hard times the last couple of weeks, indicated it was just a temporary setback on the road to perhaps another Super Bowl with a convincing 24–14 victory over the high-kicking Denver Broncos Sunday. On an unseasonably warm, clear afternoon, the Raiders administered a bitter dose of reality to 75,007 of the Denver faithful who had been deliriously talking of championships the last two months."

Cincinnati *Enquirer:* "Admit it. We were had. We took a seventh game of the season and made it a Super Bowl. Well, it was as boring as one."

Oakland *Tribune:* "Orange Crushed. Burnt Orange. Orange

Freeze. Have fun. It all blends together. The Oakland Raiders proved that Denver's defense, the 'Orange Crush,' isn't the real thing, just like Tang."

Los Angeles *Times:* "It has been an emotional week in the Mile High City. The citizens have been a mile off the ground as they reveled in Broncomania. 'Orange Crush' sweaters and T-shirts were a hot-selling item honoring the Denver Broncos, who were finally getting the national recognition. But the team lost."

New York *Post:* "It came a little too soon and too fast for the Broncos—the adulation, the dreams, but most of all the confidence that Oakland was a team they had in their pockets."

Washington *Post:* "An orange-clad crowd of 75,007 waited for the Great Pumpkin today. For the 15th straight year he failed to appear."

Chicago *Daily News:* "The Broncos, created separate and unequal, have spent their lifetime tasting ashes. Save for three winning years, they have lost and lost and lost some more. Then, in this their eighteenth season, they miraculously vaulted from the outhouse to the penthouse, drubbing Super Bowl champion Oakland and waking up one Sunday morning unbeaten and untied. There was only one problem: The Broncos had to play Oakland again. When they were done, they realized why it's so lonely at the top."

But the Broncos weren't finished yet.

19

THE STEELERS AND GOD AND JOEY BOSTON

Red Miller was a half-century old on Monday, October 31. After losing to Oakland the day before, he felt like one hundred, but wouldn't admit it. "I'm not down. We're 6–1. Who thought we would be 6–1 halfway through the season? Nobody. Not a person in the world. Not even me."

The Broncos had to leave the Raiders behind and forge on to face Pittsburgh and a mad, mad, mad "Mean" Joe Greene, who had come out in the middle of the week and unleashed a tirade against officials. "If I get half a chance, I'll punch one of them in the mouth. I wish a bolt of lightning would come down and strike one of their hearts out. If they get in the way, I'll just cleat 'em in the spine. I'll call them the dirtiest name I can think of. I'll talk about their mamas." He didn't like referees. Greene felt he was the victim of too much holding and too many penalties. Commissioner Pete Rozelle had decided to fly into Denver for the Pittsburgh–Denver game and fine Greene personally.

The Broncos, for the most part, weren't that outspoken. In fact, the team was becoming The God Squad. More and more of the players had gotten religion, literally.

Godwin Turk, a linebacker known previously for being a rowdy type, had found Christ, he said, and cleaned up his act. "The dudes on this team talked to me about God—you know there are a lot of them into religion—but I didn't pay no mind. I figured I had gotten this far all on myself. I'd pray in the pregame meeting and afterward, but it didn't mean nothing."

Then, during the Broncos' training camp, he suffered a knee injury. "I didn't know whether I could come back, and I didn't even know if I wanted to. Then I was sitting in the whirlpool, and a bunch of cats from that Christ basketball team [Athletes in Action] were up at Fort Collins, and they came in for treatment, and we started rapping. Those dudes were playing the game for the love of it and to try and get God's word across. They convinced me. I started praying." Turk claimed the knee injury "was a blessing. I told God that if he wanted me to keep playing to show me the way. If he didn't I wanted him to point me in the right direction. The knee came around. It was like God was sending me a message to straighten out. I feel like I'm a much better dude now. I can accept the bitter with the sweet. I don't want much out of life, just enough to get by. Look at Elvis [Presley]. He had everything, and it choked him."

Turk was a strange sort, to begin with. In the off-season he was a mortician and was buying a funeral home. "When I used to go to church, I couldn't take it, so I sneaked out the back and hid in the funeral home. I got interested, and I've been working in funeral homes ever since. That's another reason I didn't like Christians. When I'd be driving the hearse, the relatives would be crying and carrying on at the cemetery, but as soon as they left, they'd start fighting over who got what."

Turk wasn't alone in his life-style alteration. Craig Morton, besides being a born-again quarterback, referred to himself in midseason as "a born-again Christian. Once I met Suzie [who was about to become his wife] I began committing myself to Christ. I have an inner peace now. It has meant much to me, and I like to talk to people about it. But I don't want people to get the impression that I got the quarterback's job because of Christ. I've always believed in God, but now I've decided to give my life to Him."

Linebacker Randy Gradishar was a leader in the Federation of Christian Athletes and hosted the season's first prayer meeting, which became a weekly affair among the players. As many as thirty were attending. "Our religious beliefs are important to us," Gradishar said. "Football and religion can mix." After every game middle guard Rubin Carter always said: "First of all, I want to thank Christ for getting me through the game." The man alongside him, Barney Chavous, was a strong believer. And the list grew. More and more of the players, such as defensive back Steve Foley, would mention their thanks to God when discussing football.

Chuck Colson, a Watergate star who had converted to Christianity, came to speak to the squad one day after practice, and more than half attended. "I've never been around such a religious-oriented squad," Red Miller said. "I think it's good for everyone to have their own beliefs." He left it at that. The coach was not the most religious member of the team. His religion was football, and it was a twenty-four-hour-a-day-job. And it was making him a household name in the city, except to one shoeshine boy.

"Hey, do you know who's up on the stand?" the shoeshiner said to his compatriot at the next stand in the airport.

"No."

"Why, that's Red Foley, coach of the Broncos."

The Pittsburgh Steelers were having problems when they came to town. Several players had held out at the outset of camp for more money; others were upset with the coach; nothing seemed to be working right. Pittsburgh owned a 4–3 record and was not as dominant as in previous years. Despite being only the same team that had won back-to-back Super Bowls. So the Broncos were catching them at an appropriate time in the season, it would appear.

The fans came out cautiously that Sunday afternoon. The Black Plague of Oakland had moved on, but they were wondering if Pittsburgh would continue the misery. There was no worry. Denver won convincingly, 21–7. The Broncos swept to a 21–0 lead by halftime and turned completely conservative, holding on for the victory. Rick Upchurch, who had been bottled up all year, returned punts for 167 yards, a club record, and a touchdown. Quarterback Morton was back in style and threw a touchdown pass to Haven Moses, and Rob Lytle finished off a nice drive with a one-yard scoot. Pittsburgh came in with problems and only magnified them, committing mistakes all afternoon. Terry Bradshaw was sacked six times.

Afterward, Morton looked out of place in the dressing room. Instead of a football uniform, he wore a tuxedo. Sneaking out the back door, he stopped for a moment. "Got a plane to catch. My rehearsal dinner is tonight. In Dallas." And the next evening he was married and drove off in a carriage. It was appropriate for a man on a Cinderella team.

The Broncos came through their infamous month of Sundays with a 3–1 record. They had split with Oakland, beaten Pittsburgh, and won on the road at Cincinnati. "If you could see that we could come out of that part of the schedule with three wins, you know a lot more than I do. Those three teams are all annual playoff contenders, and long ago when we first looked at the schedule, we knew these four games would have a great bearing on our success or failure. It's a big thing to get out of that part of the schedule with a 7–1 record," Miller said privately.

In Las Vegas, meanwhile, Joey Boston was trying his best to figure out the Broncos. Boston looks exactly like you'd expect a guy named Joey Boston to look like. Dark blue shirt, tinge of gray in the hair, Italian heritage. A Joey Boston has to be either a hit-man for the mob or a bookmaker. This Joey Boston is a bookmaker. But a legal one. He takes bets for the world's largest race and sports lounge, which is an uptown title for a bookie joint. Boston operates the Stardust Hotel Sports Book on the Vegas strip. He won't say how much the book takes in annually, but Boston admitted that the Stardust handled $1.5 million on the last Super Bowl and was expecting $2 million this time around.

"That is, if Oakland and Dallas play in the big game. They're your glamour teams. Now if Denver makes it, we wouldn't have as much play. Denver ain't a glamor team—except in Denver."

But Boston was familiar with the Broncos. "I been keeping an eye on them all season, but they been confusing me. I thought after they lost to Oakland they would just dry up and blow away. I thought maybe Craig Morton was getting back to his old ways. Then they popped Pittsburgh. Of course, the Steelers were missing the best linebacker in the game. But Pittsburgh has those internal problems. And you got to think Denver is hungry. I watch that linebacker Randy Gradishar—the one from Ohio State—and he'll be slapping guys on the head—whomp, whomp—after a play. Denver's got it going, so I got to put that all into my line."

Boston sets the line—the betting line—that is used as a gauge almost everywhere. "When I figure Denver I have to throw in a couple of things. You start with a power rating of the teams. That's the first thing. Then the referees have been going with the home teams on calls this year. And you always give the home team two points. In Denver, there is the climate and altitude that other teams are unaccustomed to, and, from what I hear, when those seventy-five thousand fans yell, it's a deafening roar. So I'll go two and one-half for Denver's home-field advantage and maybe three."

Denver's next game was against San Diego, and Boston had the Broncos favored by four in the Sports Lounge. "You know the thing that bothers me about a place like this? It's like a supermarket for the tourist. Person comes up to me and sees a four next to the Denver Broncos and wants to know if he gets four points if he bets on Denver. Then we've got the kickoff time listed for the game, and they want to know what the eleven means. Then you got your wise guys—the professional bettors. But they don't know it all. Give you an example. I've got Denver favored by four over San Diego Sunday. That's the perfect number. This is a great betting game. The wise guys are all taking San Diego and the points, and the public is coming in here getting on Denver because they've become a good team, and everyone saw San Diego get kicked by Detroit last week while Denver was beating hell out of Pittsburgh.

"Well, the wise guys are all wrong. Denver is my two-star special. The Broncos will win easily."

But they didn't.

20

TIGHT TRIO

Craig Penrose laughed out loud. "Every time San Diego lines up, we will know what's coming. We did the same things last year." The defensive unit came out of a meeting and agreed with the young quarterback. "We don't need to look at the films," a linebacker said. "I can't believe it."

Maybe it was because the San Diego offensive coordinator was Max Coley, who held the same job with the Broncos the year before. "He hasn't changed a thing. It's predictable," Penrose said.

But, in San Diego, Coley was disagreeing. "I brought some of the offense with me, sure, but any time you move, there are different thoughts by different people about the offense. So much of our plan was new to me. I wouldn't say we're doing the things we did in Denver."

Miller, however, was saying privately: "Unless San Diego changes some things this week, we should know what they are doing." One of his assistants put it more bluntly. "We can get out our old films and see the San Diego offense. It's just different people running it."

A hint of ill feeling crept into Coley's voice as he sat there in gym shorts. "The weather is nicer here, and we are going to get it going. I wish Denver well, except against us. I know a lot of people in Denver had bad feelings against me, but whenever you're in the limelight, there are going to be people who don't like you."

A few months earlier Coley had talked over a meal in a

midtown Denver restaurant about the frustration of his firing. Ralston had gotten rid of Coley to take some of the pressure off himself. It didn't work. "I tried to get John to do things, but he never listened. He thought he would figure a way to get through it all. He didn't." In fact, Coley had stormed off the practice field one day in 1976 and quit, but Ralston talked him into coming back. The players could see that Ralston was losing touch with even his own men.

"I know how that defense—the 'Orange Crush'—is. It's tougher than nails. I saw plenty of it when I was there. But I think it's even better this year. It's one of the best, if not the best, in the whole league."

The Broncos arrived at the Islandia Hyatt House in San Diego early in the afternoon on Saturday and were greeted by another orange-clad throng. It was becoming customary on the road. Each week the Broncos picked up additional fellow travelers. The travel agents generally booked groups to San Diego because of the tourist attraction aspect, but this year the interest had been extremely high. As one plane crossed over the Colorado border headed for California, a man stood up and said: "Let's get drunk now and not sober up until we get back. Go Broncos." Everyone agreed and ordered drinks. The tour was staying at the same motel as the Broncos and already was well into its liquor when the team arrived. Two young men were being plied with free drinks. They looked like sailors, and they were. "We're from Denver, and we haven't slept this week. It's kind of a wake-a-thon in honor of the Broncos. Hey, Haven, would you sign my T-shirt?"

The bay next to the hotel was full of sailboats when one of the players glanced out. "That's where we should be tomorrow, not on the football field." It was a lazy time. The players went out and sat by the bay and took their drinks. "Oh, to be on top of the division and to be in San Diego. It's a grand feeling," one shouted, and the players toasted his statement.

A fog rolled in Saturday evening, and the players stayed in at the motel. Backup quarterback Norris Weese settled in a chair in the lounge and ordered a beer. The players weren't supposed to be in the bar, "but this is close enough to the restaurant. "And I'm not going to play, anyway. Got on my lucky sweater, though," he told a couple of fans who asked for his autograph. "Haven't lost when I've worn it. Wore it on the trip to Seattle during the exhibition season, and now I take it on the road all the time. This sweater is undefeated."

Assistant coach Babe Parilli strolled by and caustically eyed Weese, who promptly retired for the evening. The assistant coaches took over the bar, mingled with the orange fans, and drank the night away. Bob Gambold finally drifted out at closing, telling the bartender: "Piece of cake tomorrow. Mark my words." The Broncos were developing confidence.

But they weren't so sure of themselves late Sunday afternoon—even though it looked like a Denver-dominated crowd. Some two thousand had come for the game from Colorado, and they made more noise than the other forty-three thousand. Besides, the seats in San Diego are painted orange, and several thousand were empty. "I feel right at home," said wide receiver Haven Moses. In more ways than one. He had played at San Diego State, but never had a good game in his homecoming. Up in the stands the fans from Denver were loose. "I wouldn't miss a game for the world," said one. "I've suffered since the beginning, so I should be enjoying this."

Outside at the elevator a woman appeared in a wheelchair. Both legs were in cast. A man, apparently her husband, was pushing the chair. "My God," said an onlooker, "who would come to a football game with both legs broken?"

And then the man noticed something. Underneath the jacket of the woman was . . . an Orange Crush T-shirt.

The Broncos got all they wanted from San Diego, though. The Chargers had used some trickery—a halfback pass for a touchdown and a fumble recovery early that was run in for another to take a 14–10 lead. The miracle Broncos seemed to be out of them when they took over on their 46-yard line with 2:37 left in the final quarter.

After two incompletions, the Broncos got a break when San Diego defensive back Mike Williams was called on a controversial interference against Moses. The Chargers argued while Denver set up at the San Diego 30.

On third down again, Morton flipped to Otis Armstrong, who struggled to the 13-yard line for another first down. The

two-minute warning came, followed by a holding penalty on
Denver. The Broncos got the yardage back on a pass and then
a sweep by Lonnie Perrin, but it was fourth down and five
at the Chargers' eight. Morton signaled for a time-out and
walked over to Miller on the sidelines.

"Swing pass right to Armstrong," Miller offered.

"I don't like it," Morton said and suggested a flair to Odoms.

"Okay, if you believe in it. Just make it happen," Miller said,
with the hint of a threat behind the words.

Odoms, however, was snowed under as he broke down the
left sidelines. Wide receiver Moses had sprinted in the same
direction to take the coverage on Odoms away and then saw
the intended play break down. He was the secondary receiver
in this situation, but was surrounded at the left corner of the
end zone. Immediately he realized there was room over the
middle, so Moses cut across the back of the end zone.

Morton waited, protected in style, as if he were in a garrison
surrounded by troops. He waited . . . searching for something
to open. He waited longer. They had to be coming, he thought.
Suddenly he spotted Moses's cut, saw him escape from the
San Diego cornerback, and threw. Moses caught the pass in
the shadow of the goalpost. Touchdown. Denver was up, 17–
14, following the extra point.

Miller greeted his quarterback at the sidelines with a hand-
shake. "Way to work, Craig. You did it, all right."

This, Morton thought, is the most important offensive play
of the season. We have finally proven that the offense can come
back.

A few moments earlier Rik Smith, the Chargers' public relations director, had stood just outside the end zone and offered:
"We are going to lose it. I know it. We've been beaten down
at this end of the field so many times, and it's about to happen
again."

But the Chargers still had a chance. On the first play, sub
quarterback Bill Munson, who had replaced James Harris, who
left with a sprained ankle, was under a heavy rush by Lyle
Alzado and threw the ball out in the flat. Denver's Tom Jackson
grabbed the wayward toss and had nothing but wide-open
spaces to the goal. But at the 32, the ball popped from his

hands, squibbed on the ground and San Diego recovered. Up
in the stands a Denver fan who had given San Diego and five
points cried out: "Oh, my God! What have you done, Jackson?"
(The next week Jackson received a letter, apparently from another irate gambler: "Dear Nigger: The next time you intercept
a pass, stick it up your ass. Maybe it will stick." Jackson said:
"I guess he'll have a strong letter to follow.") San Diego took
over again for a final chance, but Munson was being helped
off the field. His leg was broken. So Harris limped back on—
he was in miserable shape—and lined up in shotgun formation.
He nevertheless completed two long gainers, but was faced
with a fourth down with sixteen seconds to go and out of field-
goal range. Harris tried to pass to Dwight McDonald, but it
was long and sadly, for the Chargers, fell to the turf.

Do you believe in magic? The Broncos had pulled it out.
In the tunnel, one hollered out: "Nothing can go wrong now.
We came back from death." Haven Moses, with a pair of touchdown passes, was a natural for the headline writers: "Moses
led the Broncos out of the wilderness and to the promised
land!" "I've never had such a good game here. It couldn't have
come at a better time," he said. On the bus away from the
stadium, Alzado said: "Forget the Cardiac Cardinals. How
about the Cardiac Broncos."

Tommy Prothro, the San Diego coach, stood in an empty
corner of his dressing room, propped up against the wall, and
chain-smoked. "I really felt like we deserved a better fate,
but that's the way it goes. That's all I got to say."

Now at 8–1, the Broncos prepared for Kansas City. And they
were loose. In practice on Thursday Bucky Dilts did a dance
for the squad on the artificial-turf portion of the practice field;
shaving cream mysteriously appeared in kicker Jim Turner's
helmet, and the coaching staff came up with a trick play that
looked like it had been diagrammed by a near-sighted plumber.
"We're enjoying it," said Tom Jackson. "It keeps us from being
uptight."

But there was some uptightness about the status of quarterback Craig Morton. He had just gotten married, and he came
down with food poisoning. "I told Suzie that was some first

meal she served me," Morton said. He took a lot of ribbing, but Morton's wife claimed it was the flu.

In the Crown Center Hotel in Kansas City another orange gathering awaited. A bar had been set up in the middle of the lobby, and the fans were well into it before the Broncos showed up. "When are they getting here?" a lady wondered. "If I drink another bloody Mary, the Broncos will have to pick me up off the floor." A few feet over a guy was talking to an assemblage. "Nothing can stop us now. I came over because I don't want to miss a second of it. I'm eating it up." The Broncos came through the doors, saw the group, and quickly got on the elevator. "You don't want to stay too long around those people these days. They'll kill you out of love." Billy Thompson had to pause, though, because of a local sportscaster. The question was, with cameras whirling: "Are the Broncos really for real? What has made the difference?" Thompson smiled. The question came again and again: "We're together."

But the Broncos didn't have it completely together the next afternoon at Arrowhead Stadium. The Broncos scored in the second quarter, but fumbles and a pair of missed field goals had cost Denver other opportunities. Kansas City added a touchdown just before halftime, and Red Miller was steaming when he entered the locker room. "We've come too far to be beaten by a team like this." The Chiefs were disorganized. Head coach Paul Wiggin, the most popular man in the city, had been fired, and assistant Tom Bettis was trying to hold the pieces together. The third quarter was played without incident—neither team scored. Then Denver put together a drive in the final period, with Morton hitting Haven Moses, who had become his favorite target, on a 23-yard touchdown. Moses and Chiefs cornerback Gary Green bumped; Green fell down; and Moses caught the ball and coasted the remaining seven yards. The M & M Connection—Morton and Moses. So Denver was clinging to a 14-7 lead.

Time was running out when K. C.'s Ted McKnight grabbed the kickoff and threatened to go the distance, but Bernard Jackson finally tripped him by the leg at the Chiefs' 41. After little success, the Chiefs lined up in punt formation. From the sidelines Miller was yelling, "Fake, fake. Get ready for it."

Fourth down and 17 at the 48 with 2:15 left. The up-blocker, Mark Bailey, took the snap instead of punter Jerrell Wilson, then stuck the ball between the legs of linebacker Ray Burks, who had lined up just behind the line of scrimmage in a normal blocking position. The play has become known over the years as the "Boomerooski," and is popular among certain college teams. Burks hesitated, then took off, left, with the ball. Denver linebacker Larry Evans had the angle on him, but missed the tackle, and then Burks, a lumbering 217-pounder who had never carried the ball before, escaped from Jim Jensen and evaded another tackler before being caught by Denver's Louis Wright at the one-yard line. Wright was the last hope, and Burks tumbled in the end zone. But the officials marked the ball a yard away.

Miller thought the Chiefs had scored. In fact, he had turned at the final moment and yelled, "Extra point team." He started mulling over extra-period strategy and wondered if the downfall of the Broncos had arrived. Then an assistant coach walked over and said, "Sure were lucky then." Miller turned and saw the ball on the one. He wiped his forehead and gasped.

On the field Wright told linebacker Tom Jackson: "That's one tackle I really didn't want to make. I kept hoping someone would stop that guy. They didn't, and I said, 'What the hell. You only live once.' "

This was the game. Halfback Ed Podolak thrust at the heart of the Broncos' defense on first down. No room available. Fullback Bailey then clubbed at the same spot and was stopped right there. The Chiefs were still at the one-yard line.

Denver defensive coordinator Joe Collier called a wide-out defense from the sidelines. Jackson would, on the play, charge from the outside rather than trying to stuff up the middle. He did and was waiting when tight end Walter White took the ball on a reverse. White was stopped for a six-yard loss. "Nice gamble," Miller said to Collier.

On fourth down and goal, with just 30 seconds showing and a crowd of 54,040 holding their frosty breaths, quarterback Livingston threw toward the back of the end zone. Henry Marshall was enveloped. The ball smacked the goalpost.

And Denver was 9–1.

Red Miller was happy afterward, especially considering that Oakland had lost to those testy San Diego Chargers. Denver was back on top, alone, in the AFC West. But Miller was also happy that he had escaped detection during the game. On a play designed to draw the defense offsides, the Broncos were called for a false start. Miller rushed to the middle of the field, which isn't allowed. "I saw him there and said: "Get off the field, coach," Randy Gradishar said. Miller offered: "I didn't realize where I was. One of the officials looked at me, and I said, 'Hello, there,' and got off the field. Before the referee understood what had happened, Miller was gone.

At 12:30 A.M. the final flight to Denver was leaving Kansas City. A lone orange-shirted fan boarded the plane. There were only six passengers. He sat down in the first seat. "I got so excited there at the end I got separated from my tour group and never found them. Missed my plane. But it was worth it. I met a Chiefs cheerleader. I promised to take her to the Super Bowl, and she said, 'Sure. But I am.' Hey, stewardess, could I have about five beers back here?"

Long after the game, Emmitt Thomas, who has been "there" for the Chiefs, said: "It's a feeling. Championship teams have it. We used to have it here. Denver has it now."

The Broncos worked out early Thanksgiving and then went home for dinner, but not before Miller had pulled off a trick. "Hey, guys, listen up before we quit. Because of the way we've been playing, a meat company is giving everyone a free turkey. You can pick it up at 637 Huron Street." Several of the veterans were cheering. "It's better than the ham we got last year. All right." Jim Jensen, a second-year player, and Otis Armstrong, a long-time veteran, showed up for their free turkeys. At the address was an empty warehouse.

On Thanksgiving Miller's wife, Nancy, gathered the family around for a special meal. Everyone was home for the first time this year—Red and his daughter, Lana, and son, Steve, and Mrs. Miller served dishes from every part of the country in which they had lived.

But the time for giving thanks was short-lived. Baltimore was ahead, and like Denver, had lost only one game in ten starts. The winner would have the best record in football. The Sack Pack of Baltimore vs. the Orange Crush of Denver.

Outside on game day supporters of the Denver symphony were collecting money. The symphony was having problems. There had been a lockout, and a group was trying to raise five hundred thousand dollars to save the symphony. Broncos fans contributed six thousand dollars and three "Orange Crush" buttons.

And just like the two previous weeks, the Broncos were in for the time of their lives.

With 7:30 remaining in the game, just one point separated the two. Denver had scored twice, and Baltimore parlayed a touchdown and a field goal in the third quarter to go with an earlier three pointer, to make it 14–13.

Bert Jones, the outstanding young quarterback for Baltimore, was guiding them again after an interception off Morton. The Colts immediately moved to Denver's twenty-four and threatened to cure Bronco fever. On third down and two, however, the Colts were offsides and backed up to the twenty-nine. Jones came out throwing toward running back Don McCauley. Denver linebacker Tom Jackson had surmised that McCauley would be the receiver, so he had laid off just far enough to give the impression of an opening. At the last instant, though, he slipped in and captured the pass. Jackson was off. Fear swept through the stands that Jackson might, as he had against San Diego and in a Green Bay game two years earlier, drop the ball. But Jackson was thinking that "whatever you do, fool, don't lose the ball. Grip it." He did score and flung the ball into the South Stands while more violence erupted around him.

The Colts returned throwing, but had to punt. Denver moved into Baltimore's territory, but a fourth-down sneak by Morton was short. Jones then threw as far as he could on first down. The ball sailed well over Raymond Chester's hands and into the arms of Louis Wright at the Broncos' thirty-two. He weaved and bobbed like a man trying to catch up with the last bus home, finally reached Baltimore's nine with 1:26 to go. A play later Denver was at the four, and in the press box assistant coach Paul Roach said over the telephone hookup with Miller: "Quarterback keeper."

Miller grabbed reserve tight end Ron Egloff, told him to inform Morton of the play, and then reacted: "Wait, Ron. Paul, that damn play isn't going to work here."

"Maybe not," Roach said from upstairs, "but it's the only play I could think of."

"Well, why not?" Miller replied.

Morton indeed kept and scored. But he wound up at the bottom of a pile and had to be carried off. Nevertheless, the Broncos were at the top of the pile at 10–1.

"I hope that guy writes me another letter," Jackson said later. "I held on without sticking the ball up my butt."

Miller said: "I don't know if we are the best team, but we've beaten some teams that had claim to being among the best."

That they had, but it had taken three finishes to achieve it.

After the Baltimore game Fred Gehrke, Miller, and their wives went to Emerson Street East, a restaurant with a sports motif. They wanted a quiet dinner. But as soon as they entered the door they were spotted, and people all over the massive room got up and gave them a thunderous ovation. "There's orange everywhere. There's no use. You can't escape," Miller said to Gehrke.

A man walked up and handed Miller a Navajo Indian rug. "I've been trying to get this to you." It was light blue with an orange Bronco insignia in the middle. Miller added it to his collection.

The next morning the Broncos' front office staff met with owner Gerald Phipps. The talk was what to do about the play-offs. Miller wouldn't hear of attending the meeting. "You're going too fast. Let's wait." So the others met behind Miller's back.

"We've got to start planning," Bob Peck said to the group. "We can't wait until the last moment. There are a lot of things to be considered."

"This is strange," Phipps said. "We've never gotten to this point before. Does anybody know what we have to do?"

Nobody really did, but they would soon find out what the playoffs were all about. Denver would clinch the division in just a few days.

21

LET THEM EAT CAKE

The pastor's message in the weekly newsletter of the Epiphany Lutheran Church had an odd twist:

"Taking St. Paul completely out of the context," wrote pastor Kemp Segenhammar, "and using his words to fit the occasion, here are some that are appropriate, '. . . I do confess, indeed I cannot deny, but confess . . .' that even as much of a football fan as I am, I never thought I would ever write about the Broncos or any other team for that matter in the *Newsletter*. But, as the writer of Ecclesiastes has said, 'There is a time for everything under heaven,' and it seems appropos to say how much fun it is that the Big Orange is doing great. After living here six years and seeing how painful the process of losing can be, it was a welcome change."

The Lutheran minister was not alone in his feeling about the Broncos, especially after the Broncos returned from Houston with a 24–14 victory, clinching the playoffs and the Western Division title. The club was 11–1, the best record in the NFL, and the city's total attention and imagination had been captured.

The city council met on the Monday night after the victory over Houston and set aside forty thousand dollars for playoff expenses. With problems like smog and water rights demanding the discussion of the city's legislative body, the major emphasis of the meeting was on the football team. Talk circulated that coach Red Miller would be run for governor.

And everyone was trying to get a piece of the action, make

some money off the Broncos. A poster including the defensive players was printed rapidly and sold by the thousands throughout the city. One man, to counteract the "Orange Crush," had designed a poster similar to the soft-drink logo called "Orange Rush." "I can't get anyone to buy it. It's a natural. We can all make a fortune off this." Another guy started bottling "Chateau de Orange," and was selling it on the streets. A downtown department store came out with coffee mugs, overpriced at four dollars, emblazoned with a story from the *Rocky Mountain News* about the Broncos' clinching the playoffs.

And the letters, more than one thousand a day, were pouring into the Broncos' office. Players such as Craig Morton had to hire private secretaries to handle the volume. And the telegrams were coming in from everywhere, literally:

"Congratulations, Broncos—John Denver and the guys Down Under." Denver, who had changed his name to fit the city, was in Australia filming a TV special, but had heard about the triumph over Houston.

At the practice field it was a zoo. The Broncos' workout field is separated from the general offices by some 100 yards, and between the two the fans camped daily—each with a new Bronco-related item. Miller emerged from behind the orange door and was met by a guy with a turquoise ring. "Made this just for you, coach. See, it's in the shape of a football. Try it on." Miller thanked him, walked another couple of feet and was met by another man. "Hey, coach, I got a dog that can center a football." "You got to be kidding." "Oh, no. Let me show you." "Well, I've really got films to look at it." "It won't take but a minute." "All right. Somebody get Mapes [center Bobby Maples]. I want him to see this." So the man and his dog, of no familiar variety, went out on the practice field with a small football, and Miller waited. The dog peed on the grass. "He'll do it," the man said. "It just takes him a few minutes to get going." So Miller waited. Finally the dog did indeed center the ball through his legs. "That's great," Miller said and shook his head. "Can you believe some of these people?"

About that time two elderly women walked through the hallway past the dressing area, looked into the room where forty-five players stood, mostly naked, frowned, and said: "We're looking for the coach." "Well, he's not in here, lady. Can't you see we're trying to get dressed." Aside, the player said: "You can't even take a shower in private anymore." The woman had a cake—orange with a football field on top. "This is really nice, ladies. We appreciate it." The women walked off, and Miller said: "This is only the fourteenth cake we've got today. Everyone must want us fat." Bob Peck, the PR man, said that the "people don't realize that the players and the coaches have work to do. Everyone wants to present the players and Red with something, and they get mad if they don't get to speak to them personally." One of the secretaries was the recipient of the cake. "My family has had orange cake every night for the last two weeks."

Miller still hadn't negotiated the distance to his office. A man had painted his station wagon orange and asked the coach to sign it. "Could you get all the players out here. I want everyone's name on it." "Well, you get them as they come out. They're pretty nice about it."

The man had just decided on the spur of the moment to paint the car. "But won't that hurt the resale value?" he was asked. "I wouldn't sell this car for anything."

A few yards down a woman with twelve kids around her walked over to the coach and offered several drawings of football players. "I painted these. Would you mind signing them for these boys? They're your biggest fans."

"Sure, sure," Miller said. At the rate he was progressing it would be dark by the time he reached the office. Especially since four television cameras from all the local stations were awaiting him on the grass. "Shit," Miller said. "Well, what are you gonna do? Okay, mens, let's get it over with." The same questions four times. "Yes, it was great to beat Houston." "No, I don't think there will be a letdown." "Yes, we're excited about the playoffs." "No, I don't think that people in the NFL are putting us down now." It's a take.

And Miller approached the orange door at the office. But wait. Here is a kid. "Coach Miller, would you sign my T-shirt?"

"Okay, son."

And here they come again. A man with a bumper sticker. "This is gonna get me rich. Hey, coach. Would you pose for a picture with this bumper sticker?"

It said: "I'm dreaming of an Orange Crushmas."

Finally . . . inside the door, Miller looked out the window at the gathering. "I have to keep remembering that these people have never had anything good happen before, but sometimes you get a little tired of it."

But Miller was starting a museum in his basement. He had an orange telephone, an orange commode seat, an orange lamp, orange T-shirts, orange sculptures, orange plaques, etc. "When I get old and forget what this was all about, I'll just go down to my museum in the basement, sit there, and relive all these moments. It can never be like this again."

Someone walked in the door with still another cake. Miller escaped through another door.

But not everyone came out of it in good shape, according to one report.

Two men, who wouldn't permit themselves to be named, had come up with a great plan for making a buck—or a thousand off the Broncos.

"You know, if we could come up with the right orange stuff to sell at the Broncos' games, we could clean up," one said.

"For sure," said his friend.

"I got it. Confetti."

It was as if he had just said, "Penicillin."

So they got on the telephone and ordered five 100-pound bags of confetti. They then purchased five thousand cellophane bags. The confetti arrived before the San Diego game, along with the cellophane bags. Then they had to get a vendor's license, $8.25 apiece. On Friday night before the game they put two ounces in each bag and Scotch-taped them. Only it didn't work. The celophane was too clingy.

So they jumped in a car and went to a grocery and purchased four thousand sandwich bags. The confetti went in all right, and they laughed while working all night.

People were in orange everywhere. The two friends were ready to make a killing. "Get you orange confetti here. A buck a bag."

But nobody bought. Confetti is not something tangible to keep.

At halftime they shouted, "Get your confetti. Fifty cents a bag."

The game ended. They took inventory. From their four thousand bags, they sold one hundred at fifty cents a bag. They divided the fifty bucks among the eight vendors.

"We lost a bundle."

"For sure."

A man turned to his friend and said things were going so good he couldn't remember when the Broncos were losers. "It seems like this has been going on for years."

"Yeah, what did we do before the madness set in?"

—People went to church in Denver on Sunday.

—Toys, not T-shirts, were purchased as Christmas presents.

—Broncos were invited to sign autographs at supermarket openings for two hundred dollars an hour.

—Pepsi-Cola was a big soft drink in town.

—Sports lovers spent December skiing in the mountains.

—Businessmen sat around at lunch talking about the stock market.

—Newborn babies weren't being posed in their first picture with orange T-shirts on.

—Television viewers in Denver watched "Andy Hardy" movies on Sunday.

—Nobody wondered what Tom Jackson ate for breakfast.

—Nobody worried about how to raise the price of playoff tickets.

—Few cared what the press back East wrote.

—Husbands and wives would talk to each other about things like getting new furniture.

—Some crimes did occur on Sunday in Denver.

—Families would pick up the phone on Sunday and call the folks back home.

—Bookies were trying to find idiots to bet on the Broncos.

—Few would put up money for the office pool.

—Farrah Fawcett-Majors's posters were popular in Denver.

—And sixty-two thousand capitalists weren't getting ugly-rich marketing every product known to man with the words orange or Broncos on it.

What had been the basis for all this, the town working itself into a fitful coma?

The defense was good to begin with. The addition of Bernard Jackson at strong safety, a steal of a trade, added considerably, along with the maturity of the four linebackers and the return to form by Lyle Alzado from his knee injury. Offensively, the Broncos had dealt Steve Ramsey for Morton. At the outset, it seemed like an even swap—one mediocre quarterback for one older mediocre quarterback. But Morton adjusted his style—which had been to force passes and try to make the big play—and provided leadership that had been lacking at the position. Mike Montler and Andy Maurer were good pickups for the offensive line, guys who had found a "home." And Bucky Dilts had developed into an excellent punter. The rest of the offense had gotten into the flow, and the philosophy of the offense, according to one player, is, "Don't fuck it up for the defense."

Miller had been the major influence, though. He brought in new offensive coaches with fresh ideas, and he had preached togetherness to the squad so long they started inviting each other over to their houses. They believed in themselves probably more so than Miller himself believed in them. Plus there had been fortunate circumstances and luck. The Broncos had remained healthy throughout while their opponents hadn't. The St. Louis Cardinals were going through a miserable period before the opening game, and Terry Metcalf was hurt. O. J. Simpson was injured when Denver played Buffalo. Kansas City was hurting. Oakland was caught surprised, and a couple of early interceptions turned the game around. Pittsburgh was without its best defensive player, Jack Lambert, and was caught with internal troubles. The Broncos played their worst game against the worst team, Seattle, and survived. Cincinnati was forced to use a lame quarterback. The Broncos had gotten breaks and made their own breaks, and the pieces fit.

Some teams, as the expression goes, can't win for losing; the Broncos in 1978 couldn't lose for winning. All the breaks were going their way. Their turn had come. It was a long time coming.

But San Diego was looming ahead, and the Broncos remembered that they had barely beaten the Chargers in the previous encounter. Since then, Dan Fouts, a holdout all season, had rejoined the team and was at quarterback, and San Diego had knocked off Oakland to help the Broncos win the division. Max Coley, the former Denver offensive coordinator, had talked to Fred Gehrke after his club beat the Raiders and said he deserved a case of scotch for the feat. So Gehrke sent him a case. He went out and purchased twelve bottles, like the ones served on airplanes. "I will remember that when we play you again," Coley laughed.

The Chargers came in with three straight victories and were thinking upset. It didn't work out that way, however. San Diego did carry a 9–7 lead into the fourth quarter, and the seventy-five thousand were wondering. Here it was December and a warm day, and Denver was losing.

But Jim Turner soon kicked a 36-yard field goal. On the play Norris Weese placed the ball down with the laces facing the wrong way, but quickly whirled them, and Turner hesitated before lazily floating the ball over the crossbars. Just 6:39 remained.

On San Diego's next possession, Fouts was racked by Denver's Paul Smith, the ball squirted out and Joe Rizzo recovered. Three plays by Denver from the Chargers' 46, and the kicking team was on. The snap went to Weese, a blocking back, and he jetted through on the left side, following what looked like forty-two blockers. Weese was pulled down 21 yards later, and Denver had possession at the 20 with only two minutes left. The Broncos were getting back at the Chargers for the trickery they pulled in San Diego.

Shortly after, Rick Upchurch lined up in the backfield for the first time during the season, grabbed the handoff from Morton and circled the right side unbothered for a 19-yard touchdown.

On the final play Fouts passed to Ricky Young in the flat, and he took off for the goal line at the other end of the field. But he slipped a the two-yard line and was downed just a yard shy at the gun.

"Thank goodness," said a writer in the end zone as darkness fell over Mile High Stadium.

"Hey, it wouldn't have mattered if he had scored. Denver still wins," said another.

"My ass," said the first guy. "I had a middle on the game," a bet on each team at different odds, so it was possible to collect on both wagers. "I had Denver and gave seven points for two hundred fifty dollars, and then later in the week the line went to nine points, so I took San Diego and the points. I make out like a bandit. Collect the whole thing. Five big ones. Go Broncos." Everyone, even the skeptics, were finally joining in—for whatever the reason.

But the triumph was not without a bad side effect. Late in the contest, unknown to the crowd, Morton had landed extremely hard on his left hip. He shrugged the pain off as just a slight, worrisome bruise, but that injury would come to haunt the Broncos.

Only one regular-season game remained. Against Dallas. Some were calling it a Super Bowl preview.

22

CRAIG AND THE COWBOYS

It had taken the Broncos twenty-six quarterbacks to finally discover one that was successful. Frank Tripucka started the parade, and Craig Morton was now the grand marshal. No matter what they did in the finale, the Broncos would finish with their best season and their first trip to the playoffs. So it was somewhat ironic that Morton would be facing, in the final regular-season game, the team that had cast him aside. The Dallas Cowboys had given him up in 1974; the New York Giants gave up on him in 1977, and currently he was the toast of Denver. In the midst of Morton's hoorah, a report came out of New York that he was being sued by a bank because of failure to pay a thirty-thousand-dollar loan. Fans started calling the newspapers and the Broncos wanting to start a fund for Morton, a man making one hundred fifty thousand dollars a year. A TV station, in fact, did begin accepting money to help Morton out of debt. But the matter got stickier. The Internal Revenue Service announced that Morton had not paid several thousand dollars in back taxes. The timing could not have been worse, but Morton shrugged it off. "As soon as the season is over I'll take care of it all. It's not what it seems." Morton had been in financial trouble before. Side businesses had gone bankrupt, and he hadn't handled his money well. But he thought all of that was behind him when the latest matter cropped up. Besides, the deep bone bruise in his hip was causing severe problems. He sat in the whirlpool for hours daily, trying to relieve the pain. And now he was to face his old team.

At least he thought he was. Red Miller had decided privately that Morton would play only briefly in the Dallas game. It was meaningless, except for the record, and the coach didn't care to risk his quarterback with the playoffs upcoming.

However, the Dallas media billed Sunday's affair as the game of the century, with Morton versus the Cowboys. And, more so, Morton versus Roger Staubach. Staubach had ousted Morton as quarterback in Dallas, and the press had created a rivalry between them. It has some basis, but, actually, they were friends.

They first met at the 1965 College All-Star game. Morton was coming out of the University of California as an All-American and headed to the Dallas Cowboys as a first-round draft choice. Staubach also was a Cowboys draft choice, but had been picked as a future player in the tenth round. He couldn't play pro ball immediately. Having graduated from the Naval Academy, Staubach had a tour of duty ahead. Both Staubach and Morton played in the all-star game, but Staubach was elected captain by his teammates and was the starter. It was a signal of things to come.

In the early years at Dallas, Morton was a caddy for Don Meredith, but not happy. He started three games in 1967, and "I learned more in those games than I did the first two years put together. I don't agree with Tom Landry's theory that it takes five years to be a quarterback in this league." Meredith finally did give it up, and Morton was his heir apparent in 1969. But Staubach had left the service and come to camp. They were a strange duo—Morton, from California, the man with the golden arm and the laid-back life-style; Staubach, Mr. Midwestern, with the scrambling ability.

At camp Morton was fined for breaking curfew, and Staubach made sure he was the last man off the practice field. It was easy to tell who eventually would win the strict Landry's heart. But Morton was the starter. The Cowboys marched to the Super Bowl after the 1970 season, and Morton became the goat when his pass bounced off a receiver's fingertips and was intercepted.

Baltimore soon kicked a field goal that won. On the side, Morton had torn up his shoulder in Atlanta—getting a ligament transplant from one of his toes ("I may be the only guy you know with athlete's shoulder")—been mugged in New York outside of P. J. Clarke's, and gone bankrupt in California.

The next season Landry announced for all to hear: "We have two starting quarterbacks." Staubach was to start one Sunday, Morton the next. But Morton knew he was headed nowhere. Staubach, however, pulled a groin in his first start, and Morton took over. He became the number one quarterback in pass standings in the league, but Landry still hadn't decided. At one point he alternated the two every other play. Finally, Landry decided on Staubach with the club at 4–3. The team won ten straight and the Super Bowl, and Staubach was named MVP in the title game.

Morton had a last opportunity. In 1972 Staubach broke his collarbone, and Morton led the team to the playoffs. But he was jerked in favor of Staubach against San Francisco, and the scrambler pulled off a miracle rally. The next week, in the conference championship against Washington, Landry chose Staubach again, but the Cowboys lost. Morton demanded to be traded. Midway through 1974, he got his wish, going to the New York Giants for a draft choice. But Morton and Staubach parted in good nature. "Few people realize this, but Craig did something for me once that I'll never forget," says Staubach. "My mother died, and I had to miss practice all week. He practiced with the first team, but I came back and played in the game, and we won. Afterward Craig stood up and said I should get the game ball. That meant a lot. People have tried to put a barrier between us, but it doesn't exist."

Morton may have gotten his desire, but the deal only ruined his reputation. The Giants were pitiful, so Morton floundered with them. He forced passes, trying to make things happen, and he looked only the worse for it. The boos were constant, so New York happily traded him to Denver in 1977 for Steve Ramsey—who didn't last out the camp with the Giants and went into private business in Dallas.

So now Morton would be returning to meet that Dallas team. "I feel much better going in with this team. I definitely want to beat them, but a lot of people want to pit me against the Cowboys, and that's not it. There is no real vindication in me. I have no animosity against Dallas. I still have a lot of friends on that team, and I care about the Cowboys. I have pleasant memories of my career in Dallas. The major thing is that we want the victory to give us thirteen—which only a few teams in the history of pro football have achieved—and we want to maintain our momentum going into the playoffs. Those reasons far outweigh any personal match.

"So much has been made of the duel between me and Roger that you can't just forget it. I'm trying, though. I have a great deal of respect for Landry. He taught me a lot about football. But a lot of the stories by the media have made much of a situation that wasn't really there."

He was enjoying his time in Denver. "This is fun. I've always enjoyed football, but I've never had as much fun as this year. Red wants you to stay loose and enjoy playing the game. There is almost no negativeness. When we're reviewing films, we almost never hear criticism. And we're made to feel a part of the total picture of winning—as if it depends on us.

"In Dallas, you were expected to be a part of a successful operation. There wasn't much fun. I'm not knocking it because it has proven successful, but we always had the feeling that even when we won on Sunday, we weren't doing it good enough. We would come out of film review, and every week someone would say, 'I wonder if we won that game.' You couldn't tell by listening to the coaches. I just couldn't continue that. I didn't want to play for the Cowboys anymore."

The season the Broncos were having had surprised him. "I really didn't have a feel for how well the team would do. I didn't know any of the players. All I'd hear was the team needed an offensive line and a quarterback. I could tell very quickly that Red Miller was instilling a winning feeling among the players. It was good that we were picked to be 7–7 or 8–6 because there was no immediate pressure on us. And we've just built together. It took the offense a while, but we were fortunate to have a defense that gets a lot of turnovers. So we've tried to remain patient, and it has worked."

It apparently had worked for Morton. At the Broncos' Quarterback Club meeting that week he was named the team's top offensive player. And the defense, which had complained about the lack of individual recognition, pepped up when five were named to the Pro Bowl. "It feels nice," said Billy Thompson at his home in the hills leading to the mountains. "But I was the same player last year, and I didn't get picked. It's because of the team." The others selected were Randy Gradishar, Lyle Alzado, Tom Jackson, and Louis Wright.

Super Bowl was a major topic all week because both Dallas and Denver were heading their respective conferences, the Broncos with a 12–1 record, Dallas 11–2. At a luncheon in Dallas Tom Landry said: "Sure this will be a possible Super Bowl preview." When Miller heard Landry's statement he cringed: "I'm not talking about that."

On the Saturday the Broncos left for Texas an "Orange Rally," naturally, was held at the Marriott Hotel in southeast Denver. Orange everywhere once again. RTD, the rapid transit system, sent a freshly painted bus labeled "Bronco No. 1," and the mayor christened it with an Orange Crush bottle.

In the parking lot were an orange Corvette, an orange truck, and an orange van, and overhead flew an orange plane. An orange cake that weighed 100 pounds was brought out, and thousands of orange balloons were released as the Cherry Creek (not Orange Creek) High School played a medley of, naturally, *Star Wars* and *Rocky*. A small dog was held aloft on a platform. He was wearing an Orange Crush T-shirt.

A couple of TV sportscasters were on hand to lead the parade. And both said they had to make no apologies about objectivity over the airwaves. "To hell with that," said John Rayburn. "We've been getting letters saying we're not giving big-city coverage. Whoever said a big city attitude always had to be presented. The fact is we have a neighborliness, like in small towns. I don't see a damn thing wrong with it. For those who do, I present them with a big raspberry." And from Gary Cruz: "I've been accused of getting overexcited. I'm a very emotional person. I don't see why I can't be perfectly objective and be a fan, too." The announcers were asked for autographs because, despite the understanding, no Broncos were present. There was, however, a tape-recorded message from Red Miller.

"We're excited," he said, and nobody could hear anything else.

In the background Debra Montoya said she idolized the Broncos. "We have an eighteen-month-old who raises her hand and yells, 'Yea' with a Bronco touchdown."

"Far out, man. Great team," said Mike Schaefer. Mike is ten.

Even the mayor, William McNichols, had kind words. "Win, lose, or draw against Dallas, this is the best doggoned team in the country. God bless them."

And two-year-old Scott Hansen had a red banner with nothing but red smears on it. He explained they stood for Cowboys blood. They were starting young.

Down in Dallas about three hundred orange-cladders waited outside the hotel for the Broncos' buses.

"Shit, this is great. I love it," said one man swigging from a Coors. "Where are they?"

A man came out and announced the plane was twenty minutes late landing.

"Let's go order another case."

Inside, at the bar, another group sat and watched a college game on television.

Two girls, rather chubby, sat over in the corner alone.

"I would give anything to meet Bob Swenson," one said.

"No," said the other. "I want Steve Foley. You ever seen him in person? There's the one." They were sisters, in their twenties, living at home. Their parents had paid for the trip—maybe hoping they would find Texas husbands.

The Broncos came in. Unfurled over the hotel lobby was a banner "Broncos Best Damn Team Ever. Go to Hell, Dallas."

A Texan walked into the lobby and said: "Who are these people? They act like the war just ended."

But much of the followers' laughter was drowned the next day in sorrow and beer. The Broncos fell to Dallas in a lackluster contest that neither team seemed to care about.

As Miller had said, Morton played only a series and retired to the bench. He never came back. Craig Penrose, fighting the flu—"I feel like crap"—first gave it a go and then was followed by Norris Weese. The teams didn't want to show a whole lot, saving themselves for the playoffs. But Dallas, by virtue of caring a little bit more, if nothing else, punched out a pair of methodical touchdowns—one in the first half and another in the third quarter. The difference would have been bigger, but Efren Herrera, Dallas's kicker, missed three field goals in the first half. The Broncos did seem to be staring past Dallas toward the first playoff game Christmas Eve against— as they had already discovered—Pittsburgh. Dallas heard after the game that it would be meeting Chicago in the opening round.

Horrified that Morton had played only briefly, Dallas writers descended on Miller and demanded an explanation. "The hip was bothering him more than we thought it would. We had planned to play him more." So what's a little white lie. Morton's hip actually looked like it had been attacked by the Black-and-Blue Plague.

On the other side of the stadium, Landry said the game hadn't meant much. Both clubs finished at 12–2, the best records in the league, and each had revealed little, if this was indeed a forewarning of the Super Bowl.

Only one Cowboy ventured to say anything strong about the outcome. Linebacker Tom "Hollywood" Henderson said he couldn't see "how Denver went 12–2. Craig must have made that difference. Maybe they got the big plays and turnovers that they didn't get today.

"But if this is a preview of the Super Bowl, then I'm going out and buy me a new house."

He would be reminded of those words.

The regular season was over.

And for some Broncos fans the loss was just the beginning of the day's troubles. When a contingent from Denver returned to the Dallas airport that night for the flight home, they were informed that the airplane had been overbooked, and they would have to wait. They then watched as Colorado governor Dick Lamm, who had become a late follower of the team for political advantages, boarded the plane with his own entourage. The fans had been bumped by the state's leader.

"I wouldn't vote for him if he was running for dogcatcher," said one of the irate onlookers. "Can you believe we have to stay here because the governor decided to take this plane?"

The next day Governor Lamm invited the irked fans to be his guest at a brunch before the playoff game. Few took him up on the offer.

Meanwhile, the Adams County Board of Commissioners presented Miller with a resolution on his return to Denver. The Broncos' offices are located in the county outside Denver. "We suffered with you through the heartbreaks, and now we're sharing your joy," said Commissioner Jim Covey, who had gotten out of a sickbed for the presentation.

"If you win the Super Bowl, we'll even reduce the taxes on your building."

23

THE SINGER AND THE GENERAL

Each Denver Broncos player was spending his free moments leading up to the playoffs in a different manner. Relaxation is a personal thing. It could mean a good book or Christmas shopping or just lying around. But Jon Keyworth and Tom Glassic had their own outlets. Keyworth liked to sing; Glassic re-created famous battles.

Before the 1977 season, the only time Keyworth sang was in the shower. In early September, though, the Broncos' fullback decided to diversify himself and bought a restaurant with a friend. One night, prior to the opening, he began talking with the band he had hired, and Keyworth found himself singing along. The band worked up a few arrangements with the player, and on the initial evening of operation Keyworth fooled everyone by getting up and doing several numbers.

"The more I do it, the more I enjoy it," Keyworth was telling a few of the other players he had invited over one night. Each was celebrating his birthday in December, as was Keyworth, so he held a small party and surprised them with several songs. The singing helped Keyworth take his mind off his injured knee. He had been hurt earlier in the season at Cincinnati (a torn ligament in the knee), and it seemed he would be out the rest of the way. But Keyworth shunned the diagnosis and was back playing before the playoffs. "You can't keep me out of them. I've waited for this."

He got up to warble. His voice was a cross between Waylon Jennings and Tom Jones, with a dash of Elvis's mannerisms and the movement of Mitch Ryder and the Detroit Wheels. And the crowd, especially the other players, loved it. Even Bobby Maples, a down-homer from Texas, climbed up on the stage for a duet late in the evening.

"I would rather stand out in the middle of Mile High Stadium in front of seventy-five thousand people naked, except for my helmet, than get up on stage, but I'm getting used to it," Keyworth told Maples.

In fact, Keyworth was in the midst of cutting a record, called, appropriately enough for the Broncos, "Make Miracles Happen." "It talks about being in the pits and pulling yourself up to accomplish something. It's a saga of the Broncos. This year has been a miracle." Soon afterward Keyworth had a local hit. Denver people were buying anything with a Broncos attachment.

"I may have found something, but football is still my occupation, and I'm not going to worry about singing anymore until we get to the Super Bowl."

Glassic, a starting guard, was in another realm with Napoleon, Bismarck, Wellington, and Robert E. Lee.

The second-year player had developed into a military science and history buff in college at the University of Virginia and believed that tactics of famous battles had helped him on the football field. "Don't get me wrong. Football isn't a military operation. But studying the classic campaigns gives one a point of view concerning tactics and helps in identifying strengths and weaknesses in an opponent and coming up with something that will work."

Glassic had been a collector of miniature soldiers—toys, if you must—since he was a child, and owned thousands. He had hand-painted British, French, and Prussian models and been joined in the venture by his roommate and former college teammate, Paul Tanulonis. Leading up to the Pittsburgh playoff game, Tanulonis and Glassic each placed four hundred of their troops on the floor of the apartment and matched strategies.

"There are specific rules as to the movement of troops. And you have to use the tactics of the time period the soldiers represent. If you send your cavalry against an infantry square, history tells you it won't succeed. But if your cavalry catches the infantry moving in the open, you know from the history of various campaigns that the infantry can be considered wiped. out. You start thinking of ways to attack and defend, how to press an advantage and how to record," Glassic said.

"The more you read and study military history, the more you understand the thinking of the great generals and why they succeeded or failed."

The former dean's-list student and English major didn't get total relief from his hobby, however. Before the Pittsburgh game, just as in previous weeks, he swallowed a "seasick" pill to calm a nauseous feeling.

The rest of the squad had their own preferences. Craig Morton and his wife were sampling several of Denver's restaurants. Lyle Alzado was out daily talking to youth groups. Glenn Hyde, a reserve tackle, showed up at the Colorado Mine Company to talk football with the regulars. And coach Red Miller was playing ragtime piano at home for his wife.

Keyworth and Glassic, however, would need some side interests before the season had ended. Keyworth would become the victim of a purported death threat, and Glassic was rapidly losing weight—eventually falling from 254 to 223 (too small for an offensive lineman) because of problems with his tonsils.

24

PLAY ON IN THE PLAYOFFS

The line was as far as the eye could see outside McNichols Sports Arena. It was the Monday before the first playoff game ever in Denver's history, and several hundred people were trying to obtain the last few tickets. Naturally, all seventy-three thousand season ticket holders had renewed their seats for the Denver–Pittsburgh game, but a few had been saved for the general public. "I probably won't get any," said Jack Simpson, "but at least I came here and tried." They had been there most of the night. The air was downright cold. "It's worth staying here," said Mrs. Mary Deadmon. "I'd give anything to see the playoff game." Shortly before 8:30 A.M. the windows were opened, and shortly after 8:30, the tickets were gone. So many left with what they came with—nothing.

The Broncos' coaches were up most of the night also. They huddled in a meeting room at the airport when they got back from Dallas and then moved to the club headquarters. Burning the midnight oil in his office, Miller said: We've haven't got too much time. We've got to cover a lot of things to get ready for Pittsburgh.

"It becomes sudden death now, and we've come too far to turn back."

But concern was evident. Linebacker Randy Gradishar had sprained an ankle in the Denver game, and his status was questionable. He soaked the foot all Monday afternoon in the Broncos' training room while the other players soothed their wounds at home. "We've got all winter to get well," Miller told his players Tuesday. But the Broncos, who had avoided major injuries all season, were strapped with several important maladies. Besides Gradishar's ankle, Craig Morton was still hobbling on a bruised thigh. Otis Armstrong hadn't shaken off a sprained ankle which had kept him sidelined since the Kansas City game. Bernard Jackson had a broken thumb and Billy Thompson had a severely bruised shoulder. At practice Bernard Jackson tried to catch a pass and winced. "It's making a left-hander out of me," he told Thompson, who was dressed out, but couldn't practice. Morton, who had the deep bone bruise said, "The leg still looks gruesome, but it's getting better. It loosened up on me today." Armstrong said, "Nothing is going to stop me from playing. I want a merry Christmas." And Gradishar tried to jog but had to stop. "It's tender," he told trainer Allen Hurst. As Gradishar walked off, Hurst told an assistant: "No chance. He can't play."

A day later Miller walked through the clubhouse handing out cookies. When practice had ended he had received cookies from a fan for the players—each one was in the shape of a football player with a jersey number corresponding to a member of the squad. Louis Wright looked down at his and moaned: "I think I got stuck with a Bucky Dilts. I'd rather have a quarterback cookie." But he munched away. Wright was excited. "I never been on any kind of team that played in the playoffs or in a bowl game."

Wright would be tested against Pittsburgh's premier wide receiver, Lynn Swann. "He's one of the best. I'm going to bump him and stay close. I got some tricks up my sleeve for him. But he's making me lose some sleep this week."

Paul Smith had waited the longest for the playoffs—ten seasons. He sat in the lounge of the locker room and said that sometimes he doubted "if I'd ever get to a game like this. So there's no question that I'm psyched up." A few feet to his side, wide receiver Jack Dolbin said he would be treated rudely. "Pittsburgh has a physical defense. All guys are tackles. And they'll clothesline me and tackle hard if I catch a couple."

Morton said the Pittsburgh game "will be the toughest we've played all year. But I think our mood is about the same it's been. In the first game our game plan worked just about as well as we could expect. We realize this is a tough team to run against, and I think it will be a low-scoring game." Although he had been involved in fifteen previous playoff games with the Dallas Cowboys, for Morton, "this is the most exciting because we're really sharing it with the people of Denver who have waited so long. And I've been a part of this kind of enthusiasm. Red is really making it fun, even this week. He has gotten close to the players but still earns their respect. Take that walking around handing out cookies today."

Miller called the practice that day "the best one we've had all year. The concentration is there, and the players are enthusiastic."

Meanwhile, the PR department was gearing up for the largest press entourage in Denver sports history. The auxiliary press box at Mile High Stadium would be used, and the Coors beer executives, who normally use it, were moved out. The writers began arriving at the Regency and were each issued an "Orange Crush" survival kit—a T-shirt, a six-pack of Orange Crush, a story of the hoopla in the city, and orange buttons.

It was another ploy by the local Orange Crush distributors. A writer from Pittsburgh looked at the stuff and said: "I wish the name of the defense was Coors Crush. I could use a six-pack of that. What am I going to do with orange soda? You can't even mix it with anything."

In Pittsburgh, speculation began that quarterback Terry Bradshaw was having problems. He had been belted in the neck in the Steelers' final game, and one reporter said he wouldn't play. Miller was receiving daily reports from Pittsburgh. "Bradshaw hasn't thrown a pass this week," he said quietly. But Chuck Noll, the Pittsburgh coach, offered that Bradshaw was throwing and would indeed participate.

The city's insanity reached new heights. Almost every billboard in town had a statement about the game. "Orange Milkshake, 59 Cents. Help Wanted. Apply Inside." "Broncos Breakfast." "Broncos to the Super Bowl." No car was without a Broncos bumper sticker. No conversation ended without a mention of the team.

Miller walked into his office and found an orange Santa Claus, complete with orange and blue candy canes. And in midweek an orange Christmas tree suddenly appeared in the waiting room of the Broncos' offices. All around town orange Christmas trees were being sold by the hundreds. A man put a manger scene in front of his house with players' likenesses depicting the Christian characters. A woman called a TV station and suggested that everyone put orange lights on their houses for Christmas Eve. Bob Kurtz, the sportscaster at the ABC affiliate, came on each night with a new orange item—orange garbage cans, orange flower arrangements, orange pizzas, orange perfume.

A man came into the *Rocky Mountain News* offices and asked for a photographer quickly. "What's so important?" asked the city editor.

"I've just finished painting my van orange, and I've got a Bronco scene on the side of it," he said.

"No thank you," said the city editor.

Christmas had been mostly forgotten. The game would be played on Christmas Eve, and kids' toys were not important. In fact, there is usually a crush at the department stores on Christmas Eve, coming on a Saturday this year, but advertisements were warning people to shop Friday for last-minute gifts. Orange Christmas wrapping paper was the biggest seller.

"I can't believe this," said Broncos kicker Jim Turner. "When we won the Super Bowl with the New York Jets, the people got excited, but that was a drop in the bucket compared to this, and we still haven't even played the game yet."

Paul Howard, the Denver guard, was thinking more about Joe Greene of the Steelers. He lay awake at night and planned his strategy. Greene had once smacked him in the crotch during a game, and he expected some more illegal tactics. "I've got to approach him the way I would anybody else. I got to play him hard." In Pittsburgh Greene was settled on a sofa. "You tell the people of Denver we aren't coming out there to lose. We got our act together now. We know what it's all about. And I ain't going to be mean. I'm going to be good."

The Steelers had their final workout in Pittsburgh on Thursday, amid occasional snow flurries, and flew into Denver at noon Friday. About two thousand were joining the caravan, including owner Art Rooney, the grand old man of football who had waited more than three decades for his first playoff game. "If we weren't playing Denver, I'd be pulling for them. I know how it is. Our people have become complacent, but there was nothing like that first year, and it's been the same way—if not more—for Denver this season."

The Broncos worked out at Mile High Stadium on Friday, and Gradishar, the key of the defense, looked terrible. There seemed no possible way he could play. The ankle hadn't healed. The players were loose, but punter Bucky Dilts looked around at them and said: "I wonder if we aren't just whistling in the dark. Maybe we're a lot more scared than we're letting on."

Gradishar remained quiet, watching.

Then the Steelers took over. Stadium gates were locked tight. Wanderers tried to peer under a fence and over a wall, but Pittsburgh wasn't letting on.

Miller cruised into the Regency for a press conference, said he thought Gradishar would play, and then told an associate: "No way. But you can never tell about a guy like him. We'll put Turk in there probably."

Denver was installed as a two and one-half-point favorite, but by now, the Denverites thought nothing could go wrong. They arrived orange-eyed and ready on Christmas Eve afternoon. Several Broncophiles had brought portable television sets and radios to augment their own view.

And they were provided with an extra bonus. The Baltimore–Oakland game, scheduled early in Baltimore, was shown on the outdoor scoreboard TV screen. It was headed into overtime, and the cheers rose and died each time the Raiders made an error.

Upstairs, NFL officials and NBC executives were trying to make a decision. The other playoff game was running long, so they elected to hold up the Denver game for a few moments. But they couldn't wait any longer. "Oh, hell, we've waited eighteen years. We can still wait a few more minutes," said a fan in the second deck.

But the game began. A writer said: "Can you imagine that? The people watching on television in Denver can't even see the Broncos in the playoffs." But soon enough the Raiders had

won. Boos filled Mile High Stadium. Players looked around
and wondered what had occurred.

As usual, Denver lost the toss. But Pittsburgh ran aground
at its 25 and was forced to kick. Denver also failed to move
and returned the favor. The Steelers were stopped short again
and went into punt formation. The Broncos put ten men up
to test punter Rick Engles, a high-school teacher for most of
the season who had just been signed by Pittsburgh because
of an injury. John Schultz soared through a hole in the middle,
blocked the ball, and fell on it at Pittsburgh's 17. Denver had
the turnover. Just three plays later Rob Lytle cruised through
a hole on the left side and scored Denver's first playoff
touchdown.

The rest of the country missed the touchdown because NBC
was just tuning in the game. The Steelers came back out, and
on the first play Randy Gradishar made the tackle. Before the
game Miller had talked guardedly to him about playing; Gradishar refused a pain-killing shot, and he agreed to give it a
try. Gradishar played the entire game.

The first quarter ended, 7–0, and the Broncos appeared to
be in command. But Franco Harris, the Steelers' running back,
started roaring and became the first NFL player to go over
1,000 yards in playoff games with a 14-yard scoot. The Steelers
reached Denver's two-yard line, but a pair of bursts were
stopped by Gradishar, and then Bradshaw, who was playing
after all, took matters into his own hands and leaped over center, like an Olympic diver doing a half twist with a jackknife
finish.

The Steelers quickly got the ball back and were moving once
more when Harris took a handoff and stabbed at the left side.
Lyle Alzado unloaded on him, and the ball slithered on the
ground. Gradishar swept it up at the Pittsburgh 43, but never
had a solid grip. The ball bounced to the turf again, and Tom
Jackson took over from there. He clutched the ball and cas-
caded to the 10-yard line. On the first play, Otis Armstrong,
making his first appearance in over a month because of an
ankle injury, flowed right and skipped into the end zone. But
4:15 remained in the half, and Pittsburgh had plenty of time
to counter.

The Steelers traversed the complete field with Harris handling the majority of the work, down to just under two minutes to go. Denver wanted to run out the clock with the score tied, 14–14. But then a volcano named Mean Joe Greene erupted. He slugged Denver offensive guard Paul Howard in the solar plexus. On NBC the play was shown repeatedly. The official didn't detect the punch, but Howard had. He lay on the ground and had to be helped off the field. Tempers were flaring and on the very next play, Greene got into a tussle with center Mike Montler. Greene hit the Denver center, who responded but missed. The officials did see this one and assessed Pittsburgh 15 yards in penalty.

The gun sounded and Miller charged off after the departing referee with Greene right behind the Denver coach. Pittsburgh assistant George Perles got into a shouting match with Miller in the shadow of the South Stands. A small riot was developing, but saner heads prevailed, and the teams retired to their dressing rooms. Miller's first thought inside was retaliation, as he was about to speak. Then he hesitated. "Let them play that way. Let's get back at them by beating them. We'll hurt them where it does the most good—in the wallet. All right, mens."

Calm was prevalent in the second half as Denver accepted the kickoff. Soon Denver was threatening at the Pittsburgh two, but three slashes at the line produced nothing. On fourth down Miller turned to Joe Collier, the defensive coordinator, asked what he thought, and elected to go for the touchdown. But Jim Jensen was tripped up and landed just short of the goal. Pittsburgh took over, but went nowhere, and Denver got the ball back at the Steelers' 41. Then Morton waited—getting protection from his offensive line that ofttimes was "missing"—and picked out tight end Riley Odoms, isolated on rookie linebacker Robin Towes. Odoms caught the ball on the run over his shoulder at the six-yard line and bounded toward the goal. With three and one-half minutes expired in the third quarter, Denver stepped back on top, 21–14.

And the quarter ended thusly.

Then, because of a defensive coverage mixup, Bradshaw was able to hit Dave Stallworth at the Broncos' 26, and he sprinted to the two. On the next play Bradshaw rolled right and could have run the ball in, but chose to throw to right tackle Dave Brown in the back of the end zone on a tackle-eligible play. Tied again, 21–21.

Denver came again, but was stopped at the Pittsburgh 27. Jim Turner strolled out—with Norris Weese, who had been injured on a punt play and was gimpy-legged—and kicked a solid 44-yard field goal. So Denver was up, 24–21, with 7:17 to go.

Pittsburgh had to throw, and it proved costly. Bradshaw passed the ball to his left, but Tom Jackson, sitting and waiting at the Steelers' 40, jumped in, tipped the ball, and brought it down with his right hand, ending up at the Steelers' nine behind three blocking teammates. He already had a fumble recovery and an interception for the day. "I've never seen a black Santa Claus," said a fan upstairs, "until just now." At the conclusion of the play, Denver's Paul Smith did a silent dance at mid-field.

On fourth down, after a mistake by the officials on a pass that they thought was tipped illegally but wasn't, Turner kicked a 25-yard field goal. But Denver couldn't sigh yet.

Bradshaw went to the air again, and, guess who was there— Jackson! who caught the ball at the 50 and moved 17 yards downfield. On second down Miller sent in a running play, but Morton shook it off. "We can beat them on top. They're gonna blitz, so Jack should get single coverage," he told the players in the huddle. And Jack Dolbin went off on a fly pattern, and Morton threw as pretty as you please, with Doblin gathering the ball in just over the goal and just beyond cornerback Jim Allen.

It was all over. Denver had won its first playoff game. On the sidelines owner Gerald Phipps laughed out loud. Havoc reigned in the streets outside. City buses were stopping to ask the score. People leaving downtown for their homes on Christmas Eve were stopping to toast drinks with each other.

A bearded man left the stadium as if he were walking through an unseen maze, finally colliding with a chain fence. Two hulking fans picked him up and carried him off.

Two Pittsburgh followers were shouting: "Fuck all of you. I don't like this town at all."

A youngster skipped along exclaiming, "We're the champions. We're the champions. What a great Christmas present."

It was merry Crushmas in Denver.

"They had better enjoy it now, because it's never going to be like this again," said Pittsburgh quarterback Bradshaw. "Four years from now, if they're still winning here, this will die down. We used to have crazy fans, maybe not as much as this, but crazy. But things will settle down here. The fans will get conservative, wear suits."

As they walked off the field, Paul Howard reached Joe Greene. "You're an All-Pro. You don't have to play like that. You're too good for that."

Greene looked at him. "I don't like to be held."

They didn't shake hands.

25

HAPPY NEW YEAR

The snow was coming down at Interstate Dog Track, 40 miles outside Denver, and the crowd was small. The bettors were studying their books, trying to figure out what dog to back. "Your attention, please," the PA announcer said. "We're about to give away two tickets to the Broncos' playoff game Sunday against Oakland. Here's the lucky number."

All eyes left the books. Two tickets. That was better than winning the daily double.

In the newspaper a man offered his house for fifty-four thousand dollars. Included with the house were two tickets to the football game. The house was gone before the morning was out. A man was selling a '54 Buick for six hundred dollars, an ad stated. The Buick didn't run (the transmission was missing), but four tickets for the game were included. The Buick was sold.

A madhouse all over town. Christmas is a time for resting up, but not in Denver. Christmas Day citizens gathered over turkey and dressing and talked about their Broncos. The TV's and radios spouted words about the game. "A Christmas Carol" was pre-empted for filmed highlights of the Pittsburgh game.

Red Miller awoke Christmas morning to find a banner outside his house, stretching across the length of the lawn. "Broncos Are No. 1." He spent two hours taking the banner down and went inside to open his gifts. A pair of house shoes—"Thank God they're not orange," he told his wife, Nancy—and other assorted trinkets. And then it was off to work again. "Oakland.

Oakland," Miller said, as he walked out the door.

That night Miller woke Nancy. She thought he was having an attack, when she looked over at him. Miller was still asleep in a dream world, but was clapping his hands and hollering: "Let's go. Let's go. Get 'em." She rolled over and went back to sleep.

Playing Oakland for the American Conference championship. Now, that was a dream for the Broncos. For so many years Denver had looked up to Oakland, tried to emulate them. And here they were, about to play each other for the right to go to the Super Bowl. They had split in regular season games and would be playing a third time.

And Broncomania—which had been a local "disease" all season—was spreading all over the country. In California a writer penned: "It's the funny little team from Colorado against the world champions. There is a lot of sympathy here for the Broncos. There is no sympathy for the Raiders." A restaurant owner in San Diego, who fed the Denver executives every time they came to town, was flying to Denver for the game.

Don Smith, a former Broncos publicist with the Pro Football Hall of Fame, said, "Suddenly here are the Broncos, who have never been on top and who until the last four or five years were the butt of jokes. Suddenly, they are winning, and winning outstandingly. They have to be the sentimental favorites of the teams. The others have won before." He said sales of Bronco souvenirs at the Hall of Fame had picked up considerably over the last six weeks. "Frankly, they haven't been one of the big sellers until recently."

Linebacker Tom Jackson said everyone "who's been an underdog will be rooting for us. They want to see Cinderella get her slipper back."

Val Pinchbeck, assistant to the president of the AFC in New York and a former member of the Broncos' staff, said attention had been building in that city because of increased television exposure of Broncomania and because of Craig Morton, a former Giant.

A man in Phoenix drove nonstop to Denver Christmas Day to buy tickets for the Oakland game; a student at Bowdoin

College boasted that he was the first student on campus with an Orange Crush T-shirt, and a New York businessman had become a Denver fan because "we need heroes here."

Meanwhile, Joe Ciancio, director of parks and recreation, was preparing security measures. He told city officials at a meeting: "Because of the rivalry between Oakland and Denver, we had better put on extra security guards." But the city was making no plans to protect the goalposts. At late-season games guard dogs had been brought out at the end of each game, but not this time. "They can have the goalposts," the mayor said to his cronies. "We're not going to punch people around. If we win, they're entitled to celebrate."

The Broncos early in the week were installed as the underdogs, by three and one-half points. Linebacker Joe Rizzo saw the information and shouted out: "That's great. From what I hear, I think they may be a little overconfident."

In Oakland, the Raiders were acting confident, if not overconfident. On Tuesday the sprinkling rain settled in and never let up. Behind a row of hedges that hadn't been cut in years, at a field near the airport and a garbage dump, the Raiders practiced. Madden closed it to the world and informed a writer from Denver he couldn't talk to anyone or come to practices.

After practice several of the players gathered at a nearby motel bar. Kicker Errol Mann chugged a beer. "We're going to Denver to win. But we have respect for that team. Don't think we don't."

John Matuszak, the big offensive lineman who had bumped around in his career and finally settled in with Oakland, sat at the bar and played music trivia. "Who did this song?" and he hummed a few bars. Nobody listened. "Hey, we're not talking about the game because we have nothing to say. We'll go out there and show them with our actions."

Ted Hendricks, a tall, gangling linebacker, settled into a chair. "If we play without making mistakes, it won't even be a game. Denver won't be in it. That's the truth. And that's all there is to it. We won't be embarrassed like we were in that first game, and it should be more like the second one. I've got a phone call."

The people of Oakland weren't getting very excited about the contest. "The people have been through this before," said one of the players at the bar. "When we go to the Super Bowl, then they will get excited."

But Ricardo, the bartender, had a thought. "I want to see Denver win. Those people deserve it. These players are getting fat and sassy. But Denver won't beat Oakland. No way. What do you think, Margie?"

A buxom waitress walked over. "I don't care. They're always grabbing anyway. Who gives a shit about football? I just want to get off."

The rain continued for three days, but Madden said: "It's not bothering us. We're in good shape to play. We know what we have to do to beat Denver. It's just a question of doing it."

Then Madden posed a philosophical statement: "Nobody at the beginning of the season talks about winning the Super Bowl. Everyone wants to go to the Super Bowl. Getting there is the thing."

In Denver Morton was still bothered by the bone bruise deep in his left hip, so Monday he checked into a hospital. The Broncos admitted that Morton was receiving overnight care, but indicated he would be back on the field the next day. He wasn't. In fact, Morton didn't leave the hospital until late Thursday. But the Broncos weren't announcing it. Morton laid in the hospital and began to wonder if he would play. The leg hadn't improved by midweek. He saw a brief item about his visit to the hospital, but thought how funny it was that the press wasn't making a big deal about the possibility that he wouldn't even be able to play. Later he was told by the Broncos about the coverup campaign. Publicly Miller was saying: "Morton will play. No question about it." Privately the Broncos were preparing young Craig Penrose. Quarterback coach Babe Parilli told Penrose on Thursday: "There's a very good chance Morton won't play. You've got to be ready."

The Raiders didn't know what was going on. The press corps that descended on Denver just assumed that Morton was being rested—much like Joe Namath had when the Jets were in the playoffs and Namath had the bad knees. "I had to practice all week for Joe before the Super Bowl, so I know what Penrose is going through," Parilli said.

The Broncos were hoping Oakland would put the ball in

the air, but it wasn't expected. The Raiders had won the second meeting by running with the ball, so that's what the Broncos were preparing for.

Meanwhile, firemen for the Denver Fire Department issued a challenge to a fire engine company in Oakland, wagering one hundred and fifty dollars on the game, with the losing company promising to pay the burn treatment center in the opponent's city. "We are confident," said Lt. Frank Baleria of the Oakland Fire Department. "We've won all our bets before."

But a lot more was being wagered on the game. In Las Vegas Joey Boston said the majority of the money was coming in on Oakland. "The public is betting Denver, the smart money is on Oakland."

The game was scheduled for noon New Year's Day, so there were going to be some hung-over fans. The remaining six hundred tickets went on sale Monday morning and were gobbled up within fifteen minutes.

There was some concern because of the unusual early starting time on a Sunday that churches' services would be affected. But most weren't concerned.

"We're not going to paint the cross orange," said one minister. "I always say, 'First things first.'" But the minister did add that the church would hold two services, one at 11:00 preceded by one at 9:30 A.M. We'll have a huge 9:30 A.M. throng and a very quiet 11:00 A.M. service." He added that he would conduct a lengthy second service only if "I want to die young."

Even though the Broncos, like the Raiders, had closed their practices, there still was an area on one street through which fans could watch. And so the fans had showed up as if waiting for a traffic accident.

The crowds waiting for the players outside the locker room had increased considerably. And inside the office, nineteen-year-old Jill Hardy was pulling at her hair. Her job was to answer the phones. The daughter of Carroll Hardy, the director of player personnel, she admitted that daddy had played a dirty trick on her. There were twelve lines into the Broncos' office. Two hundred were needed.

"They're always going—from eight in the morning on. Weird calls? There are too many weird calls. Everyone thinks he should be the coach. They have a play for Coach Miller that they think will beat Oakland.

"The weirdest call? That would be hard. I guess maybe it was the one from this high school team. They said they had originated the 'Orange Crush' idea, and the Broncos had stolen it from them. They didn't think that was right. To make up for it they wanted the Broncos to send playoff tickets to the football team, the coaches, and all the teachers at the school."

There was a sign in front of Jill. It read: "God Grant Me Patience."

Miller came wading through the mess. "We want to be accommodating, but I think it's better for our concentration if there weren't so many people around. But the players seem to be taking it in stride." Miller was still putting up a facade on Wednesday about Morton. "He'll put on the pads tomorrow." But he wouldn't.

In Oakland, defensive tackle Dave Rowe shaved his beard. "When we beat Denver, the mustache will go, and when we win the Super Bowl, I'll shave my head."

Linebacker Floyd Rice said he already had a celebration planned. "After we beat the Broncos I'm going to get a can of orange pop, turn it over, and empty it. Slowly."

Morton finally checked out of the hospital, but was in severe pain. He still didn't know if he could go. He couldn't work out, and the coaches intensified their preparation with Penrose considerably.

The Raiders flew into town late Friday, and the cameras were poised at the airport. But none of the players would say a word. If a question was posed to them, they looked at the interviewer and went on. "Well, they didn't make any friends here tonight," said a man working on the plane. "As if they had any to begin with."

On Saturday, New Year's Eve, the Broncos practiced at Mile High Stadium, then were followed in by the Raiders as a light, swirling snow began to fall over the city. Throughout the year the Broncos had played in nothing but nice weather, but the possibility of a snowstorm for the biggest one was real. The

Raider players wore silver and gray, but Ken Stabler was outfitted in red pants and a red sweatshirt—as if he were a man not to be touched by the other players. Madden came off the field and said the noise wouldn't faze his team. "We've led the league in boos the last couple of years. As long as they keep them in the stand it's Okay."

His team had been to the big one. The Broncos hadn't. "Once you win the Super Bowl, you can define the prize. You know what the prize is. You want to keep it and/or get it again very strongly."

Madden normally wears a short-sleeved shirt when he coaches on the sidelines, but the weather was threatening. "I don't know if I will wear one. If we had played today, it would be a gutsy call."

Miller, meanwhile, was telling the final Quarterback Club meeting of the year that the Broncos "have come too far to stop now. We're going to give the Raiders a hell of a game. I promise you that. We will not be outplayed. We may be beat." He got a standing ovation.

Much was being made of the fact that, according to the Chinese calendar, 1977 was the Year of the Snake—as in Ken Stabler, the Snake. But the new year would be the Year of the Horse, as in Broncos. How appropriate for a game on January 1. However, the Chinese calendar wouldn't go into effect for several more weeks.

A biorhythm expert said Craig Morton would be on a triple high while Stabler was supposed to be down physically and emotionally and up intellectually. "Quarterbacks don't throw biorhythms, though," a Raider said.

While both teams retired early New Year's Eve, the press corps partied into the night at the Regency at an AFC party, with the conference insignia in ice. The party ended about the time the ice turned to water. It was snowing outside.

New Year's Day, 1978, broke clear, but cold. Everyone was up early, because of the noon game.

A man with an orange van ferried the press corps from the motel to the stadium. "Get in, boys, got a stewardess in back. Fix your favorite drink."

A writer from *The New York Times* ordered a bloody Mary and said: "I don't care who wins, but I wouldn't mind staying in this van all day."

By the time the van reached the stadium, it was already full—as if the people had come straight from their New Year's Eve parties to the game. The buzz they got the night before was just continuing. A man in a gorilla's mask walked around in front of the crowd. "Oh, I see Al Davis is here," said somebody in the third row. And those around him started throwing empty beer cups at the gorilla.

The teams came out, and Morton looked like an old man. He was limping hard on the side. "I don't think he's gonna play," said Joe Sanchez of the Denver *Post,* who covered the team. "I think we've been had." So all eyes turned to Morton. He tried to throw a few passes, but couldn't complete anything. In the locker room Miller had helped Morton put his shoe on and was certain the quarterback couldn't play.

Denver won the toss, and Morton, who had told Miller he would try, limped on to the field. But Denver didn't accomplish anything the first series.

Oakland had the ball for the next eighteen plays and almost nine minutes, and if the air was cold before, now it was freezing. The Raiders ran the ball. At one point nine consecutive rushes pushed Oakland to the Denver six-yard line. Then, on first down, a run produced three yards, and a second one zero. On third down Stabler threw, but his receivers were covered, and the ball had to be thrown away. So Errol Mann came on for a 20-yard field goal, and Oakland was up.

It took Denver just two plays from scrimmage to retaliate. Morton sought out and found his favorite receiver, Haven Moses, racing down the right sidelines with single coverage. Moses caught the ball at the Oakland 39, and safety Skip Thomas tried unsuccessfully to grab him by the shoulders. Moses skirted free, whirled, and headed for the goal without trouble. He didn't react immediately. "I thought I might have stepped out of bounds." But a referee ruled touchdown, and Moses celebrated.

Oakland came right back, as the second period began, and was within 12 yards of a touchdown. But the drive ran aground.

A field goal was requested. Chip shot. But, oddly enough, holder David Humm turned the laces of the ball back *toward* Mann instead of away from him. The 29-yarder hit the right pole squarely and caromed back to the field.

Denver moved once more, but ended up with a 40-yard field-goal attempt, and Jim Turner was short. So the first half ended, 7–3.

On the opening kickoff of the second half, Oakland's Carl Garrett got free, spilled into the middle, and raced to the Denver 33 before being pulled down by Lonnie Perrin. But after a Stabler pass in the end zone was knocked down by Steve Foley, who had been a college quarterback and worked at the position that week, the Raiders had to punt.

The M & M Connection hooked up again to the Oakland 23, but Turner missed yet another field goal. On the first play of a series, Stabler and Clarence Davis failed to make a good exchange on a handoff, and Brison Manor dove on it at the Oakland 17-yard line.

Riley Odoms took a pass from Morton at the five, and juked his way to the two. Then Denver's Rob Lytle burst at the left side of the line and was whacked by Jack Tatum. The ball popped out immediately, and Raider Mike McCoy picked it up and started racing off. But the whistle had blown the play dead. There was no fumble.

Upstairs, Al Davis screamed: "What in the shit are they doing to us?"

The officials later said they had not seen the fumble, but it was indeed one and would be played and talked about all over America the next several days. During the dispute Oakland linebacker Floyd Rice shoved linesman Ed Marion, who had made the call, and got an unsportsmanlike conduct penalty. It was an automatic first down at the one-yard line. On the next play Morton rolled, or rather crept, right and pitched to Jon Keyworth, who rolled into the end zone. Denver led, 14–3.

But twenty-one and one-half minutes were remaining, and nothing is safe with the Raiders in town. They had not lost in Denver since 1962.

Denver could have put the Raiders away later in the quarter, though, but were victimized by an officiating decision. A low pass to Jack Dolbin, who got up and ran for a touchdown, was adjudged a trap. Replays showed it wasn't.

The Broncos had to go for a field goal instead, and, amazingly, the reliable old pro, Turner, missed a third time.

As the fourth quarter started, the Raiders came out roaring and got a touchdown when Stabler, under heavy fire, threw to tight end Dave Casper, who made a falling catch in the end zone. It was 14–10.

Morton then drove the Broncos, but threw an interception to Floyd Rice. Oakland returned the favor when Stabler fired to Bob Swenson, who took the ball at the 31 and danced to the 17. Two runs accounted for five yards, and then Morton dropped back to pass. He wanted to hit Odoms, but he wasn't there. So Morton held up. He put a hand down on the ground to balance himself and then looked elsewhere. Moses had just a step on Jack Tatum as he crossed in the end zone, dove for the sinking liner, and came up holding the ball aloft before throwing it into the South Stands—like throwing a piece of meat in a tank of piranha.

However, the Broncos missed the extra point when Weese, bothered by an injury, couldn't get it down. He tried to throw, but it was no good. The lead was 20–10 midway through the fourth quarter.

The Raiders weren't finished. They came roaring back with a touchdown, and Denver's impressive lead was just 20–17 with 3:16 showing.

After the kickoff the Broncos tried to use up the clock with runs, and Lonnie Perrin and Otis Armstrong responded. They picked up a pair of first downs to the Denver 39, and Oakland was out of time-outs. Morton just fell on the ball, and time ran out.

Haven Moses turned a cartwheel on the field.

It was frenzy. Seventy-five thousand people tried to get on the field. The Broncos and the Raiders tried to get off. Players hugged each other. Red Miller grabbed general manager Fred Gehrke and they became one.

It was unbelievable out there, as the Broncos finally made it to their locker room. The shouts outside were for Miller.

He finally emerged. A man grabbed his watch and took it off his hand. "Give it back, or I'm coming after you." Fans poured over the guy, and he handed the watch back. "I just wanted a souvenir."

Miller shouted "Thank all of you. You're sharing in this moment with us."

In the locker room Haven Moses and Craig Morton—who had been such a valuable twosome all year—sought each other out in the middle of the room. They embraced and kissed each other's tear-stained cheeks.

"Craig, you're beautiful," Moses said. "I love you."

"I love you, too, man. Great game."

Billy Thompson held the game ball high. "Who led us to the Promised Land?"

"Moses," his teammates chanted.

Morton collapsed, partially because of his bad hip, partially because of fatigue. A teammate rushed over to help him up. "I'm all right. Just give me a month."

Fred Biletnikoff, who had been hurt in the game, sought Moses out. "Congratulations, you had a hell of a game. Now you know what to do in the Super Bowl."

Miller was shouting: "Super Bowl, dammit. There, I've said it. I've had it bottled up inside of me for so long. But we're going, and nobody can stop us. What a great team." In a corner stood Miller's old high-school coach. Miller took a moment and went around introducing him.

"Super Bowl, it hasn't hit me yet," said Tom Jackson.

"My house is five minutes from the Super Bowl," said Steve Foley.

Then Miller got back in the act. "They said this team was too young. This team is here to stay. Shit. Hey, I wonder if we're for real now, goddamn it."

Morton still hadn't recovered when the network asked him over. He had spent most of the week in the hospital. His hip was bleeding. His left leg had swelled four inches bigger than his right. Craig Penrose, the man who would have replaced Morton, undressed. "He did not practice. He couldn't walk. I can't believe it."

(The Broncos would be fined by the league for keeping Morton's problem and stay in the hospital secret. Miller only smiled about the matter.)

"Nobody expected us to do anything. They expected 7-7, 8-6, also rans. This is just great. I never visualized this happening in New York. We're going to New Orleans. I can't believe it."

He would have to. The Broncos would be playing Morton's former teammates, the Dallas Cowboys, who won later on New Year's Day.

Mark van Eeghen walked up to Lyle Alzado. "Listen, man, all that stuff you read in the paper that said we said or were supposed to have said this, well, that's just bull. There was a lot of talking."

"I know, man," Alzado replied. He grabbed him and hugged him.

"Now go get that ring," added van Eeghen.

But not everyone was so cordial. Al Davis was still fuming over the incorrect official's call. "It was a big lie. The same thing happened in Vietnam. I don't mind that it happened. What I don't like is the explanation."

And Madden said: "I don't want to get into that. The more I talk about it, the more it sounds like sour grapes. But twenty million people saw it on TV. Let them make their own judgment. But Denver won. One call doesn't make the difference. I congratulate Denver."

But Neal Colzie said, about the officials, "Those motherfuckers weren't going to get out of this damned stadium if they gave the ball to us. Anyone with two eyes could see what happened. It was a home-field call. What a terrible way to lose a championship!"

Billy Thompson: "People say that God gave the world two miracles—the parting of the sea and the '69 Mets—but move over, Casey."

Paul Smith: "If I'm dreaming, I hope nobody wakes me up."

Outside, the people were still celebrating—swinging on the metal goalposts. First the south one fell, and then the north one. On the field, people were ripping up the turf. In the press box, Wilbur Latham, head groundskeeper at the stadium, looked out and offered up a big laugh. "As soon as we painted the stadium for the playoffs for TV, the grass died. They're saving us the trouble by pulling it up."

It was more New Year's Eve on the field. Downtown they were dancing in the streets. Horns blared. The masses shouted. A whole city celebrated.

In Dallas, the Cowboys had just finished off the Minnesota Vikings, and Tom Henderson was asked about his statement after the Dallas game. "I was just saying something in the heat of the situation. Denver has a really good football team."

Denver thought so. A town which had been going wild was going crazy. And that night they all went out and painted the town orange.

New Orleans, here they come.

18–19. Denver salutes the AFC champions. *(Above)* More than 100,000 await the Broncos' entourage. The state capitol is in the background. *(Below)* Craig Morton and Haven Moses oblige their loyal fans by signing autographs.

ORANGE

20. Denver Broncos T-shirts sold in downtown department stores like, well, hotcakes.

21. It's easy to see whom he supported.

MADNESS

22. Denver fans came in all sizes, shapes, and forms.

23. One young fan had—literally—gotten into Orange Crush and had the snake—like Kenny "Snake" Stabler of Oakland—well in hand.

24. One Denverite used his head to show his appreciation for Denver's game.

25. The protagonists meet in New Orleans. Denver coach Red Miller and Dallas head man Tom Landry were all smiles early in the week.

26. The Broncos in the Superdome look at the Super Bowl from the inside for the first time.

27. Tom Jackson has a new story for every member of the media. He was run over three times as a kid; his college team played for a turkey one Thanksgiving; he taught teammate Randy Gradishar how to use a knife. And they listened.

28. The loyalists—25,000 strong—had followed the Broncos to New Orleans, with their signs.

SUPER

29. Preston Pearson of Dallas finds running room tough against the Denver defense.

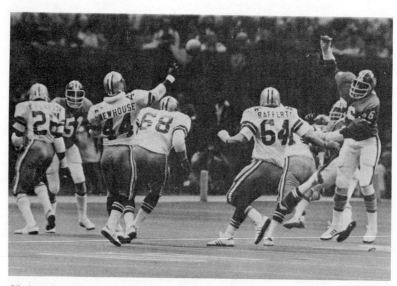

30. Just when it seems that Denver might have a comeback chance, the Cowboys catch the Broncos flatfooted, as fullback Robert Newhouse pulls up during a sweep and throws the touchdown pass that put the final nail in the coffin.

SUNDAY

31. Roger Staubach unloads for Dallas...

32....and Butch Johnson is at the end-zone doorstep to make a picture-book diving catch for a touchdown.

33. The Broncos came limping home to Denver the next day—to find snow and the final crowd at the airport. Rubin Carter *(left)*, Barney Chavous, and Paul Smith were sullen enough, but John Grant *(right)* also faced knee surgery.

34. And they cheered on for the Broncos, who, despite the loss in the Super Bowl, had provided them with the best season ever. As one sign ("Good Luck Next Year, Denver Broncos") indicated, thoughts had turned to another possible Super Bowl trip.

26

TICKET TO RIDE

Gail Stuckey, the Broncos' ticket manager, looked as if someone had smacked him in the head with a two-by-four. He turned to his wife and said, "If we get out of this alive, we'll be lucky." The problem was very basic: seventy-three thousand will not go into nine thousand. The Broncos had seventy-three thousand season ticket-holders who all wanted to go to the Super Bowl, and only nine thousand tickets were available. The Broncos had started out with close to fourteen thousand, but players, coaches, and the staff, along with VIPs, had gobbled up close to five thousand. So Stuckey had put out the word that the first three thousand priority numbers would be permitted to come that Monday and purchase thirty-dollar Super Bowl tickets. In Dallas a riot had broken out that day over tickets, and in Denver people had lined up all night at the ticket office, although unable to get tickets because they didn't fall in that small minority. Plus, the early priority ticket holders didn't like the idea of standing in line. They just wanted to be able to pick up their tickets. "I wish I had zero tickets," Stuckey said. "A ticket manager in Kansas City told me once that he hoped I never had to worry about the Super Bowl, that I wouldn't enjoy it all. Now I know what he means. If I can just get rid of these tickets, maybe I can have a free moment to think about the team going to the Super Bowl."

A man came in, said his wife was a cripple, and he would do anything for the club to get two tickets. Stuckey had to turn him down. Out in the ticket office people were jostling each other.

"My priority number is 18,031. Do I have a chance at getting a ticket?" said a Mexican-American gentleman.

"No," said the lady behind the counter. "They'll all be gone before your priority number is reached.

"It's unfair, I tell you. I've watched this team since the beginning, and I should have a right to go."

"Well, try one of the travel agents."

Another man walked in. He had an early priority number, but wanted thirty tickets. "I should have that right. I'm the team's biggest fan."

"Maybe so, but we can't give you thirty. You'll get four."

"Well, I'm going to the top with this thing."

"You do that, sir."

Another man wanted an "Orange Crush" jacket. "Sorry, sir, but we don't have any left. We're down to bumper stickers. You want some of them?"

"Yeah, I'll take anything. Got any extra tickets?"

Extra tickets was the rallying cry throughout the city. Everyone wanted a ticket to the Super Bowl. Travel agencies were trying to arrange deals, and airlines were booking extra flights. Continental Airlines, based in Denver, added several flights, but they were immediately booked solid. North Central Airlines, based in Minneapolis, had diverted six charter flights from that city, originally intended to carry Viking fans to New Orleans. Other airlines were following the theme.

But it just seemed to be causing more problems. There weren't that many tickets available; rooms in New Orleans were at a minimum, and the New Orleans Airport wouldn't be able to handle the, uh, crush of orange.

And fans were being taken for a ride in Denver. Some were paying as much as seven hundred dollars for a weekend-tour package. The New Orleans Chamber of Commerce claimed it had investigated the situation and could find no illegalities. The city seemed more concerned about getting the prostitutes off the streets.

One travel agent said the tour to the Super Bowl was more of a headache than a boon. "These fans have gone crazy." He said some of the calls he had gotten had bordered bribery. People called and said that if they could get on the tour they would swing their travel business to the agency. The agent had taken care of six hundred Broncomaniacs and had another six hundred on a waiting list—at seven hundred dollars a pop. "I'm making only fifteen dollars a person. It's a rip-off. It's the greatest rip-off of all time."

Braniff Airlines brought an orange plane off its regular route to Honolulu and announced it could take on five hundred passengers. The seats were sold out in hours.

Mike Arnold, a Denver accountant, decided to fly his own Beechcraft Queenair to New Orleans, but found out he'd be better off hitchhiking. The nearest parking space for his plane was in Mobile, Alabama.

Rent-a-cars in New Orleans were long gone. People were renting out rooms in their houses to fans from Denver. The headaches enlarged, but it didn't stop more than twenty-five thousand who were planning to make the trek south.

More problems began to surface. One tour group found out that it had been booked in Biloxi, Mississippi, about 70 miles away from New Orleans. Some people stopped payment on their checks, but most went along with it anyway. The travel agency said the problem was "regrettable," but that everything would be done to take care of the Broncos' fans.

One Denver group rented a two-bedroom New Orleans condominium for $1,175 per day.

In Farmington, New Mexico, the DeWeese family wasn't concerned about going to the Super Bowl. They would watch the game on television with their two sons—Dallas, five, and Denver, one. Larry DeWeese, a former football coach, said he had named his first son after Dallas because Cowboy Ralph Neely hails from Farmington. "Then along came a second son, and if you live in this area, you have to have one named Denver if you have one named Dallas." Now that the teams had been picked to play in the Super Bowl, "everyone is going nuts over the boys." The boys got appropriate T-shirts and helmets for the occasion.

Kerry Keyworth was planning to go, though. Wife of Broncos fullback Jon Keyworth, Kerry was a flight attendant for Continental Airlines. Hoping that the Broncos would make it to New Orleans, she had taken a leave of absence, but when she saw the number of flights being added, she volunteered to work. Between January 12 and 15, Continental had added forty flights to New Orleans. It was a move unprecedented in the airlines' history. "It might be fun to go down with a bunch of fans," Kerry Keyworth added.

Meanwhile, the Broncos were trying to keep themselves somewhat sane in preparation for the Super Bowl. Morton was on the mend, and the players were sifting through a year's worth of films of the Cowboys. "They aren't unbeatable," said Miller. "We've got to go down there and play our game."

He thought the Broncos could handle the pressure of all the media attention. They had been coming more and more over the past few weeks, and "we've stood up to it. This is a loose bunch."

In Dallas, coach Tom Landry said the Broncos reminded him of the 1966 Cowboys. "Denver has caught the fancy of people around the country. The Broncos are unique and have gone through the kind of excitement that comes to a city only once. It happened to us in 1966, when we had our first winning season and played for our first NFL Championship. The American people sentimentally are for the underdogs. We were the underdogs for a long time and naturally we picked up a lot of followers. That changes, though."

The Broncos weren't underdogs in their own city, however. The governor and the mayor had proclaimed Friday "Bronco Day" in Colorado and all city and state employees would get the day off. An immediate backlash occurred—not so much because government employees were getting a holiday, but more so because everyone else wasn't. The move was political, to gain support, but had a reverse effect, so the pair of politicos canceled the plans. A brick sailed through the window of the governor's mansion the next day. Not all Broncos fans had been satisfied.

Still, the city was planning a parade down Broadway on the Friday before the Broncos left.

On Friday afternoon more than one hundred thousand lined the downtown streets to give the Broncos a send-off tribute. "I thought you got these kind of parades when you come home from something," said assistant coach Ken Gray. "It looks like a million people to me. This is unreal."

An aide in the mayor's office was terming the crowd the biggest downtown since V-J Day. The people were overwhelming the thirty-three motorcycle policemen assigned to escort the team and its entourage along a forty-block route that was supposed to take about thirty minutes and ended up lasting more than two and one-half hours. The players rode in limousine convertibles and sports cars and wore their jerseys.

It took the first seven of the twenty-seven cars almost an hour to wind through the throng on Fourteenth Street, as fans converged from all sides for handshakes and autographs. "We love you, Broncos," a woman in her forties shouted. Patrolmen eventually gave up trying to push through the mess, and the last half of the caravan never made it to the end of the parade.

Shortly after 2:00 P.M., the procession broke up, and the players were whisked back for another practice.

The assemblage began arriving about 11:00, an hour before the motorcade was to depart from the city administration building. The "flagship" car was a white convertible Rolls-Royce carrying owners Gerald and Allan Phipps.

Coach Red Miller followed in an orange Corvette, grinning and waiving to the crowd, which included thousands of youngsters who had cut school for the afternoon.

On Seventeenth Street, office workers leaned out of offices and sprinkled the crowd with streamers. It was similar to a New York tickertape parade. All along the motorcade route, the windows of downtown buildings were filled with secretaries, businessmen, shoppers, waitresses, and salesmen craning their heads for a brief look at the Broncos.

"They're smaller than I thought they were," said a small girl to her mother. "They're cute. I'm waiting for Alzado. That's what I want to see." When Alzado's car did pass, she and others squealed as if he were a rock star. Alzado was clearly a favorite, as were Craig Morton, Haven Moses, and Red Miller. They were mobbed as the cars crawled along the downtown streets.

"I waited all these years for this. I couldn't care less," said Yellow cab driver John Clingman, who was stuck in traffic.

"We expected a good crowd, but nothing like this," beamed

an administrative aide to the mayor. "Everyone was smiling. If what the players saw today doesn't psyche that team up, then I don't know what would."

There had been no injuries or incidents, but there had been scares, primarily to the players.

Craig Morton and Haven Moses, riding in a car near the back, were dubious about the throng. "They're closing in," said Moses. "We got to get out of here."

Morton told the driver to turn at the next street, and the pair never finished the parade. "Scary," Morton said. "Remind me not to get in any more parades."

The Broncos had more worries, though. Tickets. Every distant cousin had come out of the woodwork demanding tickets for the Super Bowl from the players. They filed by ticket manager Gail Stuckey at the Broncos' offices and begged for additional tickets. But Stuckey could only shake his head.

Miller could get all the tickets he wanted. He had just been named Coach of the Year by the Associated Press, and before he was through, he would sweep every coaching award. "It shows me that the faith I had in myself as a coach has paid off, but this award is for the players." Morton had been named AFC Player of the Year.

The Broncos concluded their home workout Saturday. Miller had called Don Shula, who had taken his Miami Dolphins to the Super Bowl, and Shula told him to get the major share of work out of way before going to New Orleans because of the many distractions they would encounter once they got there.

"Our main work has been finalized. We did what we wanted to do, and we're ready to go."

On the seventh day the Broncos rested and prepared to take off for the Super Bowl.

27

THE WEEK THAT WAS

A lull hung over the bayou Monday morning. But the storm was coming. An orange storm. New Orleans was calm until midafternoon. There was almost an eerie normality to the city. The French Quarter was quiet. The airport had its usual Monday quota of passengers and all were going about their business downtown. However, the Crescent City was in the midst of a transformation as the countdown for Super Bowl XII officially began. The city wouldn't be the same for another week. Some fifteen hundred members of the media started checking into the Regency Hyatt—across the street from the Superdome.

Meanwhile, in Denver, an orange bird was headed for paradise. Gimpy Craig Morton was the first on board. Speedy Rick Upchurch was the last. In between filed the rest of the Denver Broncos, embarking on the biggest trip of their young lives. Four months before it was regarded as an impossible journey. It took two and one-half hours.

A sendoff crowd was at Stapleton Airport, and Claudie Minor signed a T-shirt for a security guard. Bucky Dilts autographed an air-sick bag for a stewardess. The Broncos were loose and relaxed as the Braniff plane finally departed a few minutes behind schedule.

Kicker Jim Turner pulled out a camera once the plane was in the air and started taking pictures of everything that moved. All the players got up. Mike Montler carried a football around and had the players sign it. "There seems to be more press on board than players," Turner mumbled. He, along with backup defensive back Randy Poltl, started handing out the latest T-shirt, their own concoction.

An announcement came over the loudspeaker asking the twenty-eight members of the press not to interview the players, to let them enjoy the flight. The Broncos cheered in unison. Most of the players played cards. Bobby Maples put on a feathered cowboy hat. "Just came back from a pheasant hunt," he grinned.

The plane finally touched down in New Orleans at 4:18. On the ground the local New Orleans media waited. Upstairs more orange-shirted people pressed against the windows, hoping for a moment with their heroes. A city official came down the stairs and explained to Bob Peck, the PR guy, that he wanted to hand each player a key to the city and make a speech. "I think you'd just better hand out the keys. They won't want to be waiting around for a speech."

The plane pulled up, and Red Miller was the first off. Billy Thompson and Craig Morton followed him down the steps. "Craig, we really did make it," Thompson said. Miller looked at all the cameras. "Hi, mens. Glad to be in New Orleans. We hope to have a good time."

It was cold and dreary in New Orleans, and the Broncos quickly boarded buses for their five-minute ride to the nearby Sheraton Inn.

The Cowboys were due an hour later, but it was after 6:00 when they finally flew in. The team's bus had broken down on the way to the Dallas airport. The same city official presented keys to the players, and Landry spoke up: "Glad to be in New Orleans." Everyone left happy. The Cowboys went off to check into a motel across the street from the airport.

Both teams were in town.

That evening Andy Maurer, who had once played for the New Orleans Saints, grabbed punter Bucky Dilts and a few of the other young players and took them off to the French Quarter. "I'm going to take care of you boys. Our big night on the town."

They stopped off first at Houlihan's, which in honor of the Broncos was serving an "Orange Crush" omelette. A few tables over sat another group of heavy young men. The two bunches eyed each other, and finally Scott Laidlaw, Tom Rafferty, Herbert Scott, and Pat Donovan of the Cowboys said hello to the Denver group. The first confrontation. There was small talk for a few minutes, and then the two groups parted. Maurer took his boys over to Pat O'Brien's for the famous Hurricane. It was crowded inside, and it was too cold to stand outside. Bucky Dilts sipped at a Hurricane. "Welcome to New Orleans," he said to a girl. "I'm your official host."

Eventually the bunch headed back to the Broncos' hotel— a thirty-minute trip through Fat City. Maurer, somewhat tipsy, swerved the car once and almost went off the side of the road. From the back of the car: "It took us all year, Andy, to get here, and you're going to wipe us out in one night."

In the French Quarter the people were beginning to take advantage of Orange Mania. "Everything that isn't nailed down is being painted orange and sold," said one storekeeper. On his shelf were several Super Bowl T-shirts. On the inside, though, the T-shirts said Sugar Bowl, a reminder of the recent bowl between Ohio State and Notre Dame.

Everybody in New Orleans was getting up. "This is a great time for our city," said Ben Levy, former executive director of the Superdome who headed up the task force to bring the Super Bowl to the city. It had been there three previous times, but all at the old Sugar Bowl on the Tulane University campus. This would be the first Super Bowl indoors.

What was this Super Bowl? Bill Petersen may have uttered the most concise summarization when he took over as head coach of the Houston Oilers and addressed his first booster group.

"I want you to remember one word and one word only.

"Super Bowl."

Super Bowl may be two words, but since 1966, it has been *the word* in the National Football League. And the game— it's only a game after all—has become an incredible phenomenon in American society. Everyone is aware of it. Norman Vincent Peale claimed that if "Jesus were alive today, he would be at the Super Bowl." Previous Super Bowls are among the top-rated telecasts in network history. It is one contest which provides football with a distinct advantage over the other sports. The World Series and the NBA title series last seven games. The Stanley Cup is another country. But the Super Bowl boils down to one day, one game, two teams. However, Duane Thomas wouldn't consider it too important. "It can't be the *ultimate*. It will be played again next year, won't it?"

Each of the first eleven games had offered a twist of its own, a handle.

Super Bowl I: Lamar Hunt came up with the name after watching his daughter play with a new toy called a Super Ball. He added the roman numeral to give the game a historical touch. The first game was the thrill of the unknown. Nobody knew what would happen since the AFL was meeting the NFL for the first time. Green Bay kicked Kansas City, 35–10, and the star was Max McGee, a substitute receiver who hadn't thought he would play and got drunk the night before the game in Los Angeles.

Super Bowl II: It marked Vince Lombardi's retirement as the Green Bay coach, but John Rauch, the Oakland Raiders' coach, walked off with the moment of the week. Tired of his mundane, worthless quotes, a writer said: "John, you have a gun pointed to your head. How do you answer? Does your team run more or pass more? Remember, you have a gun pointed to your head." Rauch replied: "I like to balance our offense." In unison, the press shouted: "Bang!" Oakland died in Miami, 33–14.

Super Bowl III: The year (1969) the AFL was recognized as a force. Joe Namath predicted victory and then led his New York Jets over the Baltimore Colts, 16–7. Lou Michaels of the Colts was asked afterward what he had learned: "I learned how to lose seventy-five hundred dollars in less than three hours." Namath proved that an athlete didn't have to remain celibate the night prior to a big game.

Super Bowl IV: Kansas City coach Hank Stram was wired for sound when the Chiefs playéd the Minnesota Vikings at the Sugar Bowl, and the film later revealed him saying: "It's like stealing." The Chiefs heisted a 23–7 triumph, and Minnesota coach Bud Grant was on his way to infamy as a Super Bowl participant.

Super Bowl V: The Battle of Turnovers. Between Dallas and

Baltimore, eleven errors were committed. The last was the most costly, an interception pick-off from Craig Morton. The Colts set up a 32-yard field goal on the final play by Jim O'Brien.

Super Bowl VI: The Miami Dolphins finished with a significant achievement: becoming the only team in Super Bowl history not to score a touchdown. The famous Duane "I'm-Not-Talking" Thomas game. Miami's Bob Griese was hauled down on one play for a 29-yard loss. Dallas rolled, 24–3.

Super Bowl VII: George Allen, coach of the Washington Redskins, had a member of his staff chart the sun in the sky over the Los Angeles Coliseum the day before the game. Garo Yepremian of Miami tried to turn a miscued field goal into a pass, and it was intercepted for the Redskins' only touchdown. "At practice I let Garo throw passes to my son. Never again," said Dolphins' coach Don Shula. Despite what seemed like a close score (14–7), Washington was never in it.

Super Bowl VIII: The least remembered of all the Super Bowls. Miami won, 24–7, over Minnesota. Minnesota lost the toss and got the field direction option. The Vikings chose to kick off into the wind, another in a long line of faulty judgments by Minnesota in Super-Bowl history. Coach Grant complained about sparrows in the shower room at the Vikings' practice facilities in Houston. Larry Csonka dragged Vikings all around the field on thirty-three carries for 145 yards. The game was the easiest to figure. The Vikings never had a chance.

Super Bowl IX: Minnesota had something to prove, was favored, and had it all over the Pittsburgh Steelers, making their first Super Bowl appearance. But the Steelers won anyway, 16–6. The Vikings had a total of 17 yards rushing and no run over four yards. Minnesota had become known as the Super Stiffs.

Super Bowl X: The most exciting game in Super-Bowl history. Dallas used a reverse on the kickoff for 40 yards, but fell behind Pittsburgh. Lynn Swann, Steelers' receiver, recovered from a concussion to make three incredible catches, but Pittsburgh went into a prevent defense, which prevented nothing. On the last play of the game Dallas quarterback Roger Staubach threw into the end zone. Everyone waited. Waited. Waited. Pittsburgh's Glen Edwards intercepted. Dallas lost, 21–17, but the game showed that Super Bowls don't have to be Super Bores.

Super Bowl XI: By now no one thought Minnesota could win. And the Vikings couldn't. Oakland 32, Minnesota 14. Blowout. Back to the bores before a record crowd of 103,438 at the Rose Bowl. Fran Tarkenton, Minnesota quarterback, interviewed himself for the network he works for, NBC. John Madden, at last, got respect.

So the Super Bowl had an interesting history. And especially to someone like Rich Jackson, who would have loved to have been in one. But Jackson didn't get the chance. It was evident in his eyes in the Broncos' motel that he was just a little bit jealous. Jackson, who had once been a member of this club, had come to visit his friend on the team, Paul Smith. The younger players, though, didn't know who he was. Smith and Jackson went up to the room, carrying a load of oranges Jackson had brought from the playground where he works after teaching physical education each day. "Tombstone," as Jackson had been called, was the first great Denver defensive lineman in the late sixties and early seventies. He had been picked to the Pro Bowl, named the Colorado Pro Athlete of the Year, and inducted into the state's sports hall of fame in 1975. But the knees had gone, and the Broncos peddled him to Cleveland in 1972. "It hurt, man, to be traded like that," he told Smith. "I had given that organization everything. But, I'm happy for you guys. Best of luck."

Tuesday morning both teams got down to business—the best they could under the circumstances. Both had breakfast and dressed for their first practice in New Orleans. But first there would be a round of interviews and pictures. The Broncos gathered at Tulane Stadium, their practice site, and awaited the horde of press. It was uncomfortably chilly, even though the NFL holds these games in warm-weather cities. Tulane Stadium was a wreck. It was rusting like an old, discarded battleship, replaced by the new Superdome. Ironically, the bonds on the old girl had just been paid off. Norris Weese, who had played in the Sugar Bowl, walked out of the locker room and looked around. "Boy, that's sad. This used to be the place every kid wanted to play in, and now, they've just let it go to waste."

Ken Gray and Red Miller were talking about a game that took place in Tulane once. Gray had been an offensive lineman for the St. Louis Cardinals when Miller was an assistant with the team. "Remember, Red. We had them down and were kicking them [New Orleans] Saints good, and they came back and beat us."

"Yeah, I remember."

The media gravitated toward Craig Morton and Lyle Alzado. For the five thousandth time Alzado was explaining his background in New York and how he wanted to help kids. He took a stocking cap off his head and looked over the assemblage. "I hope no kid has to go through what I did."

Bill Thompson sat on a bench and shivered. "They said it could be a cold day in hell before we got to the Super Bowl. Well, put an overcoat on the devil."

Bob Swenson, a Denver linebacker, said: How does my suntan look?" Another player offers that the birds in New Orleans must fly north for the winter.

The media types can't believe how loose the Broncos are. "Are you guys really this loose?"

"Yes, isn't everybody?" replied Swenson.

Louis Wright put on a fur coat someone in the crowd had and modeled for the photographers. Thompson picked up his camera—practically every player had a camera—and took a picture of a photographer taking a picture of Wright taking a picture of Thompson.

Weese sat alone until somebody walked up. "Good, are you going to interview me? I thought I would have to pay someone."

Finally the players were gathered in a group for the official team picture. Five players stuck out their tongues.

Across town at the Saints' practice field, the Cowboys filed out quietly, no shenanigans. Dick Schaap of NBC grabbed defensive lineman Randy White and tried to chide him into saying something bad against Denver. "I respect them. They beat two of the best teams in professional football, Pittsburgh and Oakland, to get here. You have to respect them." The camera stops. "Sorry, Dick. I can't say anything bad against Denver. You know how it is."

A young man with a microphone corners Tony Dorsett. "I'm

from your hometown, Tony. They flew me all this way to get an interview. Can I have a moment?"

"Sure."

"I'm here talking to Tony Dorsett, local hero, and the people would not forgive me if I didn't come home with an interview. Tony, it's been a great season following your great college career at Pittsburgh, but I would have to say that the turning point in your career had to be when you were playing little-league football, and a lot of people recognized you were going to be good, and you went off to high school and the coach took you under his wings, really made a player out of you. I guess there are a lot of people back home you would like to say hello to."

"Yes, I would like to say hello to everyone back home."

End of interview.

Efren Herrera, the kicker, was being asked about the three field goals he missed in the final regular-season game against Denver. "Won't happen again. I just wasn't in the groove that day. It wasn't anything Denver did. But I'm fine now."

And Roger Staubach said he would not "be playing against Craig Morton unless he has been switched to strong safety."

A few players, like Golden Richards, disappeared into the distance to get away from the crowd. But the reporters wanted to end it, too. It was cold outside.

Both teams worked on.

Dixie Beer was served in the press headquarters. "Tastes like warm piss," says a writer from the West Coast. "But I could develop a taste for warm piss."

The Broncos, meanwhile, weren't particularly happy with their housing. Rooms that might normally go for twenty dollars were forty dollars a shot for the Broncos, and the club hadn't gotten the three hundred promised, so Bob Peck was running around trying to secure more. The players were desperate. Peck found some rooms at ninety dollars a night. The players said they weren't that desperate.

Otis Armstrong walked into his room and saw a cockroach run under the bed. "Must be a Dallas spy." A player walked out of the dining room and said: "Well, it's good news and bad news in there. The bad news is the food isn't very good. The good news is there's plenty of it."

Red Miller walked through the lobby and headed for the newsstand. "Let me have four of those cigars right there," Miller said. "I've got some better ones you'll like here," she told him. "Don't smoke 'em, ma'am. Just chew on them, and these will do nicely." Miller wandered off through a hallway thinking that the Broncos might not win the game. He was trying to figure out a way to prevent that. "Dallas is the better team. No question about that," he was thinking. The solution hadn't come to him yet.

In Denver the camper trailers were pulling out. One caravan of twenty began the three-day trip. "We're gonna spread orange all the way from here to New Orleans," said John Williams in his camper trailer. "This is the only way to go."

It was still cold Wednesday, and the players headed for lunch before practice. The elevator started on the seventh floor, picked up two pilots, and gathered in Broncos on the way down. By the second floor, there were eleven players. And the elevator stopped between floors. Some thirty-six hundred pounds were on the elevator. The load limit is two thousand pounds. The players started yelling, and the rest of the force came to their rescue. Cornerback Steve Foley joined in on an adjoining elevator and shouted to the players; "You've only got five more minutes of air."

Bob Swenson went into the coffeeshop and purchased several bars of Marathon candy. He slipped them into a crack in the elevator. "Here, animals. This will hold you."

Mostly the other players laughed. The motel manager called for a repairman. And twenty minutes later the machinery was back in working order, and the doors opened.

"I think somebody punched the wrong button," said Randy Gradishar among the survivors. Tom Jackson looked over at Swenson and said, "It was a nice bunch to get stuck with." "I thought my life was flashing in front of my face, and it turned out to be Godwin Turk," said Billy Thompson.

The players trooped off for lunch.

Down the street Dallas coach Tom Landry was telling the press that offense "will be the key to the game. Both defenses have proven themselves worthy." Miller talked to the press and agreed with Landry, but added: "I think the game will be won in the pits, with matchups. The skilled positions can only go to work after the battles up front have been fought."

But Miller later told an associate: "I know the players think that just getting here is the accomplishment. I am having to watch that. But I want to go ahead and win it all. I don't know about them. We may figure it out!"

The French Quarter was gearing on Wednesday for the arrival. Signs saying: "This is Broncomania Headquarters" were popping up all over. "I like Denver," says a bartender. "Fresh money, and from what I understand, the people are maniacs. The Dallas people have been to the Super Bowl before, so I don't think they all go as wild. But I'm expecting a big week from Denver people. That's why I got all this orange shit all over everywhere."

One family was already celebrating. A stone's throw from downtown New Orleans lives the Ivan Foley family on Broad Place. Fifteen kids. And the offspring of the moment is Steve Foley, who once played quarterback for nearby Tulane University and is now a starting defensive back for the Broncos. Across the street from the Foleys is St. Rita's School, which was once destroyed by fire about fifteen years ago. When the parish rebuilt the school, a residence for the nuns was built on the second floor. So the convent across the street was put up for the sale. The Foleys grabbed it and threw nightly parties for the kids with jambalaya and red beans and rice.

The other Foleys had been given Super Bowl tickets by Steve and would be pulling for him.

The four starting linebackers—Joe Rizzo, Randy Gradishar, Tom Jackson, and Bob Swenson—headed off to the French Quarter that night to check things out. A bar owner on Bourbon Street recognized the group and invited them to sit down. He had his huckster at the door yell out that the "Orange Crush" was inside, and he handed each player a T-shirt with the bar's name on it. "What you fellas want?" They ordered drinks and people came in to talk. When the Broncos got up to leave, the owner handed them a bill for sixty dollars. "What's this for?" Swenson asked. "The four T-shirts and the drinks." In unison, the players grabbed the T-shirts and threw them at the guy, threw some money on the table, and stormed out.

"This is nothing but a big rip-off," Swenson said.

"I wish the game were tomorrow," Jackson replied.

"I wish it was yesterday so we could get out of town," said Rizzo. "You really think the Super Bowl is something until you get here. I don't know about you guys, but I'm getting tired of being asked the same questions over and over."

Back at the hotel Craig Morton had just returned from a fine meal downtown—he was a wine connoisseur. "It's no bother to me. The answers come easy because the questions are the same."

At the Regency Hyatt downtown on TV, the movie *Black Sunday* was being shown. It's about a Super Bowl game between Dallas and Pittsburgh, with a Goodyear blimp crashing in. A writer looked at it and said: "A blimp will have a tough time trying to get pictures of this Super Bowl."

The Cowboys think the novelty of New Orleans is wearing thin. The endless morning press conferences. Boredom is setting in. The Cowboys try to relieve some of it by going off to see the King Tut exhibit that night. Roger Staubach hollered out at the players in the lobby: "The tour has been called off, I understand, because King Tut died." The Broncos pass on the King Tut tour. "Who wants to see a bunch of old shit," says one player.

Besides, they're preparing for the Thursday arrival of the wives. And as soon as the wives get in they bitch about accommodations. Red Miller appoints a bitch coach, Randy Gradishar. "I want the players to have someone to complain to. We haven't had enough bitching this week."

Armstrong complains about the roaches in his room.

Rubin Carter bitches about not getting grits with his breakfast. Jim Turner complains about shaving cream in his kicking shoe.

The writers were picking sides by now, anything to break the monotony. Everyone had been interviewed. At a previous Super Bowl one writer went off to talk to a colony of lepers about the Super Bowl. No one is willing to risk it this year.

"It will be 47–0 Dallas," said David Israel of the Washington *Post*. "A real nothing game." In a betting pool it was 70–30 in favor of the Cowboys. Jimmy the Greek swooped into town and picked Dallas by four. The celebrities were arriving. Billy Carter, the President's brother, said he didn't even know who was playing, "but this had got to be a lot more fun than hanging around a bunch of Arabs in the White House." John Denver, among the biggest of the Broncos' fans, blew into the Regency, followed by several other celebrity types.

Police arrested eight more prostitutes, bringing the week's total to thirty-six behind bars.

Then Dennis Benkowski arrived. His wheelchair had been stolen earlier, and the Broncos replaced it and brought him to the Super Bowl as their guest.

Back in Denver the city was seething over a column written by Jim Murray, a syndicated columnist for the Los Angeles *Times*. He had suggested, with his tongue firmly implanted in his cheek, that Denver didn't belong in the Super Bowl. Those were fighting words, and the *Rocky Mountain News* was swamped with calls. A television station talked with newspaper executives. People were burning. On the back of the newspaper building an orange hand-painted sign appeared saying: Screw Murray."

Murray, meanwhile, said he had received a number of calls in New Orleans. "Those people are upset. Well, that's life."

Jon Keyworth suddenly became a household name. A call had been made in Denver threatening Keyworth's life, and FBI agents quickly put Keyworth under guard in New Orleans. A policeman stood outside his room. "Hey, Jon, we're coming after you," a player hollered through the walls. Keyworth smiled. "Why does it have to be me?" After a thorough investigation it turned out that a Denver woman was upset about her husband. Marital problems had caused her to call. It was only natural since the Broncos' were the only subject being talked about that she should use the Broncos to get back at him.

More T-shirts went on sale—now in all varieties. A woman washed one selling for one dollar, and all the lettering came off.

And the Cariotis family just loved the Broncos. They had set up shop in the lobby of the Regency Hyatt and couldn't sell all their orange stuff fast enough.

Oddly enough, though, the Cariotises lived in Dallas and were Cowboys fans. "We're definitely behind Dallas, but don't let the word get around. We don't want the people from Denver to stop buying."

The Cariotises have a business in Dallas called Sports Novelties, and they supply the area colleges and the Cowboys. But the Broncos getting in the Super Bowl really put them on top.

"We had a whole warehouse full of bright orange stuff left over from when [the University of] Texas changed its colors to bright orange," said son Steve. "I didn't know how we would get rid of that stuff. Well, here comes Denver. We sure wanted them in the playoffs, and the Broncos getting to the Super Bowl was a dream for us. And as soon as it happened, we just pulled all the orange shirts and hats out of the warehouse and stamped 'Orange Crush' on them. The Cariotises didn't miss a trick. Brother Nick had airplane reservations to both cities after the game. "Nick wants to celebrate no matter who wins, and maybe he can sell a few more shirts."

If the Broncos win, it's good for business.

If the Cowboys win, it's good for pleasure.

Late Wednesday night in the French Quarter a man wearing a hat walked into a parking garage and asked for his car. His family waited with him. The Landry daughters were in a festive mood, but the man stood silent, grim-faced.

He was Tom Landry.

Finally a woman recognized him. "You're Tom Landry, aren't you? I'm a Dallas fan, and I just want to shake your hand." Landry obliged her and went back to wait. It was ten minutes before the Landry car arrived. He never said a word. Alicia Landry stood beside her husband in mutual silence.

Landry never changed.

Miller was back in his room trying to figure out what was going to happen. "After you look at the films of them enough," assistant Babe Parilli told his cohorts, "you begin to realize how unbelievably well they are coached. There is no better coached team."

Everyone was getting into the act in Denver. In the morning newspaper there were no less than fifteen pages of orange ads, like the one that said "Fram Oil Filters: We believe in Orange Power." Or Fred Schmid, home of the red-tag sales: "This week we're having an orange-tag sale." Advertising types were waiting up nights thinking up these things.

The fans were beginning to roll in. Behind the Regency, a parking lot had been set up for vans, and it was full of orange recreation vehicles. People were sleeping in and cooking over open stoves. And the French Quarter was filled up. Reservations were in demand. A man in a blue-sequined cowboy outfit walked down the middle of Bourbon Street and bumped into an orange-clad maniac. "If the Broncos lose to your bunch, I'll name my next kid Dallas."

Inside a bar down the street, a Bronco fan sought out a Cowboy fan. "Let me buy you a drink."

"That's mighty nice of you."

"Well, I got something I want to say to you. You people keep talking about how big Texas is. If you pressed down the mountains, our state would be bigger than yours."

"But," said his friend, "if we did that, Colorado would just be a big piece of shit like Texas."

The Texas man looked up. "If it weren't for Texas money in Colorado, Colorado wouldn't be nothing."

Outside, the streets were turning aglow.

"Dallas what?"

"Denver sucks big oranges."

At the Regency old men and young women were arriving. Nice executives and their daughters, or could be someone else. In the bathroom one young woman tells another: "This is going to be my biggest grossing week, and the guy just wants me for show. And he's not really a horrible old guy."

Players were still unhappy about their own accommodations and were asking members of the press about the hotel. "Does it have hot water? If it does, it's one up on our place."

In the press room, "Attention, Super Bowl media. Attention." Two hundred typewriters stop. They're wondering if a player has been run over by a car. "Jay Saldi of Dallas is now listed as questionable because of a bruised calf. Thank you." A writer turns: "Who is Jay Saldi?"

On Thursday the practices move into the Superdome because of continuing bad weather. Inside the dome Bill Curl, the public relations director, is scurrying about. "I've got a carpenter who has stolen a TV, and I've got CBS wanting to bring through fifty Japanese television executives, and the NFL wants nobody in here while they practice. I can see the start of World War III because the Japanese didn't get to see the Superdome."

Inside, down on the field, the Broncos go through the motions. Craig Morton tests a still-tender leg. Fred Gehrke, the club's general manager, turns to Bob Peck: "I think they look like they want to win."

Denver had been designated the home team, which was just fine with both the Broncos and the Cowboys. Dallas always like to wear white, and Denver likes its orange.

Back in Denver, a band called Aura couldn't believe its fortune. Last August they had been playing at a Denver motel when a man walked up and asked if the group would like to play at a Super Bowl party. "Oh, sure," Laura Theoder, the vocalist, told him. The man handed her his card. He was Ed Garvey, executive director of the players association. "At the time it didn't mean that much, but now it does. The Broncos are in the Super Bowl." So the band was getting a free trip to see the team play.

The people of New Orleans were taking it all in. Bernard Saltalamcchia, Jr., a cab driver, said the game and the people of Denver were meaning an extra thirty dollars a shift to him. "It's all there if you want to get it, and you don't mind putting up with some Broncomania."

Some sixty thousand visitors were pouring into the city.

A waitress said her tips were up forty dollars a night. Owen Brennan, who owned a famous restaurant called Brennan's, was expecting two thousand for breakfast the morning of the game.

Meanwhile, in a French Quarter hotel, Bud Goode had his own feelings about the outcome. Goode is a football statistician who feeds an endless flow of data into a Univac 1108 computer. The room looked an office. Goode has ten NFL teams, including

Denver, as clients. "In my opinion, it's going to be one of the best Super Bowl games ever. It matches two teams which are well balanced, as opposed to last year's mismatch. Denver doesn't want to get into a scoring contest with Dallas. The Broncos want to do what they've been doing best all season— be patient and wait for a break. And then, bam."

Two astrologists in Denver had their own opinions. According to Diana Truaz and Michael Nelson, "the moon rules Denver and has a very strong position. It is the highest planet in the chart which indicates Denver's ultimate success. Dallas, however, is most likely to jump out to an early lead. The position of Uranus and Mars both indicate that Denver will take the lead, probably in the second half. Venus conjuncts the sun in the opposing sector of the chart, indicating that Dallas will underestimate the Broncos. The moon will come into a ninety-degree angle to Venus and the sun sometime in the third or fourth quarter, and when this happens Denver should take the lead and win the game, although by a small margin. No matter what happens it's destined to be an exciting game."

A large ad said: "Top money paid for Super Bowl tickets. Bring them to 1660 Lincoln Street, Suite 1526, between 8:30 and 6:30." Tickets were still in demand, especially for a group in New York who had been flown down and been told that their travel agent had no tickets. They would have to watch the game from a motel room.

Howard Witkin, the Denver builder who had been a fan all along, was more fortunate. His motel room was located in the sticks, and had no hot water, but he did have a room and a ticket to the game for himself and his wife. They went off on Friday to look at the old colonial homes and the King Tut exhibit.

"It's costing me over a thousand dollars, and I'm not really enjoying myself, but I figure it this way. This is something happening that is never going to be repeated, and I wanted to be a part of it. That's the bottom line. And it makes it all worthwhile."

Friday night was the scene of the annual Super Bowl wing-ding at a cost of seventy-five thousand dollars. Food every-where—seafood, cheese, wine, banana daiquiris in Superdome replica plastic cups. Someone asked Ethel Kennedy what she thought about the game. "I really don't know."

The party was a bore. After about an hour most of the people started wandering out to look for the action down in the Quarter.

Most of the players had gone out for dinner and returned to the comforts of their rooms. The game was less than forty-eight hours away.

Jim Murray now said: "The Denver Broncos do it with emotion. The Dallas Cowboys do it without emotion. Emotion works better five thousand feet up. Cowboys 33, Denver 14."

Jerry Magee of the San Diego *Union:* "Blessed are they, the Denver Broncos, blessed and good and tough and several other things. Their success seems predestined. It's fate. Why argue with it? Denver will win."

Jerry Lisker of the New York *Post:* "Rooting for Denver, betting on Dallas. Logic over emotion."

Will Grimsley of the Associated Press: "Big D squeezes the orange down to the pulp. Dallas 17, Denver 7."

Dan Hurby of the San Jose *Mercury:* "Denver plays with emotion, like Liza Minnelli. Dallas plays by rote, like George Hamilton. The difference will be dramatic. The Broncos to roll, 31–10."

Gil Lyons of the Seattle *Times:* "If Denver wins, they'll make Cinderella look like a pumpkin. This is a team which came from nowhere, few believed in, and which will make bumpkins out of the experts. Last year's player revolt. This year's retread quarterback. It's too much. Cinderella lives, but Dallas by 14."

On Saturday the French Quarter was a mass of people. New Year's Eve and Mardi Gras and a New York subway rush. More than twenty thousand were Bronco fans. The French Quarter was a sea of orange and blue—with Cowboy followers mixed in.

A woman in an orange blouse spied an orange sofa in an antique shop on Esplanade Avenue.

"How much?" she asked.

"Five hundred," said he.

"Wrap it up," she said.

Dolores Kerif of Denver went into the St. Louis Catholic

Cathedral and asked the priest to pray for a Denver victory. The priest, along with everyone else in New Orleans, was obliging.

One pretty Denver supporter wore a necklace of soda-pop cans—Orange Crush, of course.

In the Regency, which had set up bars every few feet, the people gathered and sang:

> I've been rootin' for the Broncos,
> All these eighteen years,
> We've been rootin' for the Broncos,
> Through all the sweat and tears . . .

A young woman, hoarse from singing, turned to someone: "We've got a little motto that goes with the song. It goes like this: Colorado has its mountains. Texas has it cactus. Denver is playing Dallas, and it's just for practice."

Both sides were dressed up in Western attire, and a cartoonist had put together a cartoon with the inscription: "There's never been a bronco that can't be rode. There's never been a cowboy that ain't been throwed."

A huckster on Bourbon Street was featuring a "neutral hat," half blue and half orange. "That way I don't get kicked in the nose."

And three young Dallas men in blue regalia showed up in town with a trio of beauties, resplendent in orange. "Hedging our bets," said one guy. "We win any way the game goes."

Thousands of supporters from both sides mingled. They sat on the patio of Pat O'Brien's in the light snow and exchanged opinions, but police reported no incidents. Someone said $300 million would be wagered on the game.

The Broncos moved through their final workout and then held the final important meetings. Curfew was moved up from midnight to 11:00, and everyone went to bed early.

Sunday the Broncos were awakened early by the screaming fans down in the lobby. A church service was at 11:30, but most of the players were up well before then. "Now it is hitting us," wrote wide receiver Jack Dolbin in his diary. "Most of us awakened in the night with a dry mouth and a nervous stomach."

The team ate together after the church service, but then the waiting began. Thompson thought he was going to claw the wall down.

But downtown nobody was waiting. The celebration carried on. Bloody Marys were selling so fast at $2.50 that extra bartenders had to be called in to meet the demand. A cold beer and a hot dog cost $3.25 after a thirty-minute wait.

"I bet I could sell this tree for $150," said an orange-shirted man standing next to one of the motel props. "Tree for sale. Buy this beautiful tree."

Dario Hutchinson stood in the middle of the mob holding a sign that said: "Needed: one ticket." "I came down here only because a friend of mine said he had tickets. He messed me up."

And it went on.

Howard Witkin found a scarce seat and said: "Well, it's almost here."

A friend walked up and said: "You won't believe it, but there's a guy out front in orange selling three tickets. I went up to him and asked how he could have three tickets left over when all the people in Denver wanted them so bad. He said it was a sad story, that he and his wife and their next-door neighbors were coming down for the Super Bowl, but his wife had died. I told him I was sorry to hear that, but where were his friends? And he said: 'Oh, they're at the funeral.'"

"You got to be kidding."

"Yeah."

But just about everything else had happened. People with no rooms and no tickets begging on the streets.

Five-o'clock start, first time in Super Bowl history, makes both teams antsy. Finally, at 3:00 the first bus from both hotels pulls out.

Outside the Superdome once more the sea of orange and blue is prevalent. And they begin filing in, find their seats, eat their tacos, drink their beer. The game that everybody has been waiting for is about to begin.

It has come down to this for the Broncos.

28

MORTON'S ETERNAL WAIT

MONDAY

Craig Morton arrived at the Denver airport an hour ahead of the scheduled departure for New Orleans. He wasn't nervous. He just wanted to avoid the anticipated sendoff crowd. He found a back route through the airport hallways and climbed aboard the plane alone. "Well, here we go," he said out loud, but nobody heard.

Outside, the other players were wading through still another mob scene. "It's not that I don't like people, but you never know what can happen when there are a lot of them jammed into one place," Morton said. "And I'm basically a private person. It can never happen, of course, but I would like to be able to get up in the morning, play football, leave the field, and go out in society and be unrecognized. But there is so much importance attached to football, and it gets so much publicity, you just have to accept the things that go with it."

As the other players strolled onto the plane, Morton pulled his leg out of the way. The injured limb was by no means fully repaired, but it was better. The daily treatments had healed it sufficiently enough that Morton didn't limp anymore, but he could feel the pain and thought to himself that another week off should suffice.

Craig Penrose, the backup quarterback, slid into an inside seat, said hello, and pulled out the cards. The routine was the same as always. The two Craigs would play Spades on the flight, and, as always, Morton would win. The veteran quarterback wasn't even thinking about Dallas or the Super Bowl. He just wanted to relax because this might be the last chance. Before he even realized it, the trip was over, and at the bottom of the steps at the New Orleans airport he was handed a key to the city, fingered it a moment, and stuck it in the flight bag over his shoulder. He was immediately overrun by media sorts, but only offered up: "I feel fine. There will be plenty of time to talk this week." And then he boarded the bus for the motel.

It wasn't swank, but the motel was fine enough for Morton. "Hey, it's got a bed, a TV, and a bathroom," he told Penrose. "I'm not planning to make it home." He already had heard the complaints from some of the players as they checked in. Most of the younger players thought the Broncos would be housed in luxurious fashion, but this hotel was a basic, functional place.

As soon as Morton unpacked, he headed back down to the lobby for a trip to the Superdome. Red Miller was doing his weekly show live from the 50, and Morton was among the guests. Morton walked down the runway and onto the field. It was his first visit to the world's largest indoor stadium. He thought how it dwarfed the Astrodome. He checked the artificial turf briefly—it was about normal—and then moved over to the sidelines. He was trying to find a particular seat. Miller had started talking into the cameras, but Morton was looking for the spot where wife Suzie would be sitting during the Big Game. He drifted up the aisle, came to the seat, and thought that it wasn't that good, considering the 50-yard line location. For a game like the Super Bowl, though, the seating in the Dome had been pushed back at midfield in order to slide in several more stands for a few extra thousand people.

He was finally called over by the show's producer, spoke briefly with Miller about "how great it is to be here, and I feel we will represent Denver well," and his turn was up. Most of the players headed off for the French Quarter. The coaching staff had more or less granted unofficial permission for the squad to get the New Orleans night life out of their system the first evening. But Morton demurred. "I've been here enough other times. Go ahead. I'll get a way back." He crossed the street to the Regency Hyatt, walked through the lobby unnoticed, and asked at the registration desk for a room number. The motel already was wild. The press troops and Boy Scout conventioneers and official types from the NFL were scurrying about, but nobody stopped the player around which the Super Bowl centered—the man who had played for both teams. Morton sailed up in the windowed elevator and knocked on Bob Stenner's door. Stenner and Tom O'Neal, also in the room, had been friends of Morton a year ago in New York. They worked as producers for CBS, which would be telecasting the game next Sunday.

"Who would ever have thought you'd leave New York, go to Denver, and wind up on a Super Bowl team?" Stenner opened.

"Stranger things have happened," Morton smiled, and the three talked about the problems of the New York Giants, Morton's old team, but mostly about Stenner and O'Neal's careers.

Two hours later Morton climbed into a cab, returned to the motel and went directly to bed. His first, unexciting day in New Orleans was over.

TUESDAY

Morton saw another stadium—the Sugar Bowl—early Tuesday morning. It was "Picture and Press Day," and the Broncos had to gather at midfield. When Morton walked out, he was shocked. He had played so many times on this field against the New Orleans Saints. A movie starring Charleton Heston, called *Number One,* the story of a fading pro quarterback, had been filmed here, and Morton had been a member of the cast while playing with the Dallas Cowboys. But now the stadium seemed only a worn, ugly remnant, he thought. Corrosion covered the steel structure. Someone told him that the sea air had helped contribute to the destruction, but Morton still thought silently: "What a waste." Nobody played here anymore. The Saints and the college bowl game had moved across town to the Superdome. But this was to be the Broncos' training site for the next several days. Morton tripped over a tattered piece of artificial turf and blew warmth into his hands. The weather was at the freezing point.

Then he got ready. Morton knew what was coming as the media approached. He could recite the questions without being asked. They would want to know about his income tax problems and the challenge of playing his former team and his relationship with Dallas coach Tom Landry and his supposed feud with Dallas quarterback Roger Staubach. In fact, Morton had called a brief meeting of the Broncos' team just before leaving Denver and told them if the questions were posed, to defer them to Morton and not to bother with them.

"Craig, what about the income tax thing?" a guy from Dallas asked. Morton smiled. Of course.

"Everybody come in close. I'm going to talk about this once and then I'm not going to discuss it anymore. It's all being taken care of. We've talked with the Internal Revenue Service, and the matter will be settled. I've paid the taxes I thought I owed, and then another amount was added on. That's about it. It's not really that important. It's not on my mind. [But the IRS problem had been on his mind. He couldn't understand how the IRS had sent him a notice about back income taxes, and the story broke the same day. He had lost some respect for the privacy the IRS reportedly keeps.] Now, any more questions?"

A reporter walked up, managed to inch toward the front of the pack, and spoke up. "Craig, could you tell what's going on about the income taxes?" Morton lowered his head. It wasn't going to go away.

The questions about the Cowboys continued to be thrown. Morton gave the same stock answers over and over, but thought to himself that the game must really be boring if this was the only angle the reporters could come up with. He hadn't even played with most of the Dallas roster. Most had arrived after his trade. Sure, he still had several friends on the club, but, he had been honest with himself thinking about the Super Bowl, and he had no axe to grind or achievement to prove. It didn't matter who the other team was. "I wish Sunday would get here," he told himself, and then wished that the team could have stayed in Denver to practice.

The press contingent eventually marched off for buses—to go off and worry the Dallas Cowboys for a while and ask the questions about Morton. Meanwhile, the Denver quarterback turned and looked over at his teammates. They were jockeying around, playing with cameras and acting nonchalantly, much like they had all season, but he had the feeling that, in this situation, the looseness was forced, that it was somewhat unreal. "We are still trying to be the same way, but it's not as natural," he thought. "But what else can we do?"

The team went through its offensive routine, although it was primarily a loosening-up day, and Morton retired early to the training room. The treatment on his wounded leg had to continue, and this was the only place where he could linger in a whirlpool and receive galvanizing machine therapy (which causes a pulsating on the injured spot and breaks up the blood clots). As he sat in the whirlpool, Morton finally realized that it was all beginning—the press coverage, the attention, the pressure of a Super Bowl week—and then he closed his eyes.

Back in the room at the motel Morton turned on the projector and watched—as he had so many times before over the past week—films of the Dallas defense. He kept searching for an answer, but it wasn't there tonight. "Teams have converted third down plays only on 17 percent of the time against Dallas," Morton told Penrose—again. "That's an incredibly low number. I don't see it, Craig. Nobody else has done anything against them. You got to run. That's the only way. If we can run, we got a good chance. Pittsburgh just ran at and over them. I don't know if we can do it." But he kept looking.

Pretty soon, though, he turned on the TV set, instead, and left thoughts of Dallas behind.

WEDNESDAY

The meet-the-press procedure had changed by Wednesday. Each morning the players would now be ushered into a room, and the media would pick out likely interview candidates. It was standing-room-only around Morton Wednesday, just as it would be from then on. "I hope someone comes up with an unusual question," he thought. Nobody did. The income tax matter had settled down somewhat, but they pressed on about the Landry-Staubach feelings of Morton. "I respect Coach Landry. I learned a lot of football under him. Roger and I respect each other, and I harbor absolutely no ill feelings about him." The responses were almost as if he were reading them off cue cards. "I can answer those questions in my sleep," he thought. "There has got to be something better to write about."

As Morton boarded the bus for practice, he glanced around at the activity in the motel and wondered: "This is supposed to be the spectacle of the year, but I sometimes think it's just making a spectacle of itself. They're making the game bigger than real life. And it's not."

The live color had been decided for the offense, a color that signifies at the line of scrimmage, when yelled out by the quarterback, an audible is being called, a change in plays. Not so oddly this week's color would be red, as in Red Miller. Practice was somewhat boring, so Miller stepped up behind the center, looked down the line, and blurted: "Crimson." Center Mike Montler took his hands off the ball, turned, and stared bleakly at his quarterback. "Is crimson supposed to mean red?" "Yes, and so does chartreuse!" Morton replied. The players broke up. Morton saw a bit of genuine looseness return to the squad.

The game plan against Dallas had been established in Denver before the Broncos left, but the daily ritual of going over it continued. The Broncos wanted totally to avoid third-down plays—when Dallas would bring in an extra linebacker or defensive back, and sometimes both. So the Broncos would try quick play-action passes and draw plays and screen passes, mixing in sweeps, counters, and bursts at the middle with the backs. But Morton was still having trouble seeing how it would succeed to a domination point. He knew Denver's defense would have to hold Dallas, get a break or two, put the Broncos in scoring position, and set a tone for the game, put the Cowboys back on their heels reacting to what Denver did.

Wednesday evening Daddy Bruce, a black man from Denver who cooked the city's finest barbecue, hosted a meal for the Broncos, trying to give them at least a brief taste of home. Morton ate quietly and returned to his room. If this had been his first Super Bowl, he might have been more excitable, but he was attempting to survive the week and figure out the solution to the Cowboys' defense. He fell asleep watching the TV.

THURSDAY

The crowd was much larger around Morton this morning in the interview room. They wanted to hear his response. The first confident phrase had been uttered by a player on either team. Cliff Harris of the Cowboys had said the previous afternoon that Morton would not last out the Super Bowl. At the question Morton's eyes perked up. He thought for a moment. "Well, maybe Cliff won't finish the game, either." He laughed, and the mood passed. Morton wasn't about to get into a contest with Harris or say something that could be interpreted as an ill wind. He and Harris were close friends, and Morton's first reaction to the statement was that Harris was just trying to rib him a bit. He didn't suspect that down the street the Cowboys were plotting to build their entire defensive game plan on getting to Morton—and hard, with Harris a major culprit.

It was raining outside, and the players heard that they were going to work out at the Superdome instead. Morton welcomed the change. The weather had been bitterly harsh in New Orleans and wasn't improving. His leg had gotten better, but he felt a slight sprain in the arm. He couldn't loosen up properly in the cold, and the arm felt heavy and uncomfortable. Practice was without incident, and the Broncos were leaving the Superdome just as the Cowboys arrived.

Inside, the CBS technicians prepared for Sunday's game, and Landry spotted a familiar face—Tom O'Neal, one of the producers. However, the Dallas coach was concerned about his presence. He knew O'Neal had been in Morton's wedding and feared he might tell the Denver quarterback what the Cowboys were doing. So O'Neal was asked to leave the building. Morton was told later and smiled. Landry hadn't changed, he told himself.

At the motel Morton greeted his wife, who had flown down that morning with the other players' wives from Denver. Penrose had moved out and joined his own wife, and Craig and Suzie sat down to talk about what had been happening. "Nothing," Morton told her.

But she was about to change that. A get-together had been planned for Thursday evening at Antoine's, one of New Orleans's most famous restaurants. The Mortons' friends had arrived from New York and Texas and California, and this would be their one shot together. So a room was reserved, and the Morton entourage passed by all the orange-clad fans who were waiting at the door of the restaurant.

The affair was the most fun Morton had had all week—and would have. They dined on lamb, tasted several wines, and talked with the thirty friends right up until 10:00 P.M., when Morton had to start scrambling back to the motel to make curfew. During the ride back, Morton realized he had gone much of the entire night without even mentioning football. It was good. He felt relaxed. Maybe that was a sign, after all, that the game was going to work itself out. They could beat this Dallas team, he thought.

FRIDAY

The doubts returned Friday morning. The Broncos had a weigh-in, and guard Tom Glassic was down from a season-starting 254 to 223 pounds. Morton wasn't demoralized when told, but it alarmed him. Glassic would be playing across from Dallas's Randy White, and White controlled what the front of Dallas's defense did. Glassic would have his hands full.

By the end of the week, the Denver quarterback was sticking close to his room. He and Suzie ordered from room service for every meal because he had tried and failed to eat in the dining room, due to the overcrowding and the thrill seekers who haunted him at every turn. Besides, he was becoming tense. It didn't worry him because he became tense two or three days before every game. This was no different. In fact, it had a settling effect on Morton. He felt he was approaching the Super Bowl like the others. His complete attention was on the game. Oh, he had been concentrating before, but now every thought, every action was in some way geared toward Sunday. He knew what the Broncos had to accomplish. They had to set a pattern early offensively, not let themselves get into a bind, remain conservative, as before, but not force the defense to be backed up the entire first half.

Then, Friday night, Morton went to the enemies' camp. Vern

Lunquist, an old broadcaster friend from one of the Dallas television stations, had asked Morton if he would come over to the Cowboys' motel and participate in a light TV session sent live back to Dallas. Morton agreed and walked into the room to find Staubach. They shook hands. "Hi you doing?" Morton asked. "Fine. How's your leg?" Staubach came back. "I'm all right." The show started, and the mood was relaxed. Staubach and Morton kidded each other, and the tone was low key, humorous, off the cuff. Nothing heavy. No pointed questions. Morton enjoyed himself. And when it was over, he went back to home base. He had waved at a few of the Cowboys' players, and managed to get through the brief interlude without a testy moment.

Suzie Morton, in the meantime, had been out with several of the Cowboys' wives she had known before they all were married. The conversation avoided any mention of the Super Bowl. This was one time not to talk about husbands' employment. When Suzie and Craig were back in their room, they ordered in prime rib, sat on the bed, ate, and watched part of a movie about a murder at the Superdome.

Morton's leg seemed fine, but he was still having slight troubles with the shoulder, although the kinks were working themselves out.

Just two more days.

SATURDAY

The brunt of the preparation was over. The Broncos went to the Super Bowl for their final light session, and Morton returned to his room to relax. He had been able all week to sequester himself away from the madness down on Bourbon and other streets. He rarely looked at the newspapers or the sportscasts, and the questions about his rivalry with Dallas had been reduced to a dull roar. Reporters were searching out other stories. Everyone in the country by now had been told the Dallas-Morton saga countless times.

Morton emerged from the motel for a while Saturday night to view the pregame made-for-TV Super Bowl special that was being aired on CBS. Morton didn't care about going, but the network was making a large deal out of presenting him with the American Football Conference's Most Valuable Player Trophy. Morton and Miller—who received Coach-of-the-Year honors—accepted their prizes and left the theater. The only thing Morton really sought was a good night's sleep. And he got it. He was able to put the game aside and dropped off quickly.

SUNDAY

Like everyone else—except the network—Morton hated the 5:00 P.M. start for the game. He didn't enjoy waiting around all day. "I'm ready to go now," he told Suzie, but the contest was still hours away. So the two watched television, talked about post–Super Bowl projects, and Morton went down to join his teammates in a pregame meal, per custom.

Then, a final meeting with the coaches and . . .

The wait was, at last, over. The buses arrived, and Morton wondered if the driver could find his way to the Superdome. All week the bus drivers had taken differing routes into the city, and, finally, the players pointed out the way. But this driver was prepared. He snaked into a back street and had the team at the door of the Superdome within 35 minutes. Morton looked out the window during the ride and was trying to picture in his mind what the outcome would be that day. He really didn't know, he informed himself. It all depended on so many things. It was a shame the two teams couldn't both be declared the champions, but, in all sports, there can be only one, he thought. Then he remembered that he hadn't played well in the Super Bowl before. What fate lay ahead?

In the locker room his stall looked the same—except for the vertical socks. "What are these for?" Morton hollered at equipment manager Larry Elliott, and was told that the Broncos had worn those type socks the first season of existence. Morton didn't know the reasoning, but figured there was a sentimental attachment. Not to Red Miller, though. The Denver coach decided that the players wouldn't wear the socks for warmups, despite the suggestion from general manager Fred Gehrke. Too many players taped the outside of their shoes, and this was no time to be worrying over strange socks.

Three players, as a symbolic gesture, donned the socks. Morton tossed his aside.

Morton heard Miller's final pregame speech of the year and spoke briefly with Babe Parilli, the quarterback coach. Parilli was excited. Morton could tell. It was as if Parilli wanted to play himself, and Morton thought that the former NFL quarterback, who had been a reserve for Joe Namath in a previous Super Bowl, probably could suit up and go out and play today, if only someone would ask.

The players walked out the runway. Morton was at the middle of the pack. He could hear the noise, but he was running last-minute details over in his mind. Then the introductions began. He hesitated and looked out at the massive crowd. Morton felt like he was in a fishbowl with people staring in. He said a silent prayer to God and then thought: "Well, we've come this far. Just one more."

The next three hours were among the longest in Craig Morton's life.

29

XXVII TO X IN XII

On the sidelines Robert Newhouse was throwing the ball. Across the way the Denver Broncos didn't notice the Dallas Cowboys' fullback. They were busy scanning the crowd.

"Isn't this something?" said rookie Rob Lytle.

"Nah, not really." said punter Bucky Dilts, also first-year man. "I played in the Sugar Bowl here last year. You'll get used to it, kid."

But there was an aura in the Superdome. Outside, for the first time that week, the sun had come out. So the mood was cheery among the seventy-six thousand who had squeezed into the Superdome. Howard and Patti Witkin settled in their 50-yard-line seats, twenty-six rows up, and looked down at the Broncos. "They look loose," Witkin said. "They don't look any different from before. Maybe they can beat Dallas." Back in Denver the bars and the restaurants were full. The city streets were empty. Everybody was watching from afar. "Give my month's paycheck to be there," a guy said at the Parlour, a small Broadway Avenue bar. "Sheeeeeeet. Let's get it going."

The captains of the two teams gathered at midfield. Harvey Martin of Dallas looked into Craig Morton's eyes. "He isn't frightened. He's concerned," Martin thought. Dallas won the toss. Martin told the defense: "If we get to Craig early, we can get him."

Martin was recalling that first meeting with Denver. "The defense is super. They knocked Drew Pearson on the sideline in that last game of the season and then yelled, 'We're Orange

Crush, we're Orange Crush.' That was my first view of Orange Crush, and it stuck with me."

Following the whirlwind of pregame pageantry, the kickoff finally came at 5:17. From the north end of the field Jim Turner kicked to Butch Johnson, who got the ball at the 15 and carried to the 29-yard line.

"All right, defense," assistant Joe Collier yelled. "Make it happen."

Tom Landry had been uncertain about the first offensive call of the game. He wanted to try some trickery, but the squad was tight. He could feel it in the pregame meetings. Run a straight play, he decided. Then, at the last moment, he changed his mind. Why not? Johnson got the ball on a double reverse, but he fumbled backward and had to scramble after the bouncing ball. He grabbed it, but Tom Jackson was right there for the tackle at the Cowboys' 20. "Take that, sucker," Jackson said to the prone Johnson. "We're gonna be coming all day." On the sidelines Landry said: "Shouldn't have called that after all."

Tony Dorsett ran at left guard, but was stopped immediately by Randy Gradishar. Then Roger Staubach hit Preston Pearson on a screen for eight yards, but it wasn't enough. Dallas had to punt.

"Orange Crush," a guy shouted in the Parlour in Denver. "Stick 'em. Hey, this is a lock."

"Good job," Miller shouted to the players as they came off the field.

The Broncos got their second break when Tom Henderson ran into Rick Upchurch as he tried to field the punt at Denver's 32. With the first penalty of the game, Denver was just short of midfield. But two thrusts at the heart of Dallas's defense lost two yards. Henderson made both tackles. Then Craig Morton went to the air for the first time, finding his favorite target, Haven Moses, for 21 yards over the middle. Denver was threatening right away. But it was stopped quickly. A run by Otis Armstrong got only one; Morton's pass was deflected, and then Randy White got through to knock Morton down for a loss of 11. Denver had to punt, and five minutes had gone by without a score. So far, so good.

Then came the play on which the whole game may have hinged. Dilts punted to the goal line, and Dallas's Toby Hill had trouble reading the spin off the left foot. The ball slipped right through his hands, and Denver's special teams ace, John Schultz, dove on it. But the ball slithered away, and Hill recovered.

"Damn. We get that one, and it's all over," said Witkin. The cheers went up in the Parlour bar and then died. "An indicator," Tom Jackson hollered on the sidelines.

Tex Schramm, the Cowboys' general manager, stood up in the press box. "God! What's going on?"

Morton thought: "That's what we needed to win."

The Cowboys were backed up to their one, but got out of trouble on first down when Staubach faked right and then passed right to Dorsett at the three. He raced out to the 16, and the Cowboys had some room. Dorsett stabbed at the middle, but fumbled. Another chance for Denver. But center John Fitzgerald jumped on the ball, and the Cowboys had gotten out again safely.

Miller turned to an assistant on the sidelines. "If we could just get one of these. Just one." Staubach went back to pass and was snowed under by Rubin Carter. The Cowboys had to punt and got their first advantage. Upchurch returned it for seven yards, but the Broncos were caught holding. So they started at the 39. Morton decided to go long, but overthrew Moses. On the next play Morton threw past Upchurch, and Tom Glassic was found holding. So the Broncos were pushed back to the 29.

The bowl was turning.

Morton dropped back and came under a heavy rush. Charlie Waters came on a safety blitz. Randy White joined in the pursuit, and Morton tried to toss the ball away. It floated lazily over the line of scrimmage and landed in the hands of Dallas's diving Randy Hughes.

The gang at the Parlour reacted horrified. Morton came off the field. Miller walked over. "Hold your head up. We'll get it back."

Morton replied: "It's a touchdown if they don't hit my arm."

It took Dallas just five plays for the first score of the game.

Staubach struck with a pass, and then four running plays finished it off. Dorsett ran off left tackle, got through safety Thompson's hands and galloped into the end zone. That moment was preserved—used later as the official lithograph of the game, with three Broncos sprawled on the artificial turf while Dorsett celebrated.

Schultz brought the kickoff 37 yards to the 40, and the Broncos were in good shape once again. But on second down Morton was under heavy pressure by Ed "Too Tall" Jones and had to unload in a hurry. The ball was tipped by Bob Breunig, and Aaron Kyle intercepted, returning from his own 46 to the Denver 35. Dallas moved to the eight-yard line in easy fashion, but Lyle Alzado stormed through on third down to pop Staubach. So Dallas went for a field goal, and it was 10–0, with the quarter almost over.

The Cowboys had fumbled three times and gotten away without tragedy. But then Morton came back with a pair of interceptions, and the Cowboys transformed them into a touchdown and a field goal. The orange maniacs sitting in the top deck of the north end zone had been silenced. Morton was beginning to realize there was no way out.

After another Denver punt, the Cowboys came again. The Broncos' defense had been on the field too long. It was beginning to show in the sweat pouring down the players' faces. Dallas went from its 43 to the Denver 19, but a Staubach-Dorsett pass was incomplete on second down. Then Staubach scrambled right, was about to be hauled down near the sidelines, and threw into the end zone. Thompson came down with the ball. The Broncos had dodged another bullet—apparently. But then the official ruled that Staubach had indeed stepped out of bounds. For the first time CBS was employing an overhead camera, placed in the ceiling of the Superdome. And its replays showed that Staubach hadn't hit the line.

"We're getting screwed. I knew it," said the guy at the bar in Denver. "You can't beat these guys."

Herrera kicked a 43-yard field goal, and Denver trailed, 13–0.

The mistakes continued. On the kickoff holding was ruled, and Denver was forced to start at its 10. Lytle picked up five yards, and Miller sent in a pass play. "We need something to break it." Miller said on the sidelines. "Maybe this will do it."

Moses got in the clear and was racing free, ahead of Benny Barnes, just short of the 50-yard line, but Morton's pass wasn't going to get there. "Oh, please," Moses muttered. But the ball fell into Barnes's clutches at the 40, and Moses jerked him down. "That was it," Miller shouted. "That puts us in the game. Dammit." And he pulled the earphones off his head. Denver held, and White punted to the Denver 36. Schultz tried to come up and make a tackle, but typical of how the game was going, the ball caromed off his helmet and was rebounded up the field to the 40, where Dallas's Bruce Huther was waiting.

Dorsett got the call on three of the next four plays and pushed the Cowboys to the 21, but Dallas stalled when a Staubach pass over the goal was tipped away by Louis Wright.

Herrera tried to make it three straight, but the ball sailed wide left. Denver had survived another onslaught, but there were more problems ahead. Morton passed up the middle to Jack Dolbin at the 42, but the sure-fingered receiver, who had not fumbled all year, fumbled. Hughes recovered and slid to the Denver 27. The Cowboys got 18 more yards, but bogged down. A swing pass lost seven, and then Staubach couldn't connect with Drew Pearson in the end zone. He then flipped the ball to Newhouse, but Bob Swenson and Bernard Jackson rushed over to make the tackle with only a one-yard net. Dallas had been stopped again. Herrera tried another field goal and missed again.

However, push was leading to shove. Earlier Morton had wondered about how he could complete passes on third down against Dallas. Everything was failing, though. So he would try again, and Riley Odoms was the target. Odoms rumbled 10 yards, but the ball, amazingly, was punched away from him. Hughes got it—the third turnover he had come up with. Dallas had the ball this time at the 28. At last, though, the Broncos, who had lived off the turnovers of other teams all season, came up with their very first. Staubach threw to DuPree, but he was speared by Steve Foley and gave up the ball. Tom Jackson, the Broncos' big-play linebacker, fell on the fumble at the 12, and Denver was hanging on.

With only forty-nine seconds remaining, the Broncos elected to run out the clock and go to the dressing room to regroup. But even that strategy failed. Rob Lytle scooped out 29 yards, and the Broncos were suddenly at the 40-yard line, with an opportunity for a last-gasp strike. So Morton threw to Odoms.

It was intercepted. Staubach trotted back out and threw to Preston Pearson at the 27. He got up to stop the clock with one second remaining, and the Denver defense stared at Herrera once more. But he missed. The half ended. The Cowboys could have been up at least 19–0 and possibly 30–0, so the Broncos were somewhat fortunate trailing by only 13–0. But the offense showed no signs of production.

Morton had been intercepted four times—a Super Bowl record. He had been intercepted only eight times all season and not once in the playoffs. Denver had only three first downs at halftime and a total of 72 yards on offense. The Cowboys had the ball twenty and one-half minutes to just nine and one-half for Denver. Denver's Wright and Gradishar had to leave the field with injuries and were being put back together in the dressing room.

The Broncos had to come up with some solutions during the break. Outside, on the field, the NFL was putting on a show with Parisian dancers. In Denver, at the Parlour, drinks were passed around for everyone. "We can come back in the second half," the guy at the bar said. "Hell, we're down only 13." In the stands Witkin got up and went out to buy some nauchos.

In Houston, Oilers coach Bum Phillips was watching the game on TV. "The thing that surprises me is that the Broncos are beating themselves, and they haven't done that all year," he told someone in the room. "But they're still in the game, as unbelievable as that seems."

In Miami, the Dolphins' director of pro scouting, George Young, thought Denver "wasn't making anything on first down in the first half, and everything else is difficult after that."

In Los Angeles Jack Faulkner, once a coach of the Broncos and the man who started orange in Denver, said the Broncos were throwing too much down the middle. "They should be throwing on first down. But you throw outside. Down the middle won't beat the Cowboys."

In the locker room Miller was trying to figure out how to alter the possibility of a runaway. "Craig, we may go to Norris Weese for a while, to see if we can open it up."

"Do whatever you think is necessary," Morton replied. He looked like a beaten man already.

Only a few minutes remained until the second half, so Miller walked over to the blackboard and wrote, under a decal that read, "Bald is Beautiful," and was left over from other days:

> 7 turnovers, 13 pts
> Tuck ball away
> hard-hit
> Take away
> defense
> 30 minutes
> kickoff returns
> settle down

He turned to the players. "You're not too tight, just too emotional."

The bell sounded. Time to go back out. "Offense, break the ice," he added.

Denver came out charged, taking the second half kickoff and putting together its longest drive of the contest, 35 yards. Otis Armstrong, on his favorite play, swept right end for 18 yards and put Denver in Dallas territory. After an incomplete pass, Morton rolled right and pitched to Jon Keyworth for six. A screen pass failed, so Denver was forced to punt. Miller knew the Broncos needed something, anything, so he passed the word to special teams coach Marv Braden. "Tell Dilts to throw." The Broncos have practiced the play all season, but never used it. Nobody was aware that punter Dilts had an excellent throwing arm. Dilts loved the idea.

But the Cowboys were expecting a fake, and Dilts, at only 5'9", was trapped in the wave of Dallas defenders. He tried to run, but was pulled down for a four-yard loss at the 45-yard line. Nothing worked. But a late flag fell, and Dallas was called for illegal procedure. Twelve men were on the field. Thus, the Broncos had a first down at the Cowboys' 36. Three plays, though, accounted for only five yards, and Jim Turner, who had been the star in the New York Jets' victory over Balti-

more nine years earlier with three field goals, came on to connect—barely—on a 47-yarder. Denver had, at last, scored.

Maybe the momentum had turned back, especially when
Johnson fumbled the kickoff and had to pounce on it at the
21. And soon the Cowboys were forced to punt back to Denver.
But, from their 35, the Broncos couldn't get going again. Morton was sacked by Martin for a nine-yard loss.

End of momentum.

A short punt presented Dallas with the ball at its 42, and
Staubach wanted it all. He overthrew Golden Richards in the
end zone and replied with still another bomb from the 45.
Johnson had raced past both Steve Foley and Bernard Jackson,
and the ball sailed just over his outstretched hands at the goal.
But Johnson dove through the air, got his fingertips on it, and
flipped into the end zone. The ball popped free, but he had
held just long enough. Denver trailed, 20–10, after the extra
point. The Broncos didn't bother to argue the call. That seemed
to be it, although only eight minutes had expired in the third
quarter.

"Wait till next year," the guy in the Parlour said. "That's
it."

But it wasn't. On first down after the kickoff, Morton threw
right at Dallas's Jones. He hit him in the chest and fell to the
rug. That was it. Morton was beginning to play just like Kenny
Stabler had in the first loss to Denver. He was completely out
of it by now. Miller saw the same thing on the sidelines and
called Weese. "It's your turn. See what you can do." Weese
had dreamed three nights before that he would be called on
and had told assistant Babe Parilli, who replied jokingly, "No
way, kid."

The Cowboys weren't prepared for the change, but had seen
Weese in the previous game with Denver. "He'll run," Martin
hollered down the defensive line. Weese gave to Lytle off tackle
for four yards. Then he passed to Jim Jensen for five. On fourth
down at the Cowboys' 17, Weese rolled right and then pitched
to Jensen, playing against his old teammates. Jensen jumped
a body and creased the defense for 16 yards to the one. On
the next play Lytle struck at the left side and scored. With
Turner's conversion, Denver was within 10 again.

"We can win this thing, gawl darnit," Miller said. "We can. We're going to win."

And the third quarter ended. Fifteen more minutes. As usual, Miller held up four fingers—as he had done all year. The players on the sidelines joined in with him. "The fourth quarter always belongs to us. It may sound high schoolish, but I want our people to think we own the quarter," Miller had said.

If the Broncos could just stop Dallas one more time and put up another score, it would be a game, a contest.

And Miller's command seemed to work. As the fourth quarter began, on third down, Staubach was plummeted by Tom Jackson, and Rubin Carter recovered for Denver at its 45.

Staubach got up slowly holding his right hand. He could tell the thumb was broken, so he grabbed a trainer, and they walked toward the locker room. "Staubach's going," a Denver player screamed. "Let's get 'em now." Morton, standing on the sidelines with his arms folded at his mid section, watched his friend walk toward the clubhouse. He put his head down.

The Cowboys had also lost Dorsett, who reinjured a knee, and the situation appeared better for Denver. Especially after Dallas was called for a face-mask penalty on first down, nullifying an eight-yard loss by Lytle. Weese threw to Upchurch for nine, and Armstrong then got the first down. Weese tried to hit Jack Dolbin, but he was out of bounds. A fling into the end zone for Upchurch was too long, and then Weese passed up the middle, after scrambling around for what seemed an eternity, incomplete to Doblin. Dilts punted into the end zone.

Danny White came on at quarterback and pushed the Cowboys to the 40-yard line before Staubach, freshly bandaged, returned to the field and took over. But he threw the ball out of bounds, and Dallas punted. On first down Weese was pressured and threw right to Odoms for a loss of one. Miller had told Morton: "Noris is doing well. Let's stick with it." Morton nodded and crossed his arms again and stuck one foot solidly—toes down—in the turf. Weese then ran for seven yards out to the Broncos' 30. On third down, the Broncos shifted into the shotgun formation. A strange oohing noise passed through the crowd. The Cowboys were well known for the shotgun, but not the Broncos.

Weese faded, and Martin stormed through. He grabbed the Denver quarterback, who was still searching for a receiver and trying to get away, and the ball floated away. Kyle, who had played up the road from Denver at the University of Wyoming, dropped on the ball.

The Denver offense came off the field. Weese snapped his chinstrap off. "Hey, Norris, we got time," Miller said. "We stop them right here, and we're in it." Just over seven minutes remained. But Weese knew it was finished. No storybook hero this day he.

Staubach huddled his players, and down on one knee he said: "Brown right. Halfback lead. Fullback pass." It was a play the team had practiced in New Orleans all week, and fullback Robert Newhouse knew it was intended for him. He had not thrown all year, but when he was a rookie, he had completed a similar pass against Detroit. Newhouse stuck his right hand in his mouth and wiped it off on his pants, hoping the Broncos wouldn't notice. He was trying to get the stickum off his hands.

Staubach called the signals, took the snap, and handed off to Newhouse, who gave all the indications of going on an end sweep. The idea was to make cornerback Steve Foley bite on the play, come up to make the tackle. Foley made a move toward the line, then thought: "This looks like a pass," as Golden Richards flew past him. Foley backtracked and tried to run down Richards just as Newhouse pulled up and threw the ball in a perfect high spiral to the end zone. Foley hadn't made up the ground. He made a desperate lunge toward the ball and Richards, but the ball landed securely in the Dallas's wide receiver's hands.

Richards was surrounded by Cowboys, and the celebration began in the Cowboys' sections in the stands.

Miller looked at Parilli. "That's it, Babe. It's all over."

Weese attempted to bring the Broncos back, moving them into Dallas territory on a variety of passes and runs. But then he overthrew Moses in the end zone, was sacked for a five-yard loss, and, finally, on fourth and 20, passed toward Upchurch at the five. Upchurch leaped, had the ball in his grasp, and let it go. It was a fitting finish to Denver's offense. They couldn't hold on all day.

The Cowboys came out with 3:14 remaining and never gave up the ball again.

Upstairs the Broncos' fans were shouting in unison: "We love you, Broncos. We love you, Broncos." Miller stared up. "They're still with us. You got to give them credit."

Schramm left his seat upstairs. "Good. That was a good one."

But most of the press thought it was a bad one, another less-than-perfect Super Bowl. Maybe it's because of the two-week period between the conference championships and the Super Bowl. Maybe it's because of the importance of the game that makes players tight and do things they normally wouldn't. Or maybe it's just the way Super Bowls are. Dallas had fumbled six times and lost two; Denver had given away four fumbles. Denver had been intercepted four times. A total of eight turnovers by a team which had been so careful not to turn the ball over in all the games leading up to the finale.

The Broncos filed slowly into their locker room. The door was closed. Miller asked for a prayer.

Then Miller spoke, and everyone's attention swirled to him. "The main thing is don't be ashamed of what happened here today. It's just one game. You've won fourteen games in this season. Be proud of it. Don't ever forget that you got us here, all of you. One game doesn't make that much difference. We lost to a great team, but you're a great team. When the people come in, act like a great team. I'm forever proud of you. We'll make it here again."

The doors opened, and the press converged.

"It hurts too much inside to cry," said defensive end Lyle Alzado. "Sure, I'm hurting inside. I don't need to cry. I feel bad enough."

Craig Morton peeled off his uniform. "There's not much to say except we lost. Dallas is a good football team. I don't know what else to say." He went off to the shower.

Bernard Jackson turned to Tom Jackson. "There were twenty-six teams watching us today. We lost the Super Bowl. So what?"

"Today," Tom Jackson replied, "they were the best in the world. They deserved to be world champions. On another day, who knows? Maybe we would be the best in the world."

There wasn't much to say in the Denver locker room. "When you are behind like that the opposition dictates what goes on," Alzado did say. "This past year we usually dictated what goes on, but today Dallas did. Butch Johnson's catch took the air out of us. I haven't seen one like that in a long, long time."

Morton emerged from the shower and was greeted by a new wave of writers. "I didn't play well today, but we accomplished a lot this season. On the first two interceptions my arm was hit. The third one I underthrew. The last one I was forced out of the pocket and threw off-balance. They took away about everything we had. We tried to get something started but . . ." and his voice trailed off.

"We beat ourselves," Rick Upchurch offered. Bob Swenson agreed. "This was a silver platter game for Dallas. A silver platter.

"We felt at halftime we should have been behind 30–0. And we weren't impressed. Heck, you give me the ball that many times, and I'll score. They threw everything in the books at us and couldn't score much. Guys were making mistakes like they've never made before."

"We'll be back someday. The fact is," said Tom Jackson, "we've got a good football team. We'll get a shot at it again someday, and when we do, we'll remember this loss. And we'll give it our best shot. If we played each other ten times, I'm not sure how many times we'd win. But today, they were the best."

Miller said that the Broncos were "not handing us our heads. They were better today, but we can walk out of here with our heads high. We knew we had to establish a running game if we could. But we couldn't. And then on third down they bring in their six defensive backs. That 4–1–6 defense is terrific.

"We thought we would get more maneuverability with Weese. We needed to break the ice and get things going. Craig couldn't quite get things going. But we've put Weese in before. There's not much else we can say. We lost the Super Bowl."

The television set was turned off in the Parlour back in Denver. Nobody wanted to watch "All in the Family." In Chicago, at the home offices of Orange Crush, an executive smiled. "That means the mania in Denver will continue," he said. The fans poured out of the Superdome and into the streets and over to the Regency Hyatt, where bartenders couldn't dispense drinks fast enough.

The Cowboys, meanwhile, celebrated. The champagne in the Broncos' locker room remained uncorked, but the champagne in the Cowboys' dressing room was being splashed about.

"I feel bad for the Broncos," said Dallas coach Tom Landry. "They beat great teams to get here and had great emotion. Unfortunately, you're only as good as your last win."

"Our number óne plan was to rush Craig. Not give him time to throw. We have a pretty good pass rush, and no quarterback can be effective when he doesn't have time."

Staubach said the win was, naturally, "super. Winning two is not easy. It was scary when we got here because it seemed as if history was repeating. So many things were the same. We stayed at the same motel. We were playing the same type team that Miami had been that year. A Cinderella team."

Staubach then talked about Morton. "I feel sorry for him. I've been there myself in a few big games. I remember a championship game against Minnesota a couple of years ago. I had a terrible second half. I could do nothing right. There's so much pressure. Maybe he began to second-guess himself. It's no fun for any quarterback when there's no time, and we didn't give him time. Jim Thorpe probably couldn't have done anything under the circumstances."

Kyle said the Broncos "didn't do anything different from what we expected. They didn't go as deep, but they had to get rid of it fast because of the pressure." Mel Renfro called this "the greatest Cowboy team ever. When I was asked in midseason, I said, 'We won't know until we get to the Super Bowl if this is our greatest team.' Now we've won it and proved this is the greatest."

Then Harvey Martin stood up in the middle of the locker room with a can of Orange Crush in his hand. He smashed the can: "Everybody knows Orange Crush is a soft drink, not a football team."

It may actually be a mood more than a football team, and one loss couldn't take that away.

In the midst of everything nobody had noticed that, at the conclusion of the game, Landry had walked over to Morton. They never had been big friends. "You're a great quarterback, Craig. Today it just wasn't there. Good luck," the Dallas coach told him.

Now Morton was thinking about that as he sat on the bus. The Broncos were leaving to go back to their motel for a post-game party.

"Wait a second, driver. Lyle Alzado isn't here yet," Miller said. Alzado was limping toward the bus, another of the many victims that had fallen during the afternoon.

"We came here together, and we're going home together," Miller said. And the bus pulled away. Denver had lost the Super Bowl, 27–10.

30

WAIT UNTIL
NEXT YEAR

Several hundred partygoers were milling around in the lobby at the Sheraton with nowhere to party. The banquet room containing the food was locked. Bob Peck's wife caught him at the motel door as he slumped in belatedly from the Super Bowl.

"They won't let anybody in to eat. The manager won't open the door."

"Dammit, isn't anything going right today?" Peck said.

Peck sought out the motel manager, who claimed Gerald Phipps's wife had ordered him to stop the party, that since the Broncos lost, there was no reason to spend a lot of money on food. The Phippses were found, and it was a hoax. Some woman posing as Mrs. Phipps had approached the manager, feeling sorry for the Broncos' owners.

So the party went on. The liquor was brought out, and the Olympic Jazz Band began to play. More than a thousand crammed into the ballroom, trying to drink away the day. The security force at the front door was supposed to check everyone for an invitation, but soon enough, that idea was forgotten when a player walked in with thirty-seven friends. Many had come to hear John Denver sing, but when he walked into the ballroom and saw the mob scene, he declined gracefully to perform.

Red Miller didn't really want to go, but thought he should make a brief appearance with his family. He went around shaking hands, and a guy in orange pants and orange jacket rushed up.

"Hey, don't feel bad, Red. Let me buy you a Red Miller drink."

"That's a tomato juice and a Miller's beer."

"You're trying to get me sick," Miller smiled.

Nancy Miller decided to stay, but Miller begged off. "I'm going up to the room."

He sat down on the bed, pulled out the statistics from the Super Bowl, and reread them. He could hear the noise from the party downstairs. For two hours he lay there, wide awake. But he never could find the answer. Finally he dropped off to sleep, clutching the stats.

Defensive back Billy Thompson passed through the party, shook hands with several teammates, took condolences from a few fans, and felt it was no time for celebrating. So he took off for a quiet dinner with relatives.

But most of the players remained. Lyle Alzado sat in a corner as the world passed by. "Don't feel bad, Lyle," a woman said. "We're still happy about what happened."

"Oh, we'll be back. I know it. Red Miller will find a way for us to get back."

NFL commissioner Pete Rozelle came into the room and appeared to be searching. He eventually found the person—Craig Morton. "Don't get down, Craig," he said. "What you accomplished this season couldn't be destroyed in one game. I was proud to see you and the Broncos get this far, and you should be pleased. The fans in Denver were the greatest, and the way they responded to your team makes it all worthwhile, and I was so happy for the Phippses. This is one of the last teams that's family owned. They're class people.

"You'll be back."

What had happened at the Superdome really hadn't sunk in with Morton yet. All he could think about was that another season was over. An empty feeling. The defeat and the personal involvement wouldn't smack him for several days.

Outside the banquet room, reserve defensive lineman John Grant was suffering. Along with several others, he had been severely injured in the game and now had to walk with the aid of crutches, contemplating an operation. As Grant approached the motel he tripped and fell. An orange-clad man helped him up. Grant apologized. "Hey, my pleasure. You guys did more for me this year than I can ever repay," the fan called as Grant went in the door.

By 2:00 A.M., most of the players had gone, but several weren't ready just yet to go to bed. They wouldn't be able to sleep. So Morton walked up to the house band, asked them to play a few more sets, and pulled a roll of bills from his wallet. "It's too soon," he told Suzie back at the table. "People want to go on."

And they did—until 5:15 A.M.

Downtown, at the Regency Hyatt, the blue and orange loyalists mingled through the night, forgetting the outcome. The last few days had brought them closer together. (Later, in a Denver newspaper, a letter to the editor from a Dallas group said: "Broncos fans, we found out, are true fans. We respect you and enjoyed being with you in New Orleans. Let's do it again sometime.")

"I don't care what they say about Texans. We love you now," said one Bronco backer. "We're gonna come back here and kick your ass next year."

"The Super Bowl is in Miami next year."

"Miami, New Orleans. I don't care where it is. We'll kick your ass. Let me buy you another drink."

Outside the bar on the escalator that rose from the first to the third floor, a man shouted: "We're number one." When he reached the top, he continued. "Hey, there were only two teams here today—out of twenty-eight. That ain't so bad." The others around him cheered. No reason to get down. They had spent so much money they felt the need to celebrate some more.

The Witkins and their tour group weren't so fortunate. They were supposed to leave New Orleans at 1:00 A.M. for the flight back to Denver, but at 4:00 they were still sitting on the runway. The air traffic was backed up for hours, and the liquor was gone. "Anybody know any songs we can sing?" someone spoke up. "Why don't you hold it down. We might as well sleep on the runway. It's cheaper here than that fleabag where we stayed." Witkin turned to his wife, Patti. "Well, we've been to a Super Bowl now. How did you like it?"

"Let's stay home and watch it on television next time."

Early the next morning the players started bringing their luggage down to the lobby. "What do we do with this stuff?" one said.

"Set it down. We'll straighten it out."

"Yeah, and my luggage will end up in Dallas."

"No escort today?" someone asked, sarcastically. All week cops on motorcycles had helped the Broncos through the city. But there was none today. The Broncos loaded up and headed for the airport, stopping for red lights. The driver had to circle the airport once before finding the proper gate. The bus ride was silent. Some of the players were thinking what a mistake it had been to house wives and relatives at the same motel. The hassles all week had diverted their attention. The Baltimore Colts had once said the same thing after a Super Bowl.

"Next time will be different. We know what we did wrong," Bob Peck told Dave Frei.

"Let's hope there will be a next time."

Gail Stuckey, the ticket manager, added: "And next time let somebody else handle the tickets." The Broncos had been able to fulfill most of the last-minute requests, but one man close to the team had to have a ticket in the worst way. Fred Gehrke had a line on one. The man was flying in the day of the game and would leave the ticket at the will-call window. Everything worked fine until Gehrke saw the man this morning. "You owe me one hundred dollars."

"What do you mean?" Gehrke said.

"I had to pay one hundred dollars for the ticket."

The Broncos' general manager ended up buying a scalped ticket.

Miller sat in the front seat of the first bus with a notebook on his lap. He was writing. "I'm tired, but there are things to do. I'm going to St. Louis next week to meet with the scouting combine. We've got to get started on next year."

Gehrke leaned over. "Why don't you take a few days off? Heck, we've been through a lot? More than anybody ever expected."

"No, we must get started."

Back in the same bus Morton sat and peered out the window.

"I'm fine. I'm just not much for Super Bowls." He had been the goat in two with two different teams. Stories were appearing in newspapers all over the nation this Monday morning to support that fact.

"It took Craig Morton fifteen years to lead the Dallas Cowboys to a Super Bowl victory," stated one.

"Morton found Christ this season, but he couldn't find Moses Sunday."

The bus pulled up to the concourse and the players were told their plane had been delayed by the heavy air traffic. However, one plane was waiting. "That's probably the Dallas plane," someone said.

A Braniff jet eventually did pull up. It was red and yellow. So much for the orange airplanes. "That's what happens when you lose the Super Bowl," said reserve tackle Hank Allison. Everyone laughed. The Broncos were lighthearted even in defeat. If they were ashamed, they weren't showing it. "We had a great season. That should be worth something," Morton said as he entered the plane. The players were making preparations for the off season. Ten of them would be going off for a week to Hawaii to film the Superteams made-for-TV competition against Dallas. Five others were heading to Tampa to play in the Pro Bowl. Lyle Alzado was working on a book with a New York writer about his life and had been asked to appear in a movie. Several players had been approached about a fast-food restaurant commercial. Most were planning lengthy trips.

The plane flew over New Orleans, and Haven Moses looked out at the city. "We'll be back. You hear me?"

Down below, it was a major case of Super Blahs. The city looked hung over. Trash blew in the streets. Grayness was in the air. People going back to work. The French Quarter cleaning up. The Superdome standing still.

Even Tom Landry appeared on the beaten side. "I'm not too chipper this morning," he told a passenger on the way down to the Regency Hyatt for his morning-after press conference. "Most of us were too tired to enjoy the party last night."

He spoke to the press. "I'm glad to be here, but we went through a lot yesterday to get here." Landry said he considered the Cowboys "lucky. You have to have luck in the playoffs. We got away with some things early in the game. If Denver had recovered the fumble, it might have been a different game. We were tight, but we settled down, and our defense played exceptional."

The conference broke up. The writers started leaving the hotel and trying to think up ways to lie about their thousand-dollar bills during the week's stay. Landry rejoined his Cowboys, and they headed for the airport. A Braniff plane pulled up. It was blue. The airlines knew how to take advantage of a situation.

In the air the Broncos were mostly silent the first two hours. There was no talk about the Super Bowl. It was as if a two-ton weight had been set aside.

Then several of the players started a pillow fight.

The players didn't expect much of a reception, but Denver had one more to go. Some one thousand waited in 16-degree weather outside the plane at Stapleton Airport. They were chanting to keep warm. "We're number two." Then the plane landed. The fans hoped the players would join them momentarily and talk about the game, but most walked on toward the luggage ramp. John Grant was slower than the others because of the crutches. He would have to postpone any off-season relaxation; knee surgery was scheduled in a few days. As the players waited for their baggage, a few did sign autographs.

"We still love you," a young fan hollered at Otis Armstrong. He kissed her and replied: "Thank you. We appreciate that."

Cher Thompson, a twenty-two-year-old student, had spent her second-semester tuition on a Super Bowl trip and had barely beaten the players back to Denver. She went to a flower stand and used her last twenty dollars to buy carnations—orange, naturally. She handed them out as the players came by.

Morton was cheered, and a tear rolled down his face. "That's what I hate the most," he said. "We wanted to win so badly for these people."

The crowd swarmed over Red Miller. He kept repeating: "Thank you. Thank you." In the background Nancy Miller watched her husband. "It's unbelievable how he answered their needs. Loyalty, that's the key word."

The Broncos were home for good.

As Red Miller climbed on the bus for the ride back to the Broncos' offices, he turned to some fans and concluded: "All I can promise you is that we'll get better."

For this season, to those fans, nobody did it better.

The Denver Broncos had come from nowhere to present the National Football League with a Cinderella team, one with a following unlike anywhere in the country. Broncomania had existed before, but only simmered, waiting to boil. In the season of seventy-seven it not only boiled, but exploded and burned. Everyone in Denver picked up the orange fever; it spread all over Colorado and the Rocky Mountains. Then Denver got into the playoffs and finally reached the Super Bowl. Orange hysteria extended across an entire country as all became aware of this mediocre team that had come from an upstart league and finally struggled for success. It was a fairy-tale year in football. And, for the Broncos, nothing could ever be the same, just as Pittsburgh quarterback Terry Bradshaw said. Denver fans will expect their team to be good now. They will anticipate another trip to the Super Bowl as a new season starts. They won't be underdogs to the nation any longer. And the world will be prepared for another orange invasion. How a city and a state reacted to its team will never be forgotten, though.

A classified ad appeared in a Denver newspaper the next morning. All it said was: "Denver still loves you, Broncos. You gave us so much, and nobody can take it away. You have made us a proud city."

Orange Madness does live on.

It's only . . . the beginning.

INDEX